ENVIRONMENTAL EDUCATION

ENVIRONMENTAL EDUCATION

Arul Jothi
M.Sc., M.Ed.
Principal, Arcot Sri Mahalakshmi Women's Teacher Training Institute,
Villapakkam, Vellore Dist.-632521 T.N.

Dr. D.L. Balaji
B.Com., M.A., M.Phil., D.Lit.,
Correspondent, Arcot Sri Mahalakshmi Educational Institutions,
Villapakkam, Vellore Dist.-632521 T.N.

Dr. Rajesh Verma
Lecturer, School of Education,
Nalanda Open University,
Patna

CENTRUM PRESS
NEW DELHI-110002 (INDIA)

CENTRUM PRESS
H.O.: 4360/4, Ansari Road, Daryaganj,
New Delhi-110 002 (India)
Ph.: 23278000, 23261597

B.O.: No. 1015, Ist Main Road, BSK IIIrd Stage
IIIrd Phase, IIIrd Block,
Bangalore - 560 085 (India)
Tel.: 080-41723429
Visit us at: www.centrumpress.com

Environmental Education

First Edition, 2009

PRINTED IN INDIA

Printed at Balaji Offset, Delhi

Contents

Preface

Environmental education refers to organized efforts to teach about how natural environments function and, particularly, how human beings can manage their behavior and ecosystems in order to live sustainably. The term is often used to imply education within the school system, from primary to post-secondary. However, it is sometimes used more broadly to include all efforts to educate the public and other audiences, including print materials, websites, media campaigns, etc. Related disciplines include outdoor education and experiential education. Environmental education has been considered an additional or elective subject in much of traditional K-12 curriculum. At the elementary school level, environmental education can take the form of science enrichment curriculum, natural history field trips, community service projects, and participation in outdoor science schools. In secondary school, environmental curriculum can be a focused subject within the sciences or is a part of student interest groups or clubs. At the undergraduate and graduate level, it can be considered its own field within education, environmental studies, environmental science and policy, ecology, or human/cultural ecology programs.

One of the current trends within environmental education seeks to move from an approach of ideology and activism to one that allows students to make informed decisions and take action based on experience as well as data. Within this process, environmental curricula have progressively been integrated into governmental education standards. Some environmental educators find this movement distressing and a move away from the original political and activist approach to environmental education while others find this approach more valid and accessible. There is a movement that has progressed since the relatively recent founding (1960s) of the idea of environmental education in industrial societies, which has transported the participant from nature appreciation and awareness to education for an ecologically sustainable future. This trend may be viewed as a microcosm of how many environmental education programs seek to first engage with participants through developing a sense of nature appreciation which is then translated into actions that affect conservation and sustainability. The father of the Indian nation and an apostle of peace, Mahatma Gandhi realized the impact of industrial development in the beginning of the nineteenth century and expressed his deep concern about ecological environment.

This book focuses specifically on the nature and quality of the evidence generated by the work in this area. This book details the various issues important to the study of environmental education, the need for putting theoretical studies to practice in view of this particular subject, and instructs teachers on how to impart environmental values.

— *Dr. Rajesh Verma*

UNIT-I

Objectives, Scope and Nature of Environmental Education

(a) Meaning, Definition and Characteristics of Environmental Education—Content

Environmental Education refers to the branch of Experiential Education that is focused on teaching students about the natural world and their relationship with it. It typically focuses on ecosystems and the role humans play in those ecosystems.

Particularly, Environmental Education focuses on the ways human systems impact the environment and the way the environment in turn impacts human society. Some Environmental Education programmes aim to change people's behaviour. Others aim to give students a balanced perspective, allowing them to make their own decisions as to the best way for humans to live sustainably.

Common Environmental Education activities include Forest Ecology, Pond Ecology, Animal Ecology, Predator/Prey, Animal Tracking, Outdoor Living Skills, Garbage Dissection, and Leave No Trace.

Increasingly, Service Learning projects have Environmental Education components to them. These activities commonly include trail maintenance, habitat restoration, control of invasive/exotic species, energy conservation projects, composting projects and gardening.

Definition and Principles of Environmental Education

According to the International Union for the Conservation of Nature (IUCN), environmental education (EE) is:

> *"... the process of recognizing values and clarifying concepts in order to develop skills and attitudes necessary to understand and appreciate the interrelatedness among men, his culture and his biophysical surroundings. EE also entails practice in decision-making and self-formulation of a code of behaviour about issues concerning environmental quality. International Union for the Conservation of Nature (IUCN; 1971)*

The 1977 Tbilisi Conference, which followed soon after the launch of the United Nations Environmental Programme (UNEP), is known to have spearheaded clarification on the nature of environmental education.

This conference resulted in a declaration which listed seven directive principles for environmental education (EE) programmes. These are summarized as follows:

- EE is a lifelong educational process that occurs at all levels of education.
- EE is about the interactions which occur in the natural, the built and social environment. It should lead to the understanding of how human interactions and political processes, together with the nature of socio-economic issues and the effect of these on environmental degradation or enhancement.
- EE is for developing attitudes and value systems which lead to socio-economic improvement through positive social interactions and the maintenance and improvement of the natural and built environment.
- EE aims to develop an individual's understanding, skills and the feelings of empowerment that are necessary for both positive behaviour towards the biophysical and social environment in everyday living, and for active participation in group efforts to find the optimal solutions for environmental problems.

- EE requires a holistic and preferably interdisciplinary approach to teaching with opportunities for diverse learning experiences, but with particular emphasis on direct experiential learning in natural, built and social environments.

Environmental education is therefore not only the concern of natural scientists, but draws from the tools and resources of a wide range of disciplines in order to demonstrate the root of current problems and suggest ways in which learners could either prevent or remedy these.

What is the Difference between Environmental Education and Education for Sustainable Development?

Preserving natural resources and minimizing **environmental** damage is the agenda of both **Education** for Sustainable Development (ESD) and traditional **"environmental education"** (EE). However, the sustainability movement has stepped beyond the traditional **environmental education** framework in at least three directions.

First, this approach urges the whole society: industry, community, and government to take responsibility for the long-term consequences of their behaviour.

Second, the ESD approach emphasizes on the importance of strategic processes in guiding social transformation.

Thirdly, it suggests that **education** is a critical strategic process for preparing a society to develop sustainably. In planning a new **environmental education** programme, three consecutive projects were conducted at Naresuan University, including: a survey on community readiness measured by local stakeholders' perspectives of the needs for EE; an analysis of current **educational** programmes in universities in Asia in terms of their applicability to achieving SD; and a review of a recently developed college-level **environmental education** programme designed to address the sustainability agenda. Reflection on the results of these analyses has led to a recommendation of several basic principles for future efforts to pursue SD through **environmental education**.

Studying the Future Through Environmental Education

Environmental education is to a large extent predicated on concern for the future; to the extent that humans fail to behave in an environmentally responsible fashion, the future may be projected to be correspondingly bleak. This is held to be true in terms of use, overuse, and abuse of natural resources, both potentially sustainable and unequivocally non-renewable, and with respect to more immediate environmental pollution considerations.

There is also great interest in "the future" as an area of study: it is often associated with global concerns. To the extent that global and/or future studies attend to environmental considerations, they become appropriate vehicles for environmental education. From another perspective, future/global studies which do not emphasize the environment are at best incomplete and are quite likely to be misleading and/or simplistic.

Are Future Studies "Scientific?"

As an area of scientific study, "futurology" found an early spokesperson in the Rev. Robert Thomas Malthus, who nearly two centuries ago published the results of studies of the evolving relationships between agricultural production and human population growth. Employing rigorous analysis of sound data, Malthus concluded that incremental, eventually catastrophic, deficits in availability of food supplies were in humankind's future.

His conclusions were based on linear projections of historically established and verifiable trends of increases in food production and human population: the former was clearly rising arithmetically, the latter geometrically.

Projections such as these are based on the assumption that the trends will continue; prediction enters the picture at the point where possible and/or probable outcomes are hypothesized, particularly with respect to interactions among projections.

Malthus's procedures provide a prime example, perhaps the prime example, of classical methods of looking at the future.

Until the quite recent past, linear projections have been the commonly employed procedure of looking at the future in situations where scientific data were available and used.

Malthus's predictions have not come true on a global scale and are at present discounted by many. At the very least, his time line has not proved true. The most significant cause of this failure was the unpredictable, spectacularly rapid advancement of technology, as exemplified by the Industrial Revolution and, more recently, the Green Revolution.

Some will argue that it is as reasonable to project rapid technological advancement as it is to project other changes in a linear fashion. Had Malthus done so, his predictions would no doubt have been appreciably less drastic, certainly not so dire. But on what basis might he have projected technological advancement?

How are Projections Developed?

To project trends, data are needed; the greater the quantity and quality of properly selected and organized data available, the greater the level of confidence that may be attached to the projections derived from them. The scientific enterprise thrives on data and has increasingly done so for half a millenium. For studies dealing with the future, it is first necessary to identify and gather the data needed for establishing trends of interest; then, these data must be "processed" in such a manner that meaningful information is derived.

The introduction of high-capacity, high-speed computer technology has provided a mechanism for dealing with such data-processing concerns. One of the first to apply these technologies to future studies was Forrester (1971), who dealt with trends in human population growth, agricultural production, capital investment, environmental pollution, natural resource depletion, and "quality of life."

His data were aggregated on a global scale; his procedure did not include a specific projection dealing with technological advancement; his conclusions were Malthusian in the "gloom and doom" sense. The better-known Club of Rome LIMITS TO GROWTH report (Meadows and others 1972) was an expansion of the Forrester study—more data, more precisely defined relationships, but not much difference in conclusions.

During the past decade, a number of additional studies using computer models to project future conditions have appeared. In general, they have attempted to sharpen their projections by subsuming more data and disaggregating it so as to approach analyses on regional, as opposed to global, levels.

The intent of disaggregation is not to deemphasize global implications of projections made, but to fine-tune the understanding and predictive power of relationships detected and projected—that is, to make them more realistic in terms of their implications for the future.

What do Recent Futuristic Projections Suggest?

That the future has been a topic of continuing public interest is evidenced by THE GLOBAL 2000 REPORT TO THE PRESIDENT: ENTERING THE TWENTY-FIRST CENTURY (Barney and others 1980a, 1980b, 1980c), developed by U.S. federal government agencies under the leadership of the President's Council on Environmental Quality and the U.S. Department of State. The report consists of projections of what might be expected to happen in terms of human populations, resources, and the environment if policies in force during the late 1970s continued.

Its stated purpose was to serve as the foundation for long-term governmental planning. The report's projections indicated the potential for "global problems of alarming proportions by the year 2000," much as have many future-oriented studies of the recent past. In this particular case, projections were made to the year 2000, but not beyond.

How Valid are Such Projections?

Because the outcomes anticipated in such studies are based on the assumption of the continuation of existing trends, the outcomes change when the trends change, whether planned or otherwise. Thus, it appears that a valid use of projections and associated predicted outcomes lies, after a set of interacting projections is made, in evaluating the desirability of the apparent outcomes, then evaluating various possible changes in trends, projections, and potential outcomes which might be forthcoming.

For example, the GLOBAL 2000 study developed projections based on continuation of existing policies, as noted above. But what if those policies were changed? It takes little imagination to realize that the projections would also change. The questions of concern are, how? and so what?

How can "Alternative Futures" be Approached?

In the past two decades, the concept of "alternative futures" has been widely explored (Shane 1973). The basic problem with linear projections is that they assume, a priori, a continuation of present trends. The associated danger is that this assumption may prepare the mind for their apparent inevitability; simply, one assumes that existing patterns will continue, so planning for the future is based on that assumption. Thus, self-fulfilling prophecies may result.

An alternative futures model will identify the directions in which current trends are leading, but it then asks the questions, "What changes(s) in our exisiting planning will change these trends, and in what way(s)?" Thus, multiple options for creating modifications in projections may be considered, and the probable results of these modifications may be projected. Use of the computer as a data processor can speed up the development of alternative futures models by allowing for the rapid manipulation of massive amounts of data.

It should be noted that all of the studies referenced above place major emphasis on resource/environment considerations; all assume that such concerns are at the heart of future studies. It is possible, by assuming that technological advancements can and will overcome problems associated with resources and the environment, to define their importance out of the problem; some future studies have done so.

Whether or not it is reasonable to make such an assumption is a deep-seated question which, unfortunately, still comes down to individual perspective—the optimist says yes, the pessimist says no. Each can support his/her position, but neither has to date unequivocally refuted the opposite one. All of this presents the teacher with a difficult set of challenges. Should he or she take an optimistic, or pessimistic, position in dealing with "the future" as an instructional area? Is it possible, or appropriate, to take a neutral position? How large a role should resource/environmental concerns play in future studies? How do future studies "fit" into existing curricula, or emerging ones? Is their omission justifiable?

Many resources in addition to those noted above are available through the ERIC system and from other sources. For example, an ERIC search through November 1984 coupling the descriptors "environmental education" and "futures of society" indicates 239 citations, 147 of which are listed in RESOURCES IN EDUCATION, with the remainder journal papers referenced in CURRENT INDEX TO JOURNALS IN EDUCATION. Judicious use of other combinations of descriptors will locate additional documents.

(b) Difference between Environment Education and Educational Environment

Environmental Education is a process of recognising values and clarifying concepts in order to develop skills and added tools necessary to understand and appreciate the inter-relationship among man, his culture and his bio-physical surrounding. It creates an overall perspective, which acknowledges the fact that natural environment and man-made environment are interdependent.

It should consider the environment in its totality and should be a continuous lifelong process beginning at the pre-school level and continuing through all stages. It should be inter-disciplinary and examine major environmental issues from local, national and international points of view.

It should utilise various educational approaches to teach and learn about and from the environment with stress on practical activities and first-hand experience. It is through this process of education that people can be sensitized about the environmental issues.

Educational Environment

A student might find a particular question threatening and intimidating in one context yet stimulating and challenging in a different context. What makes one learning context unpleasant and another pleasant?

Learning depends on several factors, but a crucial step is the engagement of the learner. This is affected by their motivation and perception of relevance. These, in turn, can be affected by learners' previous experiences and preferred learning styles and by the context and environment in which the learning is taking place. In adult learning theories, teaching is as much about setting the context or climate for learning as it is about imparting knowledge or sharing expertise.

(c) Importance, Objectives, Scope and Guiding Principles of Environmental Education

Formal Environmental Education

Though formal education is the mandate of the Ministry of Human Resource Development (MHRD), the Ministry of Environment & Forests has been interacting with the MHRD, NCERT, State Departments of Education etc. to ensure that environmental components are adequately covered at the school levels by infusion into the school curricula at various levels. The major initiatives taken by the Ministry in this direction recently are mentioned below:

Environment Education in School System

Under this project, which was initiated in 1999, an exercise to strengthen environment education in the formal school curriculum has been undertaken. During the first phase of this project, a comprehensive study was conducted to assess the status of infusion of environment content in the school curriculum in the country and to assess the effectiveness of classroom teaching. The study was conducted in all the States/ UTs of the country and textbooks of all the classes from standards I to XII were analysed. Based on the findings of the study, the textbooks in Science, Social Science and Languages of middle school level in eight States (100 schools in each State) are being modified to strengthen the infusion of environmental concepts. The modified textbooks would be used for one academic session (2002-2003) in the selected schools of the selected States on pilot basis. The concerned teachers of the selected schools would also be trained to effectively teach the modified textbooks. The States participating in this project are Andhra Pradesh, Assam, Goa, Jammu & Kashmir, Maharashtra, Orissa, Punjab and Uttaranchal. Depending upon the success of the pilot implementation, the revised curriculum may be taken up in the remaining schools. The findings of the Phase I study are also being shared with the States/UTs which are not participating in this project so that they can also environmentalise their textbooks.

Environmental Appreciation Course

Though there are several courses on environmental sciences at present in the formal system, there are no structured courses available outside the formal system for people who desire to learn about environmental issues. The Ministry has taken an initiative in this regard and it presently working out a frame work for environmental appreciation courses in consultation with IGNOU.

Environmental Concepts in Management & Business Studies

Realising that the industry Managers and leaders need to be sensitized towards environmental issues and concepts of Environmental Management so that they can play an important role in introducing environmentally sound practices in their operations, the Ministry has taken an initiative to introduce/ enhance environmental concepts in the Business/Management Education. A committee comprising representatives from Management Institutions, AICTE, UGC, Industry and MoEF is already looking into various aspects like course content and syllabi of the existing courses so that gaps could be identified and suggestion could be given for enhancing/introducing the environmental content where necessary.

Non-formal Environment Education and Awareness

Environmental Education, Awareness and Training plays a significant role in encouraging and enhancing people's participation in activities aimed at conservation, protection and management of the environment, essential for achieving sustainable development. The Ministry, therefore, accords priority for the promotion of non-formal environment education and creation of awareness among all sections of the society through diverse activities using traditional and modern media of communication. Some of the major activities undertaken in this regard are as follows:

National Environment Awareness Campaign (NEAC)

The NEAC was launched in mid 1986 with the objective of creating environmental awareness at the national level. It is a multi-media campaign which utilises conventional and non-conventional methods of communication for disseminating environmental messages to a wide range of target groups. Under this campaign, nominal financial assistance is provided to registered NGOs, schools, colleges, universities, research institutions, women and youth organisations, army units, State Government Departments etc. from all over the country for organising/ conducting awareness raising activities. These activities which include seminars, workshops, training programmes, camps, padyatras, rallies, public meetings, exhibitions, essay/debate/painting/poster competitions, folk dances and songs, street theatre, puppet shows, preparation and distribution of environmental education resource materials etc., are followed by action like plantation of trees, management of household waste, cleaning of water bodies etc. Diverse target groups encompassing students, youth, teachers, tribals, farmers, other rural population, professionals and the general public are covered under NEAC. The programme is being implemented through 28 designated Regional Resource Agencies (RRAs) for specific states/regions of the country. The list of these RRAs along with their addresses is given at the end. The applications for participation in this programme are invited every year through advertisement in major national and regional newspapers during the months of May/June. Any additional information can be obtained from the concerned regional resource agency.

Eco-clubs (National Green Corps)

The main objectives of this programme are to educate children about their immediate environment and impart knowledge about the eco-systems, their inter-dependence and their need for survival, through visits and demonstrations and to mobilise youngsters by instilling in them the spirit of scientific inquiry into environmental problems and involving them in the efforts of environmental preservation.

Since the modification of the scheme in 1993, more than 10,000 Eco-clubs had been provided grants until 2000-2001 in various parts of the country. Considering that the total number of schools covered were grossly inadequate compared to the total number of schools in the country and keeping in view the potential of this programme in sensitizing the school students. It was decided to intensify this programme to cover each and every district of the country. A programme of raising 'National Green Corps' through the Eco clubs was, therefore, launched during 2001-2002. Under this programme, Eco-clubs are being set up in 100 schools of each District of the country. 47,000 Eco-clubs have been set up so far in the country. This programme is being implemented in each State/UT through the Nodal agency appointed by the State/UT Govt.

The Government of India provides financial assistance for establishment of Eco clubs @ Rs.1000 per Eco-club, Training of Master Trainers, teacher training and distribution of resource materials.

Global Learning and Observations to Benefit the Environment (GLOBE)

The GLOBE is an International Science and Education Programme, which stress on hands-on participatory approach. India joined this programme during the August, 2000. This programme, which unites students, teachers and scientists all over the world, is aimed at school children. The students of GLOBE schools are required to collect data about various basic environmental parameters under the supervision of a GLOBE trained teacher and use it for explaining hypothesis as well as to enhance their scientific understanding of the earth. This data is also used by the scientists in their research work. The GLOBE also provides an opportunity to the students to interact not only with the GLOBE scientists but also with the students from GLOBE schools in other parts of the world. About 100 schools spread over different parts of the country have already joined this programme. The teachers of these schools have also been trained in various GLOBE protocols. An International training workshop for trainers was successfully organised at New Delhi during January, 2002. The participants at this workshop, which included representatives from Nepal and Thailand besides India, were trained in Basic and Advanced GLOBE Protocols by a training team from GLOBE Headquarters in USA.

Mass Awareness

Despite great efforts to spread environmental awareness by the Ministry through several schemes, it is felt that a large population especially in rural areas is still left out. The best way to reach out to them and make them aware of the environmental problems is through media, particularly the electronic media. "Mass Awareness" has therefore been identified as one of the thrust areas of the Ministry, not only to intensify the efforts already being made in this direction but also to launch new initiatives. The Doordarshan and few other television channels are proposed to be extensively used for telecasting environment based programmes and infomercials. Professional Media agencies which are hired to assist the Ministry in carrying out the campaign also play a major role. To encourage individual efforts in producing films/ documentaries on environment/wildlife related themes in the country, the Ministry has sponsored organisation of a film festival "Vatavaran – 2001" by Centre for Media Studies, Delhi in April 2002.

Other Awareness Programmes

The Ministry also sponsors various programmes which do not fit into straitjacketed programmes like NEAC, NGC, etc., and are aimed at creating environmental awareness among children. These include environment quiz (both written as well as televised), organization of activities for observation of special occasions such as earth day, special programmes for children, etc. These proposals which are received throughout the year from various NGOs and other agencies, are considered on merit as and when received and are supported. Few examples such programmes are:

- An international written Environment Quiz programme known as Green Olympiad conducted by TERI. It is conducted in more than 200 centers across the country. Last year the quiz was conducted in both Hindi and English and more than 70,000 school students from India, Russia and UAE participated in this competition. The regional winners were selected for the televised quiz programme named TERRAQUIZ which was telecast on National channel of Doordarshan. It was a great success in sensitizing the children about environmental issues.
- Awareness activities/events by NGOs, academic institutions etc. on the occasion of special Environment days like Earth Day etc.
- Written environmental quiz programmes in different regional languages are being started. The winners of written quiz would participate in a televised quiz programme.
- Organization of an annual Vacation Programme on Environmental Resources for high school level students namely "Vacation programme on Natural resources-building a broader constituency of support for conservation" by ATREE.

(d) Factors of Degradation of Environment—Adverse Socio—Economic Impacts of Degradation of Environment.

Environmental degradation has arisen from a combination of several inter-related **factors**. These include high population growth (estimated at 2%), poverty, dependency on agriculture and poor land management practices. The following are some of the consequences.

Soil Erosion

Soil erosionposes a bigproblem for Malawi. In 1992, for instance, Malawi lost an average of 20 tonnes of soil/ha/year (World Bank). Such excessive soil losses are worrisome because they are threatening agricultural development resulting into low yields, famine and malnutrition. Soil losses have also led to the problem of siltation which is adversely affecting all users of electricity. The Electricity Supply Corporation of Malawi (ESCOM), bemoaning the frequent power interruption, had this to say:

> *"....the main challenges besetting the corporation include the heavy presence of sand and silt in the Shire River's catchment area as a result of serious environmental degradation upstream; increased damage to plant and equipment as a result of the poor water quality....The Shire River is to-day more loaded with sand than ever before making it difficult for ESCOM to effectively generate power....and the unavoidable decision by Government to open the barrage at Liwonde due to i ncreased 1 ake 1 evels meant for a lot of sand for the river and gradual deposit of the same down the river. That is why about four months after the flooding of Nkula B, mountains of sand developed at the intake dams at Nkula, Tedzani and Kapichira power plants» (Daily Times, Wednesday, November 25,2003).*

The question is: do these problems worry us as a nation?

Deforestation

Deforestation is another **environmental** crisis Malawi is experiencing. In 1975, 47/o to Malawi was forest. To-day, 28% only is forested; 21% of which are forest reserves, national parks and wildlife reserves; and 7% is customary land. The average deforestation rate is 2.8% per annum. Tobacco and tea curing, agricultural expansion, wild forest fires and the need for fuel wood are some of the major **factors** for deforestation.

Signs of deforestation are seen many places like Ndirande, Bangwe/Mzedi Mountains, Zomba/Domasi-Malosa mountains, Thyolo mountain and m Soche Hill as well as the Phwezi-Chiweta road hilly area. Consequences of deforestation are many. But of late, droughts and severe floods have become a major concern. Several people and institutions are responsible for this state of affairs as illustrated below:

"Government negligence in guarding against felling trees for charcoal is responsible for deforestation, a group village headman said on Friday. At the awareness campaign to preserve indigenous forest in Mwanza, Group Village Headman Somisoni attributed scarcity of indigenous trees in the country to lack of commitment by government to curb illegal trade. Much is preached about preservation of natural trees but no tangible action is shown to eradicate it Culprits mostly go scot-free, tempting more people to go into the so-called money-spinning business' Somisomi said" (Daily Times, Monday, 4th August, 2003: Article by Joseph Chimbuto, "Chief blames charcoal trade on government's negligence").

Water Resources Degradation

Water resource **degradation** affects the quality as well as the quantity of water supplies. Major **factors** for **degradation** include sedimentation/siltation, biological and chemical contamination. About 50% of all illnesses in Malawi is attributed to water-borne diseases such as diarrhoea. Hazardous chemicals such as untreated industrial effluent is also becoming a major threat in urban areas. Water pollution is evident in Mudi, Naperi and Limbe rivers in Blantyre, Lilongwe, Lingadzi and Mchesi rivers in Lilongwe.

Depletion of Fish Resources

Fish resources are under threat mainly due to over fishing and destruction of fish breeding areas. In the 1970s, for example, fish production was about 70,000 tonnes per year. The figure dropped to 50,000 tonnes in 1996. Specifically, about 8,000 of the Lake Malawi Chambo was produced in 1985. Less than 1,000 tonnes per annum is produced in recent years. Clearly, the downward trend has negative effect on nutrition as well as the national economy.

Threat to Bio-diversity

Malawi is rich in bio-diversity *i.e.* wild fauna and flora. There are about 4,000 species of wild animals in the country.

However, high population growth, poverty and deforestation have contributed to a decline or extinction of wildlife species. For example, the Nyasa wild beast available in 1948 but is now extinct; elephants in the Majete Game Reserve have been extinct since 1992; the nyala, buffalo, lion, reedbuck and cheetahs are all in decline. Kasungu National Park elephants were reduced from 2,853 in 1978 to 391 in 1995 due to poaching.

Social and Environmental Policy

We, as a financial institution, are aware of our social and environmental responsibilities towards society and future generations. Our objective is to be a leading company in the Turkish finance sector by conducting our activities in accordance with a sound environmental policy.

We recognize that our operations have a direct or indirect effect on the local, regional and global environment. In this respect, we have developed our Social and Environmental Management System (SEMS). We will consider a systematic and consistent approach to reduce the social and environmental impacts of our activities.

We are committed to environmental protection and sustainable development objectives. Encouraging other institutions to pursue environmental protection and pollution prevention through our lending programmes, we will integrate and implement environmental considerations into all aspects of our operations and business decisions

We know that an integral element in the achievement of our SEMS is building awareness, acceptance and support of all employees, customers, shareholders and government institutions. We will communicate our environmental policy to all related parties through guidelines and internet. We will include environmental issues in training programmes and ensure that this policy is understood and implemented by the employees at all levels.

We will integrate environmental considerations as a part of our purchasing policy. We will work with selected suppliers to ensure that they recognize and reduce the adverse environmental effects of their products and services.

We are determined to comply with relevant national regulations and legislation on environment, health, safety and social issues, together with IFC Exclusion List and IFC Performance Standards; and monitor the effectiveness of our SEMS on a regular basis. We will regularly review our environmental policy and our performance in complying with all applicable laws and regulations. We will meet and, when possible, try to exceed the standards of relevant legislation. In cases where no regulations exist, we shall set our own standards to minimize any adverse environmental effect caused as a result of our activities or operations.

Social responsibility is and always will be of particular concern to Finansbank, as is demonstrated by our sponsorship for various foundations and organizations especially in health and education fields.

We believe that commitment to environmental and social improvement is fundamental for being a healthy society. Our Bank is going to devote undivided attention and prudence to implement and carry out this policy.

Environmental Degradation

One of the greatest challenges facing humanity is environmental degradation, including deforestation, desertification, pollution, and climate change – an issue of increasing concern for the international community. Environmental degradation increases the vulnerability of the societies it affects and contributes to the scarcity of resources.

Climate change will lead to an increase in the intensity and frequency of weather extremes, such as heat waves, floods, droughts and tropical cyclones. The people hardest hit by climate change and environmental degradation are those living in the most vulnerable areas, including coastal communities, small island nations, Sub-Saharan Africa and Asian delta regions. It is the poorest of the poor, who lack the resources to prepare, adapt and rebuild, that are most affected.

Environmental degradation can lead to a scarcity of resources, such as water and farmable.

Extreme weather events, such as severe flooding, increase the spread of waterborne diseases, such as malaria and diarrhoea.

The effects of the major environmental problems on both health and productivity are:

a. *Water Pollution and Water Scarcity:* As per the estimation of UN, more than two million deaths and billions of illnesses a year are attributable to water pollution. Water scarcity compounds these health problems. Productivity is affected by the costs of providing safe water, by constraints on economic activity caused by water shortages, and by the adverse effects of water pollution and shortages on other environmental resources such as, declining fisheries and acquifer depletion leading to irreversible compaction.

b. *Air Pollution:* As per the estimation of UN, urban air pollution is responsible for 300,000—700,000 deaths annually and creates chronic health problems for many more people. Restrictions on vehicles and industrial activity during critical periods affect productivity, as does the effect of acid rain on forests and water bodies.

c. *Solid and Hazardous Wastes:* Diseases are spread by uncollected garbage and blocked drains; the health risks from hazardous wastes are typically more localized, but often acute. Wastes affect productivity through the pollution of groundwater resources.

d. *Soil Degradation:* Depleted soils increase the risks of malnutrition for farmers. Productivity losses on tropical soils are estimated to be in the range of 0.5-1.5 per cent of GNP, while secondary productivity losses are due to siltation of reservoirs, transportation channels and other hydrologic investments.

e. *Deforestation:* Death and disease can result from the localized flooding caused by deforestation. Loss of sustainable logging potential and of erosion prevention, watershed stability and carbon sequestration provided by forests are among the productivity impacts of deforestation.

f. *Loss of Biodiversity:* The extinction of plant and animal species will potentially affect the development of new drugs; it will reduce ecosystem adaptability and lead to the loss of genetic resources.

g. *Atmospheric Changes:* Ozone depletion is responsible for perhaps 300,000 additional cases of skin cancer a year and 1.7 million cases of cataracts. Global warming may lead to increase in the risk of climatic natural disasters. Productivity impacts may include sea-rise damage to coastal investments, regional changes in agricultural productivity and disruption of the marine food chain.

Conclusion: The impact of environmental disasters can be devastating on the social, economic, and environmental systems of a country or region as well as the global ecosystem. Environmental disasters do not recognise man-made borders, and threaten the legacy left to future generations of a clean and supportive environment. Because of the interdependency of earth ecosystems international co-operation is paramount to prevent, and when disaster strikes, respond to relieve quickly and effectively the effects of environmental disasters. Thus, Governments, International organizations and communities must work together – at all levels – to lessen the risks associated with environmental degradation and its contributing factors, such as climate change, and ensure that vulnerable people are prepared to survive and adapt. At the same time, companies, organizations and individuals must also ensure that their work is environmentally friendly and sustainable.

UNIT-II

Environmental Education and Pollution

Meaning and Definition of Environmental Hazards and Pollution

Definition and Meaning

Presence of dangerous unnatural ingredients causing imbalance in the ecosystem and health hazards to human beings and animals can be called as pollution.

That is, pollution is a phenomena where natural ingredients are replaced or damaged by presence of dangerous unnatural ingredients-which have potentiality to cause imbalance to the system and to create number of health hazards to animals and human beings. Such unnatural ingredients may be gases (causing air pollution), solids / liquids (causing water, food and land pollution) or sound (causing sound pollution). All of them cause imbalance in ecosystem directly or indirectly and have potentiality to cause health hazards to human beings and animals.

Meaning

Pollution can be anything-which damages the ecosystem and destroys the delicate balance in the ecosystem. Thereby, it creates health hazards to human beings and animals besides damaging the ecosystem. For *e.g.*, industries polluting air has set imbalance in composition of air and made it unworthy to breathe-thereby causing innumerable health problems to human and animal life. Extensive use of pesticides on crops has set imbalance in ecosystems of lands besides causing drinking water pollution.

Abandon Ship Takes on New Meaning: Environmental Hazard

Officials in coastal states are worried that the high upkeep of boats in the depressed economy has mariners literally abandoning their ships in droves—a practice that could threaten the environment.

There's no official tally of cast-off boats, but an unusually high number are reportedly being dumped in waters off the coasts of Florida, South Carolina and Washington State; California is mulling a measure that would let owners surrender their vessels to the state, according to the *New York Times*. Other media reported last summer that more than 200 boats had been left in New York's Jamaica Bay. "Our waters have become dumping grounds," Major Paul Ouellette of the Florida Fish and Wildlife Conservation Commission told the *Times*. "It's got to the point where something has to be done."

The environmental hazards come from leaking oil and fuel, as well as degrading biocides, such as copper paints, that prevent barnacles and algae from attaching to the bottom of a vessel, said Miriam Gordon, California state director of the environmental group Clean Water Action. Oil and fuel contain Polycyclic Aromatic Hydrocarbons (PAHs) that can kill fish and other marine species if they spill, and copper can sink into sediment, also killing marine life.

Other problems come when a boat sinks, creating giant holes and patches in sea grass – a kind of nursery for marine life seeking food and shelter, she says. Healthy sea grass is also necessary for species that feed on fish eggs there, such as birds and ducks.

Margaret Podlich, vice president of government affairs for Boat US, an association of vessel owners based in Alexandria, Va., tells *ScientificAmerican.com* that abandoned boats are nothing new, but may be more pronounced now. "This is an old problem being exaggerated because of the economy," Podlich says. Have a boat you want to get rid of but can't sell? Give it away, Podlich says, or pay to have it properly disposed of in a landfill.

Biological Hazards, and Their Adverse Health Effects

These generally fall into two broad categories: those which produce adverse health effects through infection and those which produce adverse effects in non-infective (allergic) ways.

As regards microbiological hazards in water, substantial improvements in the health of the population have resulted historically from the supply of drinking water free from disease causing organisms such as cholera. Similar improvements can be expected in the health of the inhabitants of developing countries if microbiologically safe water is provided by avoidance of contamination, and appropriate purification including disinfection (usually by chlorination). Occasional outbreaks of waterborne infection still arise from contamination of drinking water by soiled water (usually coliforms).

There can be other opportunities for further bacteriological contamination. Thus Legionella can grow in sumps or dead legs in the plumbing system and may then be dispersed as aerosols from showers.

Recreational water which is heavily contaminated with pathogens, notably coliform bacteria has been shown to be associated with an increased risk of gastrointestinal and other infectious illness, usually self-limiting.

So-called "clinical" waste is not merely an occupational hazard of health care workers but is becoming an increasingly more important risk, for example for children finding blood stained needles.

Many allergens such as grass pollen grains, or faecal material from house dust mites may cause attacks of asthma or "hay fever" (allergic rhinitis). There is evidence that high exposure to these allergens early in life, increases the risk of suffering from asthma later on. An increasing number of studies suggest that airborne chemical pollution can act synergistically with naturally occurring allergens and result in effects on lung function at concentrations lower than those at which either the allergen or the chemical irritant on its own would have produced an adverse effect.

Conclusion

The above account demonstrates the wide range of effects that the environment may have on human health, but it is very far from exhaustive and for the sake of conciseness many hazards or their effects have not been mentioned. Moreover, the simplicity of the above has meant that very important concepts have not been discussed. These include the distinction between mere association, and causation, or the quantitative implications of understanding the difference between hazard and risk.

Finally, to keep things in perspective, we must not forgot, that as a species we are the way are because of the influence of the environment on our evolution. Problems to health arise at two levels: At the level of the individual, the environmental influences which slowly 'shape' the species may in some respect or another cause harm to some members of the species-that is how a species evolves. At the level of the species, we must remember that the process of evolution is relatively slow when compared to the rate at which man can bring about environmental change. This means that unless efforts are made to care for the environment, the human species may suffer to an extent that other species already have suffered.

- es, and Exposure Agents: Environmental Pollution (Hazards or Agents)

Environmental Pollution

Pollution : Environmental pollution is any discharge of material or energy into water, land, or air that causes or may cause acute (short-term) or chronic (long-term) detriment to the Earth's ecological balance or that lowers the quality of life. Pollutants may cause primary damage, with direct identifiable impact on the environment, or secondary damage in the form of minor perturbations in the delicate balance of the biological food web that are detectable only over long time periods.

Until relatively recently in humanity's history, where pollution has existed, it has been primarily a local problem. The industrialization of society, the introduction of motorized vehicles, and the explosion of the human population, however, have caused an exponential growth in the production of goods and services.

Coupled with this growth has been a tremendous increase in waste by-products. The indiscriminate discharge of untreated industrial and domestic wastes into waterways, the spewing of thousands of tons of particulates and airborne gases into the atmosphere, the "throwaway" attitude toward solid wastes, and the use of newly developed chemicals without considering potential consequences have resulted in major environmental disasters, including the formation of smog in the Los Angeles area since the late 1940s and the pollution of large areas of the Mediterranean Sea.

Technology has begun to solve some pollution problems (see pollution control), and public awareness of the extent of pollution will eventually force governments to undertake more effective environmental planning and adopt more effective antipollution measures.

Environmental Hazard

'Environmental hazard' is a generic term for any situation or state of events which poses a threat to the surrounding environment. This term incorporates topics like pollution and Natural Hazards such as storms and earthquakes.

I feel that this sight has no information on what I am looking for! There are five types of environmental hazards:

1. Chemical
2. Physical
3. Mechanical
4. Biological
5. Psychosocial

The term can also refer to biological hazards; a large algal bloom is an environmental hazard because it makes the lake uninhabitable for other organisms.

Types of Environmental Hazards and Disaster

Environmental Disasters by Category

Agricultural:

- Salinity in Australia
- Salinization of the Fertile Crescent
- The Dust Bowl in Canada and the United States (1934-1939)
- The Great sparrow campaign; sparrows were eliminated from Chinese farms, which caused locusts to swarm the farms and resulted in a famine which killed 38 million people.
- Africanized bees, known colloquially as "killer bees"
- Central Plains Water scheme in New Zealand
- The Osborne Reef and other similar artificial reefs made of tires
- Aral Sea mismanagement
- Dirty dairying in New Zealand
- Hedgerow removal

Biodiversity:

- Extinction of American megafauna
- Extinction of Australian megafauna
- Deforestation of Easter Island
- Destruction of the old growth forests
- Rabbits in Australia
- Red imported fire ants
- Reduction in the number of the American Bison
- Introduction of the Nile perch into Lake Victoria in Africa, decimating indigenous fish species
- The Saemangeum Seawall
- Environmental threats to the Great Barrier Reef
- 2006 Zakouma elephant slaughter
- Invasive species in New Zealand
- Ghost nets
- Grounding of SS Makambo on Lord Howe Island

Coal:

- Martin County sludge spill
- Tennessee coal sludge spill

Human health:

- Introduction of infectious diseases by Europeans causing the death of indigenous people during European colonization of the Americas
- Health effects arising from the September 11 attacks
- Goiania accident, human deaths resulting from dismantling a scrapped medical machine containing a source of radioactivity

Industrial:

- Minamata disease-mercury poisoning in Japan (1950s & 1960s)
- Ontario Minamata disease in Canada
- Itai-itai disease, due to cadmium poisoning in Japan
- Love Canal toxic waste site
- Seveso disaster (1976), chemical plant explosion, caused highest known exposure to 2,3,7,8-tetrachlorodibenzo-p-dioxin (TCDD) in residential populations
- Bhopal disaster
- Sandoz chemical spill into the Rhine river (1986)
- United States Environmental Protection Agency Superfund sites in the United States
- AZF Explosion at a Toulouse chemical factory (2001)
- 2005 Jilin chemical plant explosions
- The Sydney Tar Ponds and Coke Ovens sites in the city of Sydney, Nova Scotia, Canada, known as the largest toxic waste site in North America.
- Release of lead dust into Esperance Harbour.
- Release of cyanide, heavy metals and acid into the Alamosa River, Colorado from the Summitville mine, causing the death of all marine life within a 17 mile radius.

- Release of 20,000 gallons of lethal chemicals (metam sodium, tradename Vapam) into the Upper Sacramento River near Dunsmuir, causing the death of all marine life within a 38 mile radius.
- Release of CFC's resulting in ozone depletion
- Release of sulfer dioxide after a fire at the Al-Mishraq plant in Iraq
- The Phillips Disasters
- Villa Parisi (Brazil)
- Health issues on the Aamjiwnaang First Nation due to chemical factories
- Environmental issues with the Three Gorges Dam
- Kingston Fossil Plant coal fly ash slurry spill

Mining:

- The Ok Tedi environmental disaster in Papua New Guinea
- Collapse of a colliery waste tip in Aberfan, Wales
- Mining at Cerro de San Pedro in Mexico by Minera San Xavier
- Lead dust from the Magellan Metals mine in Australia
- Failure of a toxic waste dam at the Aznalcollar mine in Spain
- Uranium mining controversy in Kakadu National Park
- The proposed Cypress Mine in New Zealand
- The tailings dam from the now abandoned Tui mine

Oil industry:

- Environmental issues in the Niger Delta relating to the oil industry
- Lago Agrio oil field issues
- Arctic Refuge drilling controversy

Nuclear:

- Atomic bombings of Hiroshima and Nagasaki
- Chernobyl disaster
- Three Mile Island accident

- Nuclear testing at Moruroa and Fangataufa
- Windscale fire
- Fallout from the Castle Bravo nuclear test
- The health of Downwinders

Pollution:

- Proliferation of plastic shopping bags

Air:

- The Donora Smog of 1948 in Donora, Pennsylvania in the United States
- The Great Smog of 1952, which killed 4,000 Londoners
- The 1983 Melbourne dust storm
- The 1997 Southeast Asian haze
- The 2005 Malaysian haze
- The 2006 Southeast Asian haze
- Yokkaichi asthma in Japan
- Health problems due to the Jinkanpo Atsugi Incinerator in Japan
- Kuwaiti oil fires

Land:

- The Dust Bowl of Canada and the United States
- Contaminated soils in Mapua, New Zealand due to the operation of an agricultural chemicals factory
- Basin F, a disposal site in the United States for contaminated liquid wastes from the chemical manufacturing operations of the Army and its lessee Shell Chemical Company
- 2006 Cote d'Ivoire toxic waste spill
- Atari video game burial

Water:

- Selenium poisoning of wildlife due to farm runoff used to create Kesterson National Wildlife Refuge, an the artificial wetland
- The Jiyeh Power Station oil spill in the Mediterranean region

- Effects of polluted water in the Berkeley Pit in the United States
- Cheakamus River derailment which polluted a river with caustic soda
- Draining and development of the Everglades

Marine:

- The artificial Osborne Reef
- Dumping of conventional and chemical munitions in Beaufort's Dyke
- Marine debris
- Environmental threats to the Great Barrier Reef
- Nurdles
- Friendly Floatees
- The Great Pacific Garbage Patch

Natural Disaster

It is a form of tuberculosis where you die in a car and madeline kills you in the middle of the day. This understanding is concentrated in the formulation: "disasters occur when hazards meet vulnerability." A natural hazard will hence never result in a natural disaster in areas without vulnerability, *e.g.* strong earthquakes in uninhabited areas. The term *natural* has consequently been disputed because the events simply are not hazards or disasters without human involvement.

Natural Hazards

A natural hazard is a threat of an event that will have a negative effect on people or the environment. Many natural hazards are related, *e.g.* earthquakes can result in tsunamis, drought can lead directly to famine and disease. A concrete example of the division between hazard and disaster is that the 1906 San Francisco earthquake was a disaster, whereas earthquakes are a hazard. Hazards are consequently relating to a future occurrence and disasters to past or current occurrences.

Notable avalanches include:

- The 1910 Wellington avalanche

- The 1954 Blons avalanches
- The 1970 Ancash earthquake
- The 1999 Galtur Avalanche
- The 2002 Kolka-Karmadon rock ice slide

Earthquakes

An Earthquake is a sudden shaking or vibration of the Earth's crust. The vibrations may vary in magnitude. The earthquake has point of origin underground called the "focus". The point directly above the focus on the surface is called the"epicentre". Earthquakes by themselves rarely kill people or wildlife. It is usually the secondary events that they trigger, such as building collapse, fires, tsunamis and volcanoes, that are actually the human disaster. As many of these could be avoided by better construction, safety systems, early warning and evacuation planning, the term unnatural disaster *is not unwarranted.*

Earthquakes are caused by the discharge of stress accumulated along geologic faults.

Some of the most significant earthquakes in recent times include:

- The 2004 Indian Ocean earthquake, the second largest earthquake in recorded history, registering a moment magnitude of 9.3. The huge tsunamis triggered by this earthquake cost the lives of at least 229,000 people.
- The 7.6-7.7 2005 Kashmir earthquake, which cost 79,000 lives in Pakistan.
- The 7.7 magnitude July 2006 Java earthquake, which also triggered tsunamis.
- The 7.9 magnitude May 12, 2008 Sichuan earthquake in Sichuan Province, China. Death toll at over 61,150 as of May 27, 2008.

Lahars

A lahar is a volcanic mudflow or landslide. The 1953 Tangiwai disaster was caused by a lahar, as was the 1985 Armero tragedy in which the town of Armero was buried and an estimated 23,000 people were killed.

Landslides and Mudflows

These occur with some regularity in parts of California after periods of heavy rain.

Volcanic Eruptions

- An **Eruption** may in itself be a disaster due to the explosion of the volcano or the fall of rock but there are several effects that may happen after an eruption that are also hazardous to human life.
- **Lava** may be produced during the eruption of a volcano a material consisting of superheated rock. There are several different forms which may be either crumbly or gluey. Leaving the volcano this destroys any buildings and plants it encounters.
- **Volcanic ash**-generally meaning the cooled ash-may form a cloud, and settle thickly in nearby locations. When mixed with water this forms a concrete like material. In sufficient quantity ash may cause roofs to collapse under its weight but even small quantities will cause ill health if inhaled. Since the ash has the consistency of ground glass it causes abrasion damage to moving parts such as engines.
- ***Supervolcanos :*** According to the Toba catastrophe theory 70 to 75 thousand years ago a super volcanic event at Lake Toba reduced the human population to 10,000 or even 1,000 breeding pairs creating a bottleneck in human evolution. The main danger from a supervolcano is the immense cloud of ash which has a disastrous global effect on climate and temperature for many years.
- **Pyroclastic flows** consist of a cloud of hot volcanic ash which builds up in the air above a volcano until it collapses under its own weight and streams very rapidly from the mountain burning anything in its path. It is believed that Pompeii was destroyed by a pyroclastic flow.

Water Disasters

Floods: Some of the most notable floods include:

- The Huang He (Yellow River) in China floods particularly often. The Great Flood of 1931 caused between 800,000 and 4,000,000 deaths.
- The Great Flood of 1993 was one of the most costly floods in United States history.
- The 1998 Yangtze River Floods, also in China, left 14 million people homeless.
- The 2000 Mozambique flood covered much of the country for three weeks, resulting in thousands of deaths, and leaving the country devastated for years afterward.

Tropical cyclones can result in extensive flooding and storm surge, as happened with:

- Bhola Cyclone, striking East Pakistan (now Bangladesh) in 1970,
- Typhoon Nina, striking China in 1975,
- Tropical Storm Allison, which struck Houston, Texas in 2001 and
- Hurricane Katrina, which left most of New Orleans under water in 2005. Much of the flooding was due to the failure of the city's levee system.

Limnic Eruptions

A limnic eruption occurs when CO_2 suddenly erupts from deep lake water, posing the threat of suffocating wildlife, livestock and humans. Such an eruption may also cause tsunamis in the lake as the rising CO_2 displaces water. Scientists believe landslides, volcanic activity, or explosions can trigger such an eruption. To date, only two limnic eruptions have been observed and recorded:

- In 1984, in Cameroon, a limnic eruption in Lake Monoun caused the deaths of 37 nearby residents
- At nearby Lake Nyos in 1986 a much larger eruption killed between 1,700 and 1,800 people by asphyxiation.

Tsunamis

Tsunami can be caused by undersea earthquakes as the one caused in Ao Nang, Thailand by the 2004 Indian Ocean Earthquake, or by landslides such as the one which occurred at Lituya Bay, Alaska in.

- Ao Nang, Thailand (2004). The 2004 Indian Ocean Earthquake created the Boxing Day Tsunami and disaster at this site.
- Lituya Bay, Alaska (1953). See paragraph three (3) of the entry. A mega-tsunami occurred here, the largest ever recorded.
- This would also fit within Land movement category because it starts with an earthquake.

Weather Disasters

Blizzards: Significant blizzards in the United States include:

- The Great Blizzard of 1888
- The Schoolhouse Blizzard earlier the same year
- The Armistice Day Blizzard in 1940
- The Storm of the Century in 1993

Cyclonic Storms

Cyclone, tropical cyclone, hurricane, *and* typhoon *are different names for the same phenomenon a cyclonic storm system that forms over the oceans. The deadliest hurricane ever was the 1970 Bhola cyclone the deadliest Atlantic hurricane was the Great Hurricane of 1780 which devastated Martinique St. Eustatius and Barbados. Another notable hurricane is Hurricane Katrina which devastated the Gulf Coast of the United States in 2005.*

Droughts

Well-known historical droughts include:

- 1900 India killing between 250,000 and 3.25 million.
- 1921-22 Soviet Union in which over 5 million perished from starvation due to drought

- 1928-30 northwest China resulting in over 3 million deaths by famine.
- 1936 and 1941 Sichuan Province China resulting in 5 million and 2.5 million deaths respectively.
- As of 2006 Western Australia New South Wales Victoria Australia Victoria and Queensland states of Australia have been under drought conditions for five to ten years. The drought is beginning to affect urban area populations for the first time.
- In 2006 Sichuan Province China experienced its worst drought in modern times with nearly 8 million people and over 7 million cattle facing water shortages.

Hailstorms

A particularly damaging hailstorm hit Munich, Germany on August 31, 1986, felling thousands of trees and causing millions of dollars in insurance claims.

Heat Waves

The worst heat wave in recent history was the European Heat Wave of 2003.

Tornadoes

Fire: Wildfires are an uncontrolled fire burning in wildland areas. Common causes include lightning and drought but wildfires may also be started by human negligence or arson. They can be a threat to those in rural areas and also wildlife.

Health and Disease

Epidemic: An epidemic is an outbreak of a contractible disease that spreads at a rapid rate through a human population. A pandemic is an epidemic whose spread is global. There have been many epidemics throughout history, such as Black Death. In the last hundred years, significant pandemics include:

- The 1918 Spanish flu pandemic, killing an estimated 50 million people worldwide
- The 1957-58 Asian flu pandemic, which killed an estimated 1 million people

- The 1968-69 Hong Kong flu pandemic
- The 2002-3 SARS pandemic
- The AIDS epidemic, beginning in 1959

Other diseases that spread more slowly, but are still considered to be global health emergencies by the WHO include:

- XDR TB, a strain of tuberculosis that is extensively resistant to drug treatments
- Malaria, which kills an estimated 1.5 million people each year
- Ebola hemorrhagic fever, which has claimed hundreds of victims in Africa in several outbreaks

Famine

In modern times, famine has hit Sub-Saharan Africa the hardest, although the number of victims of modern famines is much smaller than the number of people killed by the Asian famines of the 20th century.

Space—Gamma Ray Bursts

Impact Events: One of the largest impact events in modern times was the Tunguska event in June, 1908.

Solar Flares

A solar flare is a phenomenon where the sun suddenly releases a great amount of solar radiation, much more than normal. Some known solar flares include:

- An X20 event on August 16, 1989
- A similar flare on April 2, 2001
- The most powerful flare ever recorded, on November 4, 2003, estimated at between X40 and X45
- The most powerful flare in the past 500 years is believed to have occurred in September 1859

Supernovae and Hypernovae

Future of Natural Disasters: The United Kingdom based charity Oxfam publicly stated that the number of people hit by climate-related disasters is expected to rise by about 50%, to reach 375 million a year by 2015.

Insurance

Natural disasters play a major role in the insurance industry, which pays for certain damages arising from hurricanes, wildfires, and other catastrophes. Large reinsurance companies are particularly involved.

Types of Pollution—Land Pollution

Land Pollution is the degradation of earth's land surfaces often caused by human activities and their misuse of land resources. It occurs when waste is not disposed properly. Haphazard disposal of urban and industrial wastes, exploitation of minerals, and improper use of soil by inadequate agricultural practices are a few factors. Urbanization and industrialisation are major causes of land pollution.

The Industrial Revolution set a series of events into motion which destroyed natural habitats and polluted the environment, causing diseases in both humans and animals.

Increased Mechanization

The increase in the concentration of population in cities, along with the internal combustion engine, led to the increased number of roads and all the infra structure that goes with them. Roads cause visual, noise, light, air and water pollution, in addition to land pollution. The visual and noise areas are obvious, however light pollution is becoming more widely recognised as a problem. From outer space, large cities can be picked out at night by the glow of their lighting, so city dwellers seldom experience total darkness.

The contribution of vehicular traffic to air pollution is dealt with in another article, but, suffice to say that sulfur dioxide, nitrogen oxide and carbon monoxide are the main culprits. Water pollution is caused by the run off from roads of oil, salt and rubber residue, which enter the water courses and may make conditions unsuitable for certain organisms to live.

As the demand for food has grown very high, there is an increase in field size and mechanization. The increase in field size makes it economically viable for the farmer but results in loss of habitat and shelter for wildlife, as hedgerows and copses disappear. When crops are harvested, the naked soil is left open to wind after the heavy machinery has compacted it. Another consequence of more intensive agriculture is the move to monoculture. This is unnatural, it depletes the soil of nutrients, allows diseases and pests to spread and, in short, brings into play the use of chemical substances foreign to the environment.

Pesticides

Herbicides: Herbicides are used to kill weeds, especially on pavements and railways. They are similar to auxins and most are biodegradable by soil bacteria. However one group derived from trinitrophenol (2:4 D and 2:4:5 T) have the impurity dioxin, which is very toxic and causes fatality even in low concentrations. It also causes spontaneous abortions, haemorrhaging and cancer. Agent Orange (50% 2:4:5 T) was used as a defoliant in Vietnam. Eleven million gallons were used and children born since then to American soldiers who served in this conflict, have shown increased physical and mental disabilities compared to the rest of the population. It affects the head of the sperm and the chromosomes inside it.

Another herbicide, much loved by murder story writers, is Paraquat. It is highly toxic but it rapidly degrades in soil due to the action of bacteria and does not kill soil fauna.

Insecticides

Insecticides are used to rid farms of pests which damage crops. The insects damage not only standing crops but also stored ones and in the tropics it is reckoned that one third of the total production is lost during food storage. As with fungicides, the first insecticides used in the nineteenth century were inorganic *e.g.* Paris Green and other compounds of arsenic. Nicotine has also been used since the late eighteenth century. There are now two main groups of synthetic insecticides-

Organochlorines

Organochlorines include DDT, Aldrin, Dieldrin and BHC. They are cheap to produce, potent and persistent. DDT was used on a massive scale from the 1930s, with a peak of 72,000 tonnes used 1970. Then usage fell as the harmful environmental effects were realized. It was found worldwide in fish and birds and was even discovered in the snow in the Antarctic. It is only slightly soluble in water but is very soluble in the bloodstream. It affects the nervous and endocrine systems and causes the eggshells of birds to lack calcium causing them to be easily breakable. It is thought to be responsible for the decline of the numbers of birds of prey like ospreys and peregrine falcons in the 1950s-they are now recovering.

As well as increased concentration via the food chain, it is known to enter via permeable membranes, so fish get it through their gills. As it has low water solubility, it tends to stay at the water surface, so organisms that live there are most affected. DDT found in fish that formed part of the human food chain caused concern, but the levels found in the liver, kidney and brain tissues was less than 1ppm and in fat was 10 ppm which was below the level likely to cause harm. However, DDT was banned in Britain and America to stop the further build up of it in the food chain. The USA exploited this ban and sold DDT to developing countries, who could not afford the expensive replacement chemicals and who did not have such stringent regulations governing the use of pesticides.

Some insects have developed a resistance to insecticides- *e.g.* the which carries malaria.

Organophosphates

Organophosphates, *e.g.* parathion, methyl parathion and about 40 other insecticides are available nationally. Parathion is highly toxic, methyl-parathion is less so and Malathion is generally considered safe as it has low toxicity and is rapidly broken down in the mammalian liver. This group works by preventing normal nerve transmission as cholinesterase is prevented from breaking down the transmitter substance acetylcholine, resulting in uncontrolled muscle movements.

Entry of a variety of pesticides into our water supplies causes concern to environmental groups, as in many cases the long term effects of these specific chemicals is not known.

Restrictions came into force in July 1985 and were so frequently broken that in 1987, formal proceedings were taken against the British government. Britain is still the only European state to use Aldrin and organochlorines, although it was supposed to stop in 1993. East Anglia has the worst record for pesticide contamination of drinking water. Of the 350 pesticides used in Britain, only 50 can be analyzed, which is worrying for the global community.

Burial

Burial is the technique used by Jews, Muslims, Christians and other religions with Abrahamic influence, to dispose off the corpse of dead humans and animals. This process leads to regular soil erosion due to loosening of soil. Also, the decomposing fluids act as poisonous herbicides, pesticides and may even lead to epidemics in surrounding areas. It leads to soil pollution, soil erosion and even water pollution.

Increased Waste Disposal

In Scotland in 1993, 14 million tons of waste was produced. 100,000 tons was special waste and 260,000 tons was controlled waste from other parts of Britain and abroad. 45% of the special waste was in liquid form and 18% was asbestos-radioactive waste was not included.

Of the controlled waste, 48% came from the demolition of buildings, 22% from industry, 17% from households and 13% from business-only 3% were recycled. 90% of controlled waste was buried in landfill sites and produced 2 million tons of methane gas. 1.5% was burned in incinerators and 1.5% were exported to be disposed of or recycled. There are 748 disposal sites in Scotland.

Landfills produce leachate, which has to be recycled to keep favourable conditions for microbial activity, methane gas and some carbon dioxide.

There are very few vacant or derelict land sites in the north east of Scotland, as there are few traditional heavy industries or coal/mineral extraction sites. However some areas are contaminated by aromatic hydrocarbons (500 cubic meters).

The Urban Waste Water Treatment Directive allows sewage sludge to be sprayed onto land and the volume is expected to double to 185,000 tons of dry solids in 2005. <!-information should be updated-> This has good agricultural properties due to the high nitrogen and phosphate content. In 1990/1991, 13% wet weight was sprayed onto 0.13% of the land, however this is expected to rise 15 fold by 2005. There is a need to control this so that pathogenic microorganisms do not get into water courses and to ensure that there is no accumulation of heavy metals in the top soil.

Air Pollution

Air pollution is the introduction of chemicals, particulate matter, or biological materials that cause harm or discomfort to humans or other living organisms, or damages the natural environment, into the atmosphere.

The atmosphere is a complex, dynamic natural gaseous system that is essential to support life on planet Earth. Stratospheric ozone depletion due to air pollution has long been recognized as a threat to human health as well as to the Earth's ecosystems.

Pollutants

An air pollutant is known as a substance in the air that can cause harm to humans and the environment. Pollutants can be in the form of solid particles, liquid droplets, or gases. In addition, they may be natural or man-made.

Pollutants can be classified as either primary or secondary. Usually, primary pollutants are substances directly emitted from a process, such as ash from a volcanic eruption, the carbon monoxide gas from a motor vehicle exhaust or sulfur dioxide released from factories.

Secondary pollutants are not emitted directly. Rather, they form in the air when primary pollutants react or interact. An important example of a secondary pollutant is ground level ozone-one of the many secondary pollutants that make up photochemical smog.

Note that some pollutants may be both primary and secondary: that is, they are both emitted directly and formed from other primary pollutants.

About 4 percent of deaths in the United States can be attributed to air pollution, according to the Environmental Science Engineering Programme at the Harvard School of Public Health.

Major primary pollutants produced by human activity include:

- Sulfur oxides (SO_x)-especially sulfur dioxide, a chemical compound with the formula SO_2. SO_2 is produced by volcanoes and in various industrial processes. Since coal and petroleum often contain sulfur compounds, their combustion generates sulfur dioxide. Further oxidation of SO_2, usually in the presence of a catalyst such as NO_2, forms H_2SO_4, and thus acid rain. This is one of the causes for concern over the environmental impact of the use of these fuels as power sources.
- Nitrogen oxides (NO_x)-especially nitrogen dioxide are emitted from high temperature combustion. Can be seen as the brown haze dome above or plume downwind of cities. Nitrogen dioxide is the chemical compound with the formula NO_2. It is one of the several nitrogen oxides. This reddish-brown toxic gas has a characteristic sharp, biting odor. NO_2 is one of the most prominent air pollutants.
- Carbon monoxide-is a colourless, odourless, non-irritating but very poisonous gas. It is a product by incomplete combustion of fuel such as natural gas, coal or wood. Vehicular exhaust is a major source of carbon monoxide.
- Carbon dioxide (CO_2)-a greenhouse gas emitted from combustion but is also a gas vital to living organisms. It is a natural gas in the atmosphere.
- Volatile organic compounds-VOCs are an important outdoor air pollutant. In this field they are often divided into the separate categories of methane (CH_4) and non-

methane (NMVOCs). Methane is an extremely efficient greenhouse gas which contributes to enhanced global warming. Other hydrocarbon VOCs are also significant greenhouse gases via their role in creating ozone and in prolonging the life of methane in the atmosphere, although the effect varies depending on local air quality. Within the NMVOCs, the aromatic compounds benzene, toluene and xylene are suspected carcinogens and may lead to leukemia through prolonged exposure. 1,3-butadiene is another dangerous compound which is often associated with industrial uses.

- Particulate matter-Particulates, alternatively referred to as particulate matter (PM) or fine particles, are tiny particles of solid or liquid suspended in a gas. In contrast, aerosol refers to particles and the gas together. Sources of particulate matter can be man made or natural. Some particulates occur naturally, originating from volcanoes, dust storms, forest and grassland fires, living vegetation, and sea spray. Human activities, such as the burning of fossil fuels in vehicles, power plants and various industrial processes also generate significant amounts of aerosols. Averaged over the globe, anthropogenic aerosols—those made by human activities—currently account for about 10 percent of the total amount of aerosols in our atmosphere. Increased levels of fine particles in the air are linked to health hazards such as heart disease, altered lung function and lung cancer.
- Toxic metals, such as lead, cadmium and copper.
- Chlorofluorocarbons (CFCs)-harmful to the ozone layer emitted from products currently banned from use.
- Ammonia (NH_3)-emitted from agricultural processes. Ammonia is a compound with the formula NH_3. It is normally encountered as a gas with a characteristic pungent odor. Ammonia contributes significantly to the nutritional needs of terrestrial organisms by serving as a precursor to foodstuffs and fertilizers. Ammonia, either directly or indirectly, is also a building block for

the synthesis of many pharmaceuticals. Although in wide use, ammonia is both caustic and hazardous.

- Odors-such as from garbage, sewage, and industrial processes
- Radioactive pollutants-produced by nuclear explosions, war explosives, and natural processes such as the radioactive decay of radon.

Secondary pollutants include:

- Particulate matter formed from gaseous primary pollutants and compounds in photochemical smog. Smog is a kind of air pollution; the word "smog" is a portmanteau of smoke and fog. Classic smog results from large amounts of coal burning in an area caused by a mixture of smoke and sulfur dioxide. Modern smog does not usually come from coal but from vehicular and industrial emissions that are acted on in the atmosphere by sunlight to form secondary pollutants that also combine with the primary emissions to form photochemical smog.
- Ground level ozone (O_3) formed from NO_x and VOCs. Ozone (O_3) is a key constituent of the troposphere (it is also an important constituent of certain regions of the stratosphere commonly known as the Ozone layer). Photochemical and chemical reactions involving it drive many of the chemical processes that occur in the atmosphere by day and by night. At abnormally high concentrations brought about by human activities (largely the combustion of fossil fuel), it is a pollutant, and a constituent of smog.
- Peroxyacetyl nitrate (PAN)-similarly formed from NO_x and VOCs.

Minor air pollutants include:

- A large number of minor hazardous air pollutants. Some of these are regulated in USA under the Clean Air Act and in Europe under the Air Framework Directive.

- A variety of persistent organic pollutants, which can attach to particulate matter.

Persistent organic pollutants (POPs) are organic compounds that are resistant to environmental degradation through chemical, biological, and photolytic processes. Because of this, they have been observed to persist in the environment, to be capable of long-range transport, bioaccumulate in human and animal tissue, biomagnify in food chains, and to have potential significant impacts on human health and the environment.

Sources

Sources of air pollution refer to the various locations, activities or factors which are responsible for the releasing of pollutants in the atmosphere. These sources can be classified into two major categories which are:

Anthropogenic sources (human activity) mostly related to burning different kinds of fuel

- "Stationary Sources" include smoke stacks of power plants, manufacturing facilities (factories) and waste incinerators, as well as furnaces and other types of fuel-burning heating devices
- "Mobile Sources" include motor vehicles, marine vessels, aircraft and the effect of sound etc.
- Chemicals, dust and controlled burn practices in agriculture and forestry management. Controlled or prescribed burning is a technique sometimes used in forest management, farming, prairie restoration or greenhouse gas abatement. Fire is a natural part of both forest and grassland ecology and controlled fire can be a tool for foresters. Controlled burning stimulates the germination of some desirable forest trees, thus renewing the forest.
- Fumes from paint, hair spray, varnish, aerosol sprays and other solvents
- Waste deposition in landfills, which generate methane. Methane is not toxic; however, it is highly flammable and may form explosive mixtures with air. Methane is

also an asphyxiant and may displace oxygen in an enclosed space. Asphyxia or suffocation may result if the oxygen concentration is reduced to below 19.5% by displacement

- Military, such as nuclear weapons, toxic gases, germ warfare and rocketry

Natural sources:

- Dust from natural sources, usually large areas of land with little or no vegetation.
- Methane, emitted by the digestion of food by animals, for example cattle.
- Radon gas from radioactive decay within the Earth's crust. Radon is a colorless, odorless, naturally occurring, radioactive noble gas that is formed from the decay of radium. It is considered to be a health hazard. Radon gas from natural sources can accumulate in buildings, especially in confined areas such as the basement and it is the second most frequent cause of lung cancer, after cigarette smoking.
- Smoke and carbon monoxide from wildfires.
- Volcanic activity, which produce sulfur, chlorine, and ash particulates.

Emission Factors

Air pollutant emission factors are representative values that attempt to relate the quantity of a pollutant released to the ambient air with an activity associated with the release of that pollutant. These factors are usually expressed as the weight of pollutant divided by a unit weight, volume, distance, or duration of the activity emitting the pollutant (*e.g.*, kilograms of particulate emitted per megagram of coal burned). Such factors facilitate estimation of emissions from various sources of air pollution. In most cases, these factors are simply averages of all available data of acceptable quality, and are generally assumed to be representative of long-term averages.

The United States Environmental Protection Agency has published a compilation of air pollutant emission factors for a multitude of industrial sources. The United Kingdom, Australia, Canada and other countries have published similar compilations, as has the European Environment Agency.

Indoor Air Quality (IAQ)

A lack of ventilation indoors concentrates air pollution where people often spend the majority of their time. Radon (Rn) gas, a carcinogen, is exuded from the Earth in certain locations and trapped inside houses. Building materials including carpeting and plywood emit formaldehyde (H_2CO) gas. Paint and solvents give off volatile organic compounds (VOCs) as they dry. Lead paint can degenerate into dust and be inhaled. Intentional air pollution is introduced with the use of air fresheners, incense, and other scented items. Controlled wood fires in stoves and fireplaces can add significant amounts of smoke particulates into the air, inside and out. Indoor pollution fatalities may be caused by using pesticides and other chemical sprays indoors without proper ventilation.

Carbon monoxide (CO) poisoning and fatalities are often caused by faulty vents and chimneys, or by the burning of charcoal indoors. Chronic carbon monoxide poisoning can result even from poorly adjusted pilot lights. Traps are built into all domestic plumbing to keep sewer gas, hydrogen sulfide, out of interiors. Clothing emits tetrachloroethylene, or other dry cleaning fluids, for days after dry cleaning.

Though its use has now been banned in many countries, the extensive use of asbestos in industrial and domestic environments in the past has left a potentially very dangerous material in many localities. Asbestosis is a chronic inflammatory medical condition affecting the tissue of the lungs. It occurs after long-term, heavy exposure to asbestos from asbestos-containing materials in structures. Sufferers have severe dyspnea (shortness of breath) and are at an increased risk regarding several different types of lung cancer. As clear explanations are not always stressed in non-technical literature, care should be taken to distinguish between several forms of relevant diseases. According to the World Health Organisation (WHO), these may defined as; asbestosis, lung cancer, *and* mesothelioma *(generally a very rare form of cancer, when more widespread it is almost always associated with prolonged exposure to asbestos).*

Biological sources of air pollution are also found indoors, as gases and airborne particulates. Pets produce dander, people produce dust from minute skin flakes and decomposed hair, dust mites in bedding, carpeting and furniture produce enzymes and micrometre-sized fecal droppings, inhabitants emit methane, mold forms in walls and generates mycotoxins and spores, air conditioning systems can incubate Legionnaires' disease and mold, and houseplants, soil and surrounding gardens can produce pollen, dust, and mold. Indoors, the lack of air circulation allows these airborne pollutants to accumulate more than they would otherwise occur in nature.

Water Pollution

Water pollution is the contamination of water bodies such as lakes, rivers, oceans, and groundwater caused by human activities, which can be harmful to organisms and plants that live in these water bodies. It occurs when pollutants are discharged directly into water bodies without treating it first.

Introduction

Water pollution is a major problem in the global context. It has been suggested that it is the leading worldwide cause of deaths and diseases, and that it accounts for the deaths of more than 14,000 people daily. In addition to the acute problems of water pollution in developing countries, industrialized countries continue to struggle with pollution problems as well. In the most recent national report on water quality in the United States, 45 percent of assessed stream miles, 47 percent of assessed lake acres, and 32 percent of assessed bay and estuarine square miles were classified as polluted.

Water is typically referred to as polluted when it is impaired by anthropogenic contaminants and either does not support a human use, like serving as drinking water, and/or undergoes a marked shift in its ability to support its constituent biotic communities, such as fish. Natural phenomena such as volcanoes, algae blooms, storms, and earthquakes also cause major changes in water quality and the ecological status of water. Water pollution has many causes and characteristics.

Water Pollution Categories

Surface water and groundwater have often been studied and managed as separate resources, although they are interrelated. Sources of surface water pollution are generally grouped into two categories based on their origin.

Point Source Pollution

Point source pollution refers to contaminants that enter a waterway through a discrete conveyance, such as a pipe or ditch. Examples of sources in this category include discharges from a sewage treatment plant, a factory, or a city storm drain. The U.S. Clean Water Act (CWA) defines point source for regulatory enforcement purposes.

Non-point Source Pollution

Non-point source (NPS) pollution refers to diffuse contamination that does not originate from a single discrete source. NPS pollution is often a cumulative effect of small amounts of contaminants gathered from a large area. Nutrient runoff in stormwater from "sheet flow" over an agricultural field or a forest are sometimes cited as examples of NPS pollution.

Contaminated stormwater washed off of parking lots, roads and highways, called urban runoff, is sometimes included under the category of NPS pollution. However, this runoff is typically channeled into storm drain systems and discharged through pipes to local surface waters, and is a point source. The CWA definition of point source was amended in 1987 to include municipal storm sewer systems, as well as industrial stormwater, such as from construction sites.

Groundwater Pollution

Interactions between groundwater and surface water are complex. Consequently, groundwater pollution, sometimes referred to as groundwater contamination, is not as easily classified as surface water pollution. By its very nature, groundwater aquifers are susceptible to contamination from sources that may not directly affect surface water bodies, and the distinction of point vs. nonpoint source may be irrelevant. A spill of a chemical contaminant on soil, located away from a surface water body, may not necessarily create point source or non-point source pollution, but nonetheless may contaminate the aquifer below. Analysis of groundwater contamination may focus on soil characteristics and hydrology, as well as the nature of the contaminant itself.

Causes of Water Pollution

The specific contaminants leading to pollution in water include a wide spectrum of chemicals, pathogens, and physical or sensory changes such as elevated temperature and discoloration. While many of the chemicals and substances that are regulated may be naturally occurring (calcium, sodium, iron, manganese, etc.) the concentration is often the key in determining what is a natural component of water, and what is a contaminant.

Oxygen-depleting substances may be natural materials, such as plant matter (*e.g.* leaves and grass) as well as man-made chemicals. Other natural and anthropogenic substances may cause turbidity (cloudiness) which blocks light and disrupts plant growth, and clogs the gills of some fish species.

Many of the chemical substances are toxic. Pathogens can produce waterborne diseases in either human or animal hosts. Alteration of water's physical chemistry include acidity (change in pH), electrical conductivity, temperature, and eutrophication. Eutrophication is the fertilization of surface water by nutrients that were previously scarce.

Pathogens

Coliform bacteria are a commonly-used bacterial indicator of water pollution, although not an actual cause of disease. Other microorganisms sometimes found in surface waters which have caused human health problems include:

- *Cryptosporidium parvum*
- *Giardia lamblia*

- *Salmonella*
- *Novovirus* and other viruses
- Parasitic worms (helminths).

High levels of pathogens may result from inadequately treated sewage discharges. This can be caused by a sewage plant designed with less than secondary treatment (more typical in less-developed countries). In developed countries, older cities with aging infrastructure may have leaky sewage collection systems (pipes, pumps, valves), which can cause sanitary sewer overflows. Some cities also have combined sewers, which may discharge untreated sewage during rain storms.

Pathogen discharges may also be caused by poorly-managed livestock operations.

Chemical and Other Contaminants

Contaminants may include organic and inorganic substances.

Organic water pollutants include:

- Detergents
- Disinfection by-products found in chemically disinfected drinking water, such as chloroform
- Food processing waste, which can include oxygen-demanding substances, fats and grease
- Insecticides and herbicides, a huge range of organohalides and other chemical compounds
- Petroleum hydrocarbons, including fuels (gasoline, diesel fuel, jet fuels, and fuel oil) and lubricants (motor oil), and fuel combustion byproducts, from stormwater runoff
- Tree and brush debris from logging operations
- Volatile organic compounds (VOCs), such as industrial solvents, from improper storage. Chlorinated solvents, which are dense non-aqueous phase liquids (DNAPLs), may fall to the bottom of reservoirs, since they don't mix well with water and are denser.
- Various chemical compounds found in personal hygiene and cosmetic products

Inorganic water pollutants include:

- Acidity caused by industrial discharges (especially sulfur dioxide from power plants)
- Ammonia from food processing waste
- Chemical waste as industrial by-products
- Fertilizers containing nutrients—nitrates and phosphates—which are found in stormwater runoff from agriculture, as well as commercial and residential use
- Heavy metals from motor vehicles (via urban stormwater runoff) and acid mine drainage
- Silt (sediment) in runoff from construction sites, logging, slash and burn practices or land clearing sites

Macroscopic pollution—large visible items polluting the water—may be termed "floatables" in an urban stormwater context, or marine debris when found on the open seas, and can include such items as:

- Trash (*e.g.* paper, plastic, or food waste) discarded by people on the ground, and that are washed by rainfall into storm drains and eventually discharged into surface waters
- Nurdles, small ubiquitous waterborne plastic pellets
- Shipwrecks, large derelict ships

Thermal Pollution

Thermal pollution is the rise or fall in the temperature of a natural body of water caused by human influence. A common cause of thermal pollution is the use of water as a coolant by power plants and industrial manufacturers. Elevated water temperatures decreases oxygen levels (which can kill fish) and affects ecosystem composition, such as invasion by new thermophilic species. Urban runoff may also elevate temperature in surface waters. Thermal pollution can also be caused by the release of very cold water from the base of reservoirs into cooler rivers.

Noise Pollution

Noise pollution (or **environmental noise**) is displeasing human-, animal-or machine-created sound that disrupts the activity or balance of human or animal life. A common form of noise pollution is from **transportation**, principally motor vehicles. The word *noise* comes from the Latin word *nausea* meaning seasickness.

The source of most noise worldwide is transportation systems, motor vehicle noise, but also including aircraft noise and rail noise. Poor urban planning may give rise to noise pollution, since side-by-side industrial and residential buildings can result in noise pollution in the residential area.

Other sources are car alarms, office equipment, factory machinery, construction work, groundskeeping equipment, barking dogs, appliances, power tools, lighting hum, audio entertainment systems, loudspeakers and noisy people.

Human Health Effects

Noise health effects are both health and behavioural in nature. The unwanted sound is called noise. This unwanted sound can damage physiological and psychological health. Noise pollution can cause annoyance and aggression, hypertension, high stress levels, tinnitus, hearing loss, sleep disturbances, and other harmful effects. Furthermore, stress and hypertension are the leading causes to health problems, whereas tinnitus can lead to forgetfulness, severe depression and at times panic attacks.

Chronic exposure to noise may cause noise-induced hearing loss. Older males exposed to significant occupational noise demonstrate significantly reduced hearing sensitivity than their non-exposed peers, though differences in hearing sensitivity decrease with time and the two groups are indistinguishable by age 79. A comparison of Maaban tribesmen, who were insignificantly exposed to transportation or industrial noise, to a typical U.S. population showed that chronic exposure to moderately high levels of environmental noise contributes to hearing loss.

High noise levels can contribute to cardiovascular effects and exposure to moderately high levels during a single eight hour period causes a statistical rise in blood pressure of five to ten points and an increase in stress and vasoconstriction leading to the increased blood pressure noted above as well as to increased incidence of coronary artery disease.

Noise pollution is also a cause of annoyance. A 2005 study by Spanish researchers found that in urban areas households are willing to pay approximately four Euros per decibel per year for noise reduction.

Environmental Effects

Noise can have a detrimental effect on animals by causing stress, increasing risk of mortality by changing the delicate balance in predator/prey detection and avoidance, and by interfering with their use of sounds in communication especially in relation to reproduction and in navigation. Acoustic overexposure can lead to temporary or permanent loss of hearing.

An impact of noise on animal life is the reduction of usable habitat that noisy areas may cause, which in the case of endangered species may be part of the path to extinction. One of the best known cases of damage caused by noise pollution is the death of certain species of beached whales, brought on by the loud sound of military sonar.

Noise also makes species communicate louder, which is called Lombard vocal response. Scientists and researchers have conducted experiments that show whales' song length is longer when submarine-detectors are on. If creatures don't "speak" loud enough, their voice will be masked by anthropogenic sounds. These unheard voices might be warnings, finding of prey, or preparations of net-bubbling. When one species begins speaking louder, it will mask other species' voice, causing the whole ecosystem to eventually speak louder.

European Robins living in urban environments are more likely to sing at night in places with high levels of noise pollution during the day, suggesting that they sing at night because it is quieter, and their message can propagate through the environment more clearly. Interestingly, the same study showed that daytime noise was a stronger predictor of nocturnal singing than night-time Light pollution, to which the phenomenon is often attributed.

Zebra finches become less faithful to their partners when exposed to traffic noise. This could alter a population's evolutionary trajectory by selecting traits, sapping resources normally devoted to other activities and thus lead to profound genetic and evolutionary consequences.

Mitigation and Control of Noise

Technology to mitigate or remove noise can be applied as follows:

> *There are a variety of strategies for mitigating roadway noise including: use of noise barriers, limitation of vehicle speeds, alteration of roadway surface texture, limitation of heavy vehicles, use of traffic controls that smooth vehicle flow to reduce braking and acceleration, and tire design. An important factor in applying these strategies is a computer model for roadway noise, that is capable of addressing local topography, meteorology, traffic operations and hypothetical mitigation. Costs of building-in mitigation can be modest, provided these solutions are sought in the planning stage of a roadway project.*

Aircraft noise can be reduced to some extent by design of quieter jet engines, which was pursued vigorously in the 1970s and 1980s. This strategy has brought limited but noticeable reduction of urban sound levels. Reconsideration of operations, such as altering flight paths and time of day runway use, have demonstrated benefits for residential populations near airports. FAA sponsored residential retrofit (insulation) programmes initiated in the 1970s has also enjoyed success in reducing interior residential noise in thousands of residences across the United States.

Exposure of workers to Industrial noise has been addressed since the 1930s. Changes include redesign of industrial equipment, shock mounting assemblies and physical barriers in the workplace.

Noise Free America, a national anti-noise pollution organization, regularly lobbies for the enforcement of noise ordinances at all levels of government.

Legal Status

Governments up until the 1970s viewed noise as a "nuisance" rather than an environmental problem. In the United States there are federal standards for highway and aircraft noise; states and local governments typically have very specific statutes on building codes, urban planning and roadway development. In Canada and the EU there are few national, provincial, or state laws that protect against noise.

Noise laws and ordinances vary widely among municipalities and indeed do not even exist in some cities. An ordinance may contain a general prohibition against making noise that is a nuisance, or it may set out specific guidelines for the level of noise allowable at certain times of the day and for certain activities.

Dr. Paul Herman wrote the first comprehensive noise codes in 1975 for Portland, Oregon with funding from the EPA (Environmental Protection Agency) and HUD (Housing and Urban Development). The Portland Noise Code became the basis for most other ordinances for major US and Canadian metropolitan regions.

Most city ordinances prohibit sound above a threshold intensity from trespassing over property line at night, typically between 10 p.m. and 6 a.m., and during the day restricts it to a higher sound level; however, enforcement is uneven. Many municipalities do not follow up on complaints. Even where a municipality has an enforcement office, it may only be willing to issue warnings, since taking offenders to court is expensive.

The notable exception to this rule is the City of Portland Oregon which has instituted an aggressive protection for its citizens with fines reaching as high at $5000 per infraction, with the ability to cite a responsible noise violator multiple times in a single day.

Many conflicts over noise pollution are handled by negotiation between the emitter and the receiver. Escalation procedures vary by country, and may include action in conjunction with local authorities, in particular the police. Noise pollution often persists because only five to ten percent of people affected by noise will lodge a formal complaint. Many people are not aware of their legal right to quiet and do not know how to register a complaint.

Radiation

Surface waters are a powerful factor that causes migration of radionuclides across the territory of Belarus. For this reason it is essential to take into due account the transit role of rivers in the transportation of radionuclides, including transboundary transfer. In watercourses and flowing water bodies concentration of radionuclides are reducing every year, but they tend to accumulate in sttatic water bodies (lakes, ponds, reservoirs, especially in bottom sediments).

Due to the accident at the Chernobyl nuclear power station (CNPS) one quarter of the country's territory was contaminated by caesium-137 (23%), strontium-90 (10%) and plutonium (about 2 %).

According to the monitoring data the radiation situation in the Dnieper-Sozh and Pripyat basins is stable. The annual average concentration of caesium-137 has decreased significantly in large and small rivers for the observed 1987-2000 period. Exceeding of the National permissible levels (NPL-96, 99) for caesium-137 and strontium-90 were not observed. However, caesium-137 concentration in surface waters are closely connected with the annual volume of river flow, as can be seen from the increase in concentrations of caesium-137 in some rivers, where water supply was lower than the perennial average values.

The data analysis of concentration of caesium-137 during the spring flood in the Pripyat basin in 1999 shows that concentration of caesium-137 in a dissolved form in the Pripyat basin (the city of Mozyr) remains at the level of the average indices for the prior period (1996-1998). Yet concentration of this radionuclide has considerably increased in dredges. This means that caesium-137 is washed out and transported by flood flow with sediments.

According to the measurements of the total radioactivity of caesium-137, transferred by rivers during 12 years (1987-1999), 85% were transferred by the Ipyt during 2 years, 81% by the Sozh during 3 years, the Besed during 4 years, the Pripyat during 6 years, and 71% by the Dnieper during 9 years. The comparison between the indices of caesium-137 transfer for the period of 1987-1993 at the end-point monitoring checkpoints on the Dnieper and the Pripyat in the Ukraine and at the monitoring checkpoints in Belarus shows that only 26% of the total transfer of radioactive caesium-137 were generated within the 30-kilometer Chernobyl zone. Thus, in the river runoff formation large watersheds had greater impact on secondary river pollution within the first few years (3-4 years) after the Chernobyl accident than surface river runoff from highly contaminated territories with relatively small watersheds.

Since the radiation situation has stabilized, transboundary transport of radioactive elements through river flow has significantly decreased. Mainly it is the Pripyat that transports radionuclides, in particular strontium-90, as they are washed out from the 30-kilometer Chernobyl zone.

Due attention is devoted to studies of the radiation state of small rivers, which are tributaries of the Pripyat (the Braginka, Nesvich and Slovechna Rivers) and the Sozh (the Lipa and the Senna) in the most contaminated areas of the Gomel and Mogilev regions. Over the years radioactivity in water tends to decrease. The exception is the dissolved strontium-90, which is a specific feature for the CNPS zone.

Annual data on the content of caesium-137 and strontium-90 (in soluble and suspended forms) in the bottom sediments and water biota suggest that bottom sediments and water biota are significant contributors to the total radioactivity of surface water systems. A tendency towards a reduction in radioactivity of bottom sediments and water biota is minor.

During spring high water and summer-autumn flood, migration of radionuclides into open water systems occurs both in soluble and in absorbed forms on organic and mineral carrieres.

The ratio between concentrations of caesium-137 and strontium-90 at the end checkpoints of the Braginka and Senna Rivers suggests that starting from1992-1993, the concentration of strontium-90 has begun to exceed that of caesium-137. That phenomenon is characteristic for surface watercourses close to the CNPS zone and is explained by an increase in migration ability of strontium-90 due to its release from active particles.

Greenhouse Effect

The earth's climate is fueled by the sun. Most of the sun's energy, called solar radiation, is absorbed by the earth, but some is reflected back into space. Clouds and a natural layer of atmospheric gases absorb a portion of earth's heat and prevent it from escaping into space. This keeps our planet warm enough for life and is known as the natural **"greenhouse effect"**. Without the natural greenhouse effect, the earth's average temperature would be much colder, and the planet would be uninhabitable. Scientific evidence shows that the greenhouse effect is being increased by the release of certain gases into the atmosphere that cause the earth's temperature to rise. This is called **"global warming**." Carbon dioxide, methane, particulate matter (especially black carbon or soot), nitrous oxide, fluorinated compounds, and ozone are some of the compounds contributing to global warming. Carbon dioxide accounts for about 81 percent of greenhouse gases released in the United States. Carbon dioxide emissions are largely due to the combustion of fossil fuels in electric power generation, motor vehicles, and industries. Methane emissions, which result from agricultural activities, landfills, and other sources, are the next largest contributors to greenhouse gas emissions in the United States and worldwide.

Continued emissions of greenhouse gases could cause a 2.5° to 10° Fahrenheit rise in temperature by the year 2100. This could lead to more extreme weather events such as droughts and floods, threaten coastal resources and wetlands by raising the sea level, and increase the risk of certain diseases by producing new breeding sites for pests and pathogens. Agricultural regions and woodlands are also susceptible to changes in climate that could result in increased insect populations and plant disease. This degradation of natural ecosystems could lead to reduced biological diversity.

Ozone Layer Depletion

Ozone depletion describes two distinct, but related observations: a slow, steady decline of about 4 percent per decade in the total volume of ozone in Earth's stratosphere (ozone layer) since the late 1970s, and a much larger, but seasonal, decrease in stratospheric ozone over Earth's polar regions during the same period. The latter phenomenon is commonly referred to as the **ozone hole**. In addition to this well-known stratospheric ozone depletion, there are also tropospheric ozone depletion events, which occur near the surface in polar regions during spring.

The detailed mechanism by which the polar ozone holes form is different from that for the mid-latitude thinning, but the most important process in both trends is catalytic destruction of ozone by atomic chlorine and bromine. The main source of these halogen atoms in the stratosphere is photodissociation of chlorofluorocarbon (CFC) compounds, commonly called freons, and of bromofluorocarbon compounds known as halons. These compounds are transported into the stratosphere after being emitted at the surface. Both ozone depletion mechanisms strengthened as emissions of CFCs and halons increased.

CFCs and other contributory substances are commonly referred to as **ozone-depleting substances (ODS)**. Since the ozone layer prevents most harmful UVB wavelengths (270–315 nm) of ultraviolet light (UV light) from passing through the Earth's atmosphere, observed and projected decreases in ozone have generated worldwide concern leading to adoption of the Montreal Protocol banning the production of CFCs and halons as well as related ozone depleting chemicals such as carbon tetrachloride and trichloroethane. It is suspected that a variety of biological consequences such as increases in skin cancer, damage to plants, and reduction of plankton populations in the ocean's photic zone may result from the increased UV exposure due to ozone depletion.

Ozone Cycle Overview

Three forms (or allotropes) of oxygen are involved in the ozone-oxygen cycle: oxygen atoms (O or atomic oxygen), oxygen gas (O_2 or diatomic oxygen), and ozone gas (O_3 or triatomic oxygen). Ozone is formed in the stratosphere when oxygen molecules photodissociate after absorbing an ultraviolet photon whose wavelength is shorter than 240 nm. This produces two oxygen atoms. The atomic oxygen then combines with O_2 to create O_3. Ozone molecules absorb UV light between 310 and 200 nm, following which ozone splits into a molecule of O_2 and an oxygen atom. The oxygen atom then joins up with an oxygen molecule to regenerate ozone. This is a continuing process which terminates when an oxygen atom "recombines" with an ozone molecule to make two O_2 molecules: O + O_3'! 2 O_2

The overall amount of ozone in the stratosphere is determined by a balance between photochemical production and recombination.

Ozone can be destroyed by a number of free radical catalysts, the most important of which are the hydroxyl radical (OH·), the nitric oxide radical (NO·) and atomic chlorine (Cl·) and bromine (Br·). All of these have both natural and anthropogenic (manmade) sources; at the present time, most of the OH· and NO· in the stratosphere is of natural origin, but human activity has dramatically increased the levels of chlorine and bromine. These elements are found in certain stable organic compounds, especially chlorofluorocarbons (CFCs), which may find their way to the stratosphere without being destroyed in the troposphere due to their low reactivity. Once in the stratosphere, the Cl and Br atoms are liberated from the parent compounds by the action of ultraviolet light, *e.g.* ('h' is Planck's constant, 'i' is frequency of electromagnetic radiation)

$CFCl_3$ + hi'! $CFCl_2$ + Cl

The Cl and Br atoms can then destroy ozone molecules through a variety of catalytic cycles. In the simplest example of such a cycle, a chlorine atom reacts with an ozone molecule, taking an oxygen atom with it (forming ClO) and leaving a normal oxygen molecule. The chlorine monoxide (*i.e.*, the ClO) can react with a second molecule of ozone (*i.e.*, O_3) to yield another chlorine atom and two molecules of oxygen. The chemical shorthand for these gas-phase reactions is:

$Cl + O_3$'! $ClO + O_2$

$ClO + O_3$'! $Cl + 2\ O_2$

The overall effect is a decrease in the amount of ozone. More complicated mechanisms have been discovered that lead to ozone destruction in the lower stratosphere as well.

A single chlorine atom would keep on destroying ozone (thus a catalyst) for up to two years (the time scale for transport back down to the troposphere) were it not for reactions that remove them from this cycle by forming reservoir species such as hydrogen chloride (HCl) and chlorine nitrate ($ClONO_2$). On a per atom basis, bromine is even more efficient than chlorine at destroying ozone, but there is much less bromine in the atmosphere at present. As a result, both chlorine and bromine contribute significantly to the overall ozone depletion. Laboratory studies have shown that fluorine and iodine atoms participate in analogous catalytic cycles.

However, in the Earth's stratosphere, fluorine atoms react rapidly with water and methane to form strongly-bound HF, while organic molecules which contain iodine react so rapidly in the lower atmosphere that they do not reach the stratosphere in significant quantities. Furthermore, a single chlorine atom is able to react with 100,000 ozone molecules. This fact plus the amount of chlorine released into the atmosphere by chlorofluorocarbons (CFCs) yearly demonstrates how dangerous CFCs are to the environment.

Quantitative Understanding of the Chemical Ozone Loss Process

New research on the breakdown of a key molecule in these ozone-depleting chemicals, dichlorine peroxide (Cl_2O_2), calls into question the completeness of present atmospheric models of polar ozone depletion. Specifically, chemists at NASA's Jet Propulsion Laboratory in Pasadena, California, found in 2007 that the temperatures, and the spectrum and intensity of radiation present in the stratosphere created conditions insufficient to allow the rate of chemical-breakdown required to release chlorine radicals in the volume necessary to explain observed rates of ozone depletion.

Instead, laboratory tests, designed to be the most accurate reflection of stratospheric conditions to date, showed the decay of the crucial molecule almost a magnitude lower than previously thought.

UNIT-III

Environmental Management and Protection

Environmental Management

Environmental management is not, as the phrase could suggest, the management of the *environment* as such, but rather the management of interaction by the modern human societies with, and impact upon the environment. The three main issues that affect managers are those involving politics (networking), programmes (projects), and resources (money, facilities, etc.). The need for environmental management can be viewed from a variety of perspectives. A more common philosophy and impetus behind environmental management is the concept of carrying capacity. Simply put, carrying capacity refers to the maximum number of organisms a particular resource can sustain. The concept of carrying capacity, whilst understood by many cultures over history, has its roots in Malthusian theory. Environmental management is therefore not the conservation of the environment solely for the environment's sake, but rather the conservation of the environment for humankind's sake. This element of sustainable exploitation, getting the most out of natural assets, is visible in the EU Water Framework Directive.

Environmental management involves the management of all components of the bio-physical environment, both living (biotic) and non-living (abiotic). This is due to the interconnected and network of relationships amongst all living species and their habitats. The environment also involves the relationships of the human environment, such as the social, cultural and economic environment with the bio-physical environment.

As with all management functions, effective management tools, standards and systems are required. An 'environmental management standard or system or protocol attempts to reduce environmental impact as measured by some objective criteria. The ISO 14001 standard is the most widely used standard for environmental risk management and is closely aligned to the European Eco-Management and Audit Scheme (EMAS). As a common auditing standard, the ISO 19011 standard explains how to combine this with quality management.

Other environmental management systems (EMS) tend to be based on the ISO 14001 standard and many extend it in various ways:

- The Green Dragon Environmental Management Standard is a five level EMS designed for smaller organisations for whom ISO 14001 may be too onerous and for larger organisations who wish to implement ISO 14001 in a more manageable step-by-step approach
- BS 8555 is a phased standard that can help smaller companies move to ISO 14001 in six manageable steps
- The Natural Step focuses on basic sustainability criteria and helps focus engineering on reducing use of materials or energy use that is unsustainable in the long term
- Natural Capitalism advises using accounting reform and a general biomimicry and industrial ecology approach to do the same thing
- US Environmental Protection Agency has many further terms and standards that it defines as appropriate to large-scale EMS.
- The UN and World Bank has encouraged adopting a "natural capital" measurement and management framework.
- The European Union Eco-Management and Audit Scheme (EMAS)

Other strategies exist that rely on making simple distinctions rather than building top-down management "systems" using performance audits and full cost accounting. For instance, Ecological Intelligent Design divides products into consumables, service products or durables and unsaleables-toxic products that no one should buy, or in many cases, do not realize they are buying. By eliminating the unsaleables from the comprehensive outcome of any purchase, better environmental management is achieved without "systems".

"Today's businesses must comply with many Federal, State and local environmental laws, rules, and regulations. It's vital to safeguard your company against compliance shortcuts. This approach leaves you vulnerable to violations of the law, in addition to missing important environmental liabilities. "Who Needs Environmental Management?

All businesses need a sound environmental policy, and effective implementation. Certain business sectors and activities have been mandated to have effective environmental management practices, limits on emissions, prevention, and emergency response systems.

World-wide as of April 2005, 88,800 organizations have achieved compliance and registration to the ISO 14001 environmental management standard. Japan has the most registrations, followed by China. USA is ranked 6th, and Canada is 12th.

The number of ISO 14001 registrations per $ GDP or population are interesting statistics. In 2001, the USA had one registration per 200,000 people or one per $6000 million of gross domestic product (GDP). This compares to one registration per 23,000 people in Japan and one registration per $900 million of GDP in the United Kingdom. For Canada as of August 1999, it is 34th in the world in terms of ISO 14001 certifications per unit of GDP, behind all major competitors, and behind such countries as Korea, Thailand, Brazil and Mexico. Clearly, North America is lagging behind the rest of the world in adopting ISO 14001.

EMAS, the European environmental standard, has achieved similar recognition and adoption. The rate of growth in ISO 14001 registrations has been exponential since its start in Dec. 1995.

Individuals also need awareness and limits on their polluting behaviours that affect others.

Need for Environmental Management

Environmental management is not, as the phrase could suggest, the management of the *environment* as such, but rather the management of interaction by the modern human societies with, and impact upon the environment. The three main issues that affect managers are those involving politics (networking), programmes (projects), and resources (money, facilities, etc.). The need for environmental management can be viewed from a variety of perspectives. A more common philosophy and impetus behind environmental management is the concept of carrying capacity. Simply put, carrying capacity refers to the maximum number of organisms a particular resource can sustain. The concept of carrying capacity, whilst understood by many cultures over history, has its roots in Malthusian theory. Environmental management is therefore not the conservation of the environment solely for the environment's sake, but rather the conservation of the environment for humankind's sake. This element of sustainable exploitation, getting the most out of natural assets, is visible in the EU Water Framework Directive.

Function and Characteristics of Environment Management

Environmental management involves the management of all components of the bio-physical environment, both living (biotic) and non-living (abiotic). This is due to the interconnected and network of relationships amongst all living species and their habitats. The environment also involves the relationships of the human environment, such as the social, cultural and economic environment with the bio-physical environment.

As with all management functions, effective management tools, standards and systems are required. An 'environmental management standard or system or protocol attempts to reduce environmental impact as measured by some objective criteria. The ISO 14001 standard is the most widely used standard for environmental risk management and is closely aligned to the European Eco-Management and Audit Scheme (EMAS). As a common auditing standard, the ISO 19011 standard explains how to combine this with quality management.

Other environmental management systems (EMS) tend to be based on the ISO 14001 standard and many extend it in various ways:

- The Green Dragon Environmental Management Standard is a five level EMS designed for smaller organisations for whom ISO 14001 may be too onerous and for larger organisations who wish to implement ISO 14001 in a more manageable step-by-step approach
- BS 8555 is a phased standard that can help smaller companies move to ISO 14001 in six manageable steps
- The Natural Step focuses on basic sustainability criteria and helps focus engineering on reducing use of materials or energy use that is unsustainable in the long term
- Natural Capitalism advises using accounting reform and a general biomimicry and industrial ecology approach to do the same thing
- US Environmental Protection Agency has many further terms and standards that it defines as appropriate to large-scale EMS.
- The UN and World Bank has encouraged adopting a "natural capital" measurement and management framework.
- The European Union Eco-Management and Audit Scheme (EMAS)

Other strategies exist that rely on making simple distinctions rather than building top-down management "systems" using performance audits and full cost accounting. For instance, Ecological Intelligent Design divides products into consumables, service products or durables and unsaleables-toxic products that no one should buy, or in many cases, do not realize they are buying. By eliminating the unsaleables from the comprehensive outcome of any purchase, better environmental management is achieved without "systems".

Recent successful cases have put forward the notion of "Integrated Management". It shares a wider approach and stresses out the importance of interdisciplinary assesment. It is an interesting notion that might not be adaptable to all cases·

"Today's businesses must comply with many Federal, State and local environmental laws, rules, and regulations. It's vital to safeguard your company against compliance shortcuts. This approach leaves you vulnerable to violations of the law, in addition to missing important environmental liabilities."

Dimensions of Environment Management

A fruitful approach to studying environmental management is the analysis of industry-government relationships. Policy is defined and translated into action in this context. We find that industrial managers legitimize government regulation of industrial water use. However, the pattern of responses suggests that some of the support may be based on economic self-interest and industry's ability to control agency action. Managers legitimize a policy-setting role for federal agencies and an enforcement role for local and state government. Across the Asian region, natural resource exploitation is accelerating dramatically as countries, cities and small communities are ever more incorporated into the global economy.

Economic reform programmes that favour domestic and global market expansion rather than a social welfare agenda, policy responses to climate change, pressures associated with population growth and intensified geographical mobility, and urbanization and commoditization, are reconfiguring patterns of natural resource use and governance at both a national and local level and are having complex effects on peoples' lives. These processes are themselves not innocent of gendered power relations: they are inflected with gender discourses that set in motion differentiated and unjust life opportunities and exclusions.

At the same time, sustainable development policy initiatives that seek to ameliorate environmental degradation and its negative livelihood effects not only bring gendered impacts and responses, they also work through and produce particular framings of gender and gendered power relations. The impact of this is apparent in the unintended consequences associated with sustainable development initiatives that target women as a homogeneous and undifferentiated social category, at times exacerbating social and gender injustices. Related to this process of globalized marketization, natural resource management is embedded in the increasing diversification of livelihoods: a process buoyed by policies that support entrepreneurialism and appear to be producing individualized portfolio livelihood strategies across Asia.

Factors Responsible for Flora and Fauna Extinction

Forest Restoration and Afforestation

Forest restoration and forest growing (afforestation) are two most active forms of the forest industry impact on biological and landscape diversity:

- forest restoration is the afforestation of those areas where forest was destroyed by felling or certain catastrophic events on forest ecosystems (fires, hurricanes, etc);
- forest growing is the formation of new forests in the territories that were not previously covered with forest. In the Dnipro Basin, new forests are most commonly grown on the lands transferred into the forest reserve after field development of mineral resources (peat, some construction materials like sand, gravel, etc) or on agricultural land plots with unproductive and eroded soil.

Forest restoration is planting or, more rarely, sowing forest species or stimulating natural growth of such species in wood-cutting areas subject to final or sanitary felling or in fire-sites. Forest growing is, as a rule, associated with forest species production.

Forest species production in the basin embraces 35-40 thousand hectares, having reduced over the latest decades due to the reduced scales of final felling. However, the reduction has not been as considerable as it could have been, as the major part of land transferred into forest reserve has been represented by low-fertility agricultural land, exhausted peatlands, etc.

In the course of forest reconstruction (recovery) a new forest community is formed by planting (sowing) desired forest species, which, at the stage of soil preparation, is accompanied with breaking the continuum of the surface soil layers, ground spreading and forest grass cover. The natural successions of forest-free area are ruptured and replaced with forest successions.

Other potential impacts on flora and fauna include: application of chemicals (herbicides, insecticides, fertilizers); introduction of alien species, sometimes even formation of pestholes and nests of diseases hazardous for surrounding forests in the places of species production.

Forest restoration and afforestation have both positive and adverse impact on biological and landscape diversity.

Thus, the formation of forest species is characterized by the following processes:

- populations of non-forest species developed on the land plots allocated for afforestation are either destroyed, ousted or suppressed;
- new communities are formed, as a rule, with the genetic material non-indigenous for the area and, therefore, having a lower adaptability, which conditions a low stability of the new forest stand;
- species of the newly-formed forest stand are of the same age, which is seldom the case in natural forest communities;
- the newly-created forest stands frequently have a homogeneous species and spatial composition, thus stands of similar composition prevail in the total mass of produced forest species;
- when soils are prepared for planting new forests, the structure of their layers and ground litter is disturbed, forest restoration can also entail damaging the populations of forest species having preserved in wood-cutting areas;

- conditions for the introduction of coenotically aggressive (invasive) non-forest species are created on mineralized soils;
- soils become more susceptible to water erosion;
- the natural dynamics of restoring or forming forest communities is interrupted and substituted with the artificial one, resulting in the termination of natural lifecycle of some succession-participating species;
- the populations of species characteristic of non-forest stages of vegetation dynamics are destroyed, ousted or suppressed;
- when new forests are formed with the introduced tree species, certain species whose gene pool is alien to the aboriginal biota may be implanted;
- the application of herbicides, insecticides, silvicides and fertilizers leads to habitat contamination with foreign substances of anthropogenic origin, sometimes threatening to the local species diversity;
- pestholes and disease nidi dangerous for the surrounding forest ecosystems sometimes germinate in the places where new forests are planted.

At the same time, forest restoration and forest growing (afforestation):

- allow to restore or create forest ecosystems in previously forestless territories much faster than in natural successions;
- ensure fast recovery and development of forest habitats stimulating the return and expansion of species belonging to forest biota complexes;
- facilitate the restoration of forest vegetation complexes and their growth (in the case of forest growing), as well as the enlargement of the area of forest biotopes;
- provide varied micro-conditions inside forest ecosystems favorable for the formation of forest biocoenoses *(habitats)* with diverse fauna and flora;
- lead to breaking the ploughed sub-soil layers hardened

by perennial agricultural use and precluding the growth of trees and coenoses (*communities)* of soil organisms;

- stimulate accelerated recovery and emerging in the landscape composition of the elements representing early stages of forest successive dynamics (natural and planted undergrowth) with innate complexes of plant and animal species;
- increases the biotope diversity on previously forestless lands;
- sometimes nurtures the improvement of feeding reserves for phytophagans.

Measures to Conserve Flora and Fauna

Global warming and climate change has become a global issues and concern within the regional and international levels. In the context of national scope, this issues had grew stronger after Indonesia had been selected to become host of the 13th Conference of the Party to the United Nation Framework Convention on Climate Change (UNFCCC COP 13). The venue took place in Denpasar, Bali. Our earth has already experienced the phenomena of global warming and climate change which leads to hazardous climate events. The Inter-governmental Panel on Climate Change (IPCC) has released numbers of research which has proved that the earth are warming and climate are changing. The IPCC is an independent scientific body under the UNFCCC.

The phenomena of hazardous climate events has an enormous impact to the environment and human livelihood. Global warming and unpattern climate changes threatened farming for food security, clean water availability, human and ecosystem health. Global warming also threatened the existence of small island nations because of the rising of sea level. Eventhough climate changes has become global issue, but there are still many communities around the world who has not known and understand what is global warming and climate changes. Many of us living in developing countries are limited to information on global warming and climate changes. For many developing countries like Indonesia, efforts to develop public awareness on global warming and climate changes are urgently needed in order to enhance public understanding on the issues. In the efforts of spreading awareness on global warming and climate change, Peka Indonesia collaborating with IISES and TMII conducted one day seminar on global warming and climate change. The seminar was conducted on January 22nd 2007 in Indonesian Miniature Garden, Jakarta with seminar theme Conservation of Flora and Fauna in the middle of changing climate and global warming The aim of this one day seminar is to spread out informations on global warming and climate change to the public especially for the staffs of Indonesian Miniature Garden. Participants will received informations on the effect of global warming to the existence of biodiversity, how we can contribute to minimize carbon emission, and how we can actively involve in the conservation of our nature environment.

Thus we can minimize the effects of global warming. On this one day seminar,.we invited Dr. Sony Keraf (former minister of environment) as a key note speaker. Dr Keraf gave presentation on the science of global warming and climate change and efforts initiate by countries in the world to adapt to climate change. We also invited 5 other speaker to give prensentation on this seminar, they are, Dr. Suryo Wiyon (Department of Agriculture, IPB), Kuswandono (Gede Pangrango National Park), Dr. Rosicon Ubaidilah (Indonesian Institute of Science), and Arif (Pelangi Foundation). These five speaker gave presentations on the topic of global warming and its effect to the earth environment, effect of global warming to flora and fauna, socializing the result of UNFCCC Bali 2007, and opportunity for public involvement to reduce the effect of global warming. The seminar was attended by 150 participant, mostly from staffs of Indonesian Miniature Garden and several from public in general. We sees that forum-forum seminar like this are still needed in order to spread out the information on global warming and climate change. We envision that through good understanding, the public will increase their awareness toward global warming and will initiate an action to contribute on reducing carbon emission, thus minimalizing the hazardous effects of global warming and climate change.

UNIT-IV

India and Environmental Issues and Policies

Environmental Problems in India

Economic Magic, Environmental Failures

But as the country's population and economy continue to grow, the need to find solutions becomes more urgent every day. Across India, concern is mounting over an ever growing list of environmental problems.

More people means increased pressure on natural resources (from water to forests), while an economy in high-gear is leaving a trail of pollution that's affecting not only India, but the rest of the world too.

Deforestation

India is witnessing a rising demand for forest-based products. This is causing deforestation and encroachment into forest protected areas, which leads to a severe loss of natural resources. It is estimated that total industrial roundwood consumption in India could exceed 70 million m per year by the end of the decade (350,000 large shipping containers), while domestic supply would fall short of this figure by an estimated 14 million m.

As the nation will have to depend heavily on imports to meet this growing demand, there is fear that this could result in loss of high conservation value forests and biodiversity elsewhere.

A Thirst for Palm Oil

India is a big edible oil consumer. In fact, it is one of the three largest importers of palm oil in the world, along with EU and China. Of these imports, 95% come from Indonesia and Malaysia, causing negative social and environmental consequences in these exporting countries.

Conversion of natural forests for cultivating oil palm is a major threat to biodiversity and livelihoods in the tropics. Most of the lowland rainforest on the Indonesian island of Sumatra has already been lost, largely because of the clearance for oil palm and pulp wood plantations.

With the global demand for palm oil expected to increase from 28 million tonnes at present to about 50 million tonnes in 2030, there are very serious concerns that this will happen at the expense of biologically and economically important forests.

Pollution

Increasing competition for water among various sectors, including agriculture, industry, domestic, drinking, energy generation and others, is causing this precious natural resource to dry up. Increasing pollution is also leading to the destruction of the habitat of wildlife that lives in waterways.

Panoramic View of Environmental Degradation in India

Environmental degradation is a result of the dynamic inter play of socio-economic,institutional and technological activities. Environmental changes may be driven by many factors including economic growth, population growth, urbanization, intensification of agriculture, rising energy use and transportation. Poverty still remains a problem at the root of several environmental problems.

Social Factors

Population: Population is an important source of development, yet it is a major source of environmental degradation when it exceeds the threshhold limits of the support systems. Unless the relationship between the multiplying population and the life support system can be stabilized, development programmes, howsoever, innovative are not likely to yield desired results. Population impacts on the environment primarily through the use of natural resources and production of wastes and is associated with environmental stresses like loss of biodiversity, air and water pollution and increased pressure on arable land.

India supports 17 per cent of the world population on just 2.4 per cent of world land area. It's current rate of population growth at 1.85 per cent continues to pose a persistent population challenge. In view of the linkages between population and environment, a vigorous drive for population control need hardly be over emphasised.

Poverty

Poverty is said to be both cause and effect of environmental degradation. The circular link between poverty and environment is an extremely complex phenomenon. Inequality may foster unsustainability because the poor, who rely on natural resources more than the rich, deplete natural resources faster as they have no real prospects of gaining access to other types of resources. Moreover, degraded environment can accelerate the process of impoverishment, again because the poor depend directly on natural assets. Although there has been a significant drop in the poverty ratio in the country from 55 percent in 1973 to 36 percent in 1993-94, the absolute number of poor have, however, remained constant at around 320 million over the years. An acceleration in poverty alleviation is imperative to break this link between poverty and the environment.

Urbanisation

Lack of opportunities for gainful employment in villages and the ecological stresses is leading to an ever increasing movement of poor families to towns. Mega cities are emerging and urban slums are expanding. There has been an eightfold increase in urban population over 1901-1991. During the past two decades of 1971-91, India's urban population has doubled from 109 million to 218 million and is estimated to reach 300 million by 2000 AD.

Such rapid and unplanned expansion of cities has resulted in degradation of urban environment. It has widened the gap between demand and supply of infrastructural services such as energy, housing, transport, communication, education, water supply and sewerage and recreational amenities, thus depleting the precious environmental resource base of the cities. The result is the growing trend in deterioration of air and water quality, generation of wastes, the proliferation of slums and undesirable land use changes, all of which contribute to urban poverty.

Economic Factors

To a large extent, environmental degradation is the result of market failure, that is, the non existent or poorly functioning markets for environmental goods and services. In this context, environmental degradation is a particular case of consumption or production externalities reflected by divergence between private and social costs (or benefits). Lack of well defined property rights may be one of the reasons for such market failure. On the other hand, Market distortions created by price controls and subsidies may aggravate the achievement of environmental objectives.

The level and pattern of economic development also affect the nature of environmental problems. India's development objectives have consistently emphasised the promotion of policies and programmes for economic growth and social welfare. Between 1994-95 and 1997-98, the Indian economy has grown a little over 7 per cent per annum: the growth of industrial production and manufacturing averaging higher at 8.4 per cent and 8.9 per environmental protection in India.

Over the years, together with a spreading of environmental consciousness, there has been a change in the traditionally-held perception that there is a trade-off between environmental quality and economic growth as people have come to believe that the two are necessarily complementary. The current focus on environment is not new—environmental considerations have been an integral part of the Indian culture. The need for conservation and sustainable use of natural resources has been expressed in Indian scriptures, more than three thousand years old and is reflected in the constitutional, legislative and policy framework as also in the international commitments of the country.

Even before India's independence in 1947, several environmental legislation existed but the real impetus for bringing about a well-developed framework came only after the UN Conference on the Human Environment (Stockholm, 1972). Under the influence of this declaration, the National Council for Environmental Policy and Planning within the Department of Science and Technology was set up in 1972. This Council later evolved into a full-fledged Ministry of Environment and Forests (MoEF) in 1985 which today is the apex administrative body in the country for regulating and ensuring environmental protection. After the Stockholm Conference, in 1976, constitutional sanction was given to environmental concerns through the 42 Amendment, which incorporated them into the Directive Principles of State Policy and Fundamental Rights and Duties.

Since the 1970s an extensive network of environmental legislation has grown in the country. The MoEF and the pollution control boards (CPCB *i.e.* Central Pollution Control Board and SPCBs *i.e.* State Pollution Control Boards) together form the regulatory and administrative core of the sector.

A policy framework has also been developed to complement the legislative provisions. The Policy Statement for Abatement of Pollution and the National Conservation Strategy and Policy Statement on Environment and Development were brought out by the MoEF in 1992, to develop and promote initiatives for the protection and improvement of the environment. The EAP (Environmental Action Programme) was formulated in 1993 with the objective of improving environmental services and integrating environmental considerations in to development programmes.

Other measures have also been taken by the government to protect and preserve the environment. Several sector-specific policies have evolved, which are discussed at length in the concerned chapters. This chapter attempts to highlight only legislative initiatives towards the protection of the environment.

Environmental Protection and Policies in India

Water

Water quality standards especially those for drinking water are set by the Indian Council of Medical Research. These bear close resemblance to WHO standards. The discharge of industrial effluents is regulated by the Indian Standard Codes and recently, water quality standards for coastal water marine outfalls have also been specified.

In addition to the general standards, certain specific standards have been developed for effluent discharges from industries such as, iron and steel, aluminium, pulp and paper, oil refineries, petrochemicals and thermal power plants. Legislation to control water pollution are listed below.

Water (Prevention and Control of Pollution) Act, 1974: This Act represented India's first attempts to comprehensively deal with environmental issues. The Act prohibits the discharge of pollutants into water bodies beyond a given standard, and lays down penalties for non-compliance. The Act was amended in 1988 to conform closely to the provisions of the EPA, 1986. It set up the CPCB (Central Pollution Control Board) which lays down standards for the prevention and control of water pollution. At the State level, the SPCBs (State Pollution Control Board) function under the direction of the CPCB and the state government.

Water (Prevention and Control of Pollution) Cess Act, 1977: This Act provides for a levy and collection of a cess on water consumed by industries and local authorities. It aims at augmenting the resources of the central and state boards for prevention and control of water pollution. Following this Act, *The Water (Prevention and Control of Pollution) Cess Rules* were formulated in 1978 for defining standards and indications for the kind of and location of meters that every consumer of water is required to install.

Air

Air (Prevention and Control of Pollution) Act, 1981: To counter the problems associated with air pollution, ambient air quality standards were established, under the 1981 Act. The Act provides means for the control and abatement of air pollution. The Act seeks to combat air pollution by prohibiting the use of polluting fuels and substances, as well as by regulating appliances that give rise to air pollution. Under the Act establishing or operating of any industrial plant in the pollution control area requires consent from state boards. The boards are also expected to test the air in air pollution control areas, inspect pollution control equipment, and manufacturing processes.

National Ambient Air Quality Standards (NAAQS) for major pollutants were notified by the CPCB in April 1994. These are deemed to be levels of air quality necessary with an adequate margin of safety, to protect public health, vegetation and property (CPCB 1995 cited in Gupta, 1999). The NAAQS prescribe specific standards for industrial, residential, rural and other sensitive areas. Industry-specific emission standards have also been developed for iron and steel plants, cement plants, fertilizer plants, oil refineries and the aluminium industry. The ambient quality standards prescribed in India are similar to those prevailing in many developed and developing countries.

To empower the central and state pollution boards to meet grave emergencies, the *Air (Prevention and Control of Pollution) Amendment Act*, 1987, was enacted. The boards were authorized to take immediate measures to tackle such emergencies and recover the expenses incurred from the offenders. The power to cancel consent for non-fulfilment of the conditions prescribed has also been emphasized in the Air Act Amendment.

The Air (Prevention and Control of Pollution) Rules formulated in 1982, defined the procedures for conducting meetings of the boards, the powers of the presiding officers, decision-making, the quorum; manner in which the records of the meeting were to be set etc. They also prescribed the manner and the purpose of seeking assistance from specialists and the fee to be paid to them.

Complementing the above Acts is the *Atomic Energy Act* of 1982, which was introduced to deal with radioactive waste. In 1988, the *Motor Vehicles Act,* was enacted to regulate vehicular traffic, besides ensuring proper packaging, labelling and transportation of the hazardous wastes. Various aspects of vehicular pollution have also been notified under the EPA of 1986. Mass emission standards were notified in 1990, which were made more stringent in 1996.

In 2000 these standards were revised yet again and for the first time separate obligations for vehicle owners, manufacturers and enforcing agencies were stipulated. In addition, fairly stringent Euro I and II emission norms were notified by the Supreme Court on April 29, 1999 for the city of Delhi. The notification made it mandatory for car manufacturers to conform to the Euro I and Euro II norms by May 1999 and April 2000, respectively, for new non-commercial vehicle sold in Delhi.

Forests and Wildlife

The Wildlife (Protection) Act, 1972, Amendment 1991: The WPA (Wildlife Protection Act), 1972, provides for protection to listed species of flora and fauna and establishes a network of ecologically-important protected areas. The WPA empowers the central and state governments to declare any area a wildlife sanctuary, national park or closed area. There is a blanket ban on carrying out any industrial activity inside these protected areas.

It provides for authorities to administer and implement the Act; regulate the hunting o. wild animals; protect specified plants, sanctuaries, national parks and closed areas; restrict trade or commerce in wild animals or animal articles; and miscellaneous matters. The Act prohibits hunting of animals except with permission of authorized officer when an animal has become dangerous to human life or property or so disabled or diseased as to be beyond recovery (WWF-India, 1999). The near-total prohibition on hunting was made more effective by the Amendment Act of 1991.

The Forest (Conservation) Act, 1980: This Act was adopted to protect and conserve forests. The Act restricts the powers of the state in respect of de-reservation of forests and use of forestland for non-forest purposes (the term 'non-forest purpose' includes clearing any forestland for cultivation of cash crops, plantation crops, horticulture or any purpose other than re-afforestation).

General

Environment (Protection) Act, 1986 (EPA): This Act is an umbrella legislation designed to provide a framework for the co-ordination of central and state authorities established under the Water (Prevention and Control) Act, 1974 and Air (Prevention and Control) Act, 1981. Under this Act, the central government is empowered to take measures necessary to protect and improve the quality of the environment by setting standards for emissions and discharges; regulating the location of industries; management of hazardous wastes, and protection of public health and welfare.

From time to time the central government issues notifications under the EPA for the protection of ecologically-sensitive areas or issues guidelines for matters under the EPA.

Some notifications issued under this Act are:

- *Doon Valley Notification* (1989), which prohibits the setting up of an industry in which the daily consumption of coal/fuel is more than 24 MT (million tonnes) per day in the Doon Valley.
- *Coastal Regulation Zone Notification* (1991), which regulates activities along coastal stretches. As per this notification, dumping ash or any other waste in the CRZ is prohibited. The thermal power plants (only foreshore facilities for transport of raw materials, facilities for intake of cooling water and outfall for discharge of treated waste water/cooling water) require clearance from the MoEF.
- *Dhanu Taluka Notification* (1991), under which the district of Dhanu Taluka has been declared an

ecologically fragile region and setting up power plants in its vicinity is prohibited.

- *Revdanda Creek Notification (1989)*, which prohibits setting up industries in the belt around the Revdanda Creek as per the rules laid down in the notification.
- *The Environmental Impact Assessment of Development Projects Notification*, (1994 and as amended in 1997). As per this notification:
- All projects listed under Schedule I require environmental clearance from the MoEF.
- Projects under the delicenced category of the New Industrial Policy also require clearance from the MoEF.
- All developmental projects whether or not under the Schedule I, if located in fragile regions must obtain MoEF clearance.
- Industrial projects with investments above Rs 500 million must obtain MoEF clearance and are further required to obtain a LOI (Letter Of Intent) from the Ministry of Industry, and an NOC (No Objection Certificate) from the SPCB and the State Forest Department if the location involves forestland. Once the NOC is obtained, the LOI is converted into an industrial licence by the state authority.
- The notification also stipulated procedural requirements for the establishment and operation of new power plants. As per this notification, two-stage clearance for site-specific projects such as pithead thermal power plants and valley projects is required. Site clearance is given in the first stage and final environmental clearance in the second. A public hearing has been made mandatory for projects covered by this notification. This is an important step in providing transparency and a greater role to local communities.
- *Ash Content Notification* (1997), required the use of beneficiated coal with ash content not exceeding 34% with effect from June 2001, (the date later was extended to June 2002). This applies to all thermal plants located

beyond one thousand kilometres from the pithead and any thermal plant located in an urban area or, sensitive area irrespective of the distance from the pithead except any pithead power plant.

- *Taj Trapezium Notification* (1998), provided that no power plant could be set up within the geographical limit of the Taj Trapezium assigned by the Taj Trapezium Zone Pollution (Prevention and Control) Authority.
- *Disposal of Fly Ash Notification* (1999) the main objective of which is to conserve the topsoil, protect the environment and prevent the dumping and disposal of fly ash discharged from lignite-based power plants. The salient feature of this notification is that no person within a radius of 50 km from a coal-or lignite-based power plant shall manufacture clay bricks or tiles without mixing at least 25% of ash with soil on a weight-to-weight basis. For the thermal power plants the utilisation of the flyash would be as follows:
- Every coal-or lignite-based power plant shall make available ash for at least ten years from the date of publication of the above notification without any payment or any other consideration, for the purpose of manufacturing ash-based products such as cement, concrete blocks, bricks, panels or any other material or for construction of roads, embankments, dams, dykes or for any other construction activity.
- Every coal or lignite based thermal power plant commissioned subject to environmental clearance conditions stipulating the submission of an action plan for full utilisation of fly ash shall, within a period of nine years from the publication of this notification, phase out the dumping and disposal of fly ash on land in accordance with the plan.

Rules for the Manufacture, Use, Import, Export and Storage of Hazardous Micro-organisms / Genetically Engineered Organisms or Cell were introduced in 1989 with the view to protect the environment, nature and health in connection with gene technology and micro-organisms, under the Environmental Protection Act, 1986. The government in 1991, further decided to institute a national label scheme for environmentally-friendly products called the 'ECOMARK'.

The scheme attempts to provide incentives to manufactures and importers to reduce adverse environmental impacts, reward genuine initiatives by companies, and improve the quality of the environment and sustainability of available resources. Besides the above attempts, notifications pertaining *to Recycled Plastics Manufacture and Usage Rules, 1999* were also incorporated under the Environment (Protection) Act of 1986.

The Environment (Protection) Rules, 1986: These rules lay down the procedures for setting standards of emission or discharge of environmental pollutants. The Rules prescribe the parameters for the Central Government, under which it can issue orders of prohibition and restrictions on the location and operation of industries in different areas.

The Rules lay down the procedure for taking samples, serving notice, submitting samples for analysis and laboratory reports. The functions of the laboratories are also described under the Rules along with the qualifications of the concerned analysts.

The National Environment Appellate Authority Act, 1997: This Act provided for the establishment of a National Environment Appellate Authority to hear appeals with respect to restriction of areas in which any industry operation or process or class of industries, operations or processes could not carry out or would be allowed to carry out subject to certain safeguards under the Environment (Protection) Act, 1986.

In addition to these, various Acts specific to the coal sector have been enacted. The first attempts in this direction can be traced back to the *Mines Act, 1952*, which promoted health and safety standards in coal mines. Later the *Coal Mines (Conservation and Development) Act* (1974) came up for conservation of coal during mining operations. For conservation and development of oil and natural gas resources a similar legislation was enacted in 1959.

Hazardous Wastes

There are several legislation that directly or indirectly deal with hazardous waste. The relevant legislation are the Factories Act, 1948, the Public Liability Insurance Act, 1991, the National Environment Tribunal Act, 1995 and some notifications under the Environmental Protection Act of 1986. A brief description of each of these is given below.

Under the EPA 1986, the MoEF has issued several notifications to tackle the problem of hazardous waste management. These include:

- *Hazardous Wastes (Management and Handling) Rules, 1989*, which brought out a guide for manufacture, storage and import of hazardous chemicals and for management of hazardous wastes.
- *Biomedical Waste (Management and Handling) Rules, 1998,* were formulated along parallel lines, for proper disposal, segregation, transport etc. of infectious wastes.
- *Municipal Wastes (Management and Handling) Rules, 2000,* whose aim was to enable municipalities to dispose municipal solid waste in a scientific manner.
- *Hazardous Wastes (Management and Handling) Amendment Rules, 2000*, a recent notification issued with the view to providing guidelines for the import and export of hazardous waste in the country.

Factories Act, 1948 and its Amendment in 1987: The Factories Act, 1948 was a post-independence statute that explicitly showed concern for the environment. The primary aim of the 1948 Act has been to ensure the welfare of workers not only in their working conditions in the factories but also their employment benefits. While ensuring the safety and health of the workers, the Act contributes to environmental protection.

The Act contains a comprehensive list of 29 categories of industries involving hazardous processes, which are defined as a process or activity where unless special care is taken, raw materials used therein or the intermediate or the finished products, by-products, wastes or effluents would:

- Cause material impairment to health of the persons engaged
- Result in the pollution of the general environment

Public Liability Insurance Act (PLIA), 1991: The Act covers accidents involving hazardous substances and insurance coverage for these. Where death or injury results from an accident, this Act makes the owner liable to provide relief as is specified in the Schedule of the Act. The PLIA was amended in 1992, and the Central Government was authorized to establish the Environmental Relief Fund, for making relief payments.

National Environment Tribunal Act, 1995: The Act provided strict liability for damages arising out of any accident occurring while handling any hazardous substance and for the establishment of a National Environment Tribunal for effective and expeditious disposal of cases arising from such accident, with a view to give relief and compensation for damages to persons, property and the environment and for the matters connected therewith or incidental thereto.

International Agreements on Environmental Issues: India is signatory to a number of multilateral environment agreements (MEA) and conventions. An overview of some of the major MEAs and India's obligations under these is presented below. These are discussed at length in the respective chapters.

Convention on International Trade in Endangered Species of Wild Fauna and Flora (CITES), 1973: The aim of CITES is to control or prevent international commercial trade in endangered species or products derived from them. CITES does not seek to directly protect endangered species or curtail development practices that destroy their habitats. Rather, it seeks to reduce the economic incentive to poach endangered species and destroy their habitat by closing off the international market. India became a party to the CITES in 1976. International trade in all wild flora and fauna in general and species covered under CITES is regulated jointly through the provisions of The Wildlife (Protection) Act 1972, the Import/ Export policy of Government of India and the Customs Act 1962 (Bajaj, 1996).

Montreal Protocol on Substances that Deplete the Ozone Layer (to the Vienna Convention for the Protection of the Ozone Layer), 1987: The Montreal Protocol to the Vienna Convention on Substances that deplete the Ozone Layer, came into force in 1989. The protocol set targets for reducing the consumption and production of a range of ozone depleting substances (ODS). In a major innovation the Protocol recognized that all nations should not be treated equally. The agreement acknowledges that certain countries have contributed to ozone depletion more than others. It also recognizes that a nation's obligation to reduce current emissions should reflect its technological and financial ability to do so. Because of this, the agreement sets more stringent standards and accelerated phase-out timetables to countries that have contributed most to ozone depletion (Divan and Rosencranz, 2001).

India acceded to the Montreal Protocol along with its London Amendment in September 1992. The MoEF has established an Ozone Cell and a steering committee on the Montreal Protocol to facilitate implementation of the India Country Programme, for phasing out ODS production by 2010.

To meet India's commitments under the Montreal Protocol, the Government of India has also taken certain policy decisions.

- Goods required to implement ODS phase-out projects funded by the Multilateral Fund are fully exempt from duties. This benefit has been also extended to new investments with non-ODS technologies.
- Commercial banks are prohibited from financing or refinancing investments with ODS technologies.

The Gazette of India on 19 July 2000 notified rules for regulation of ODS phase-out called the *Ozone Depleting Substances (Regulation and Control) Rules, 2000*. They were notified under the Environment (Protection) Act, 1986. These rules were drafted by the MoEF following consultations with industries and related government departments.

Basel Convention on Transboundary Movement of Hazardous Wastes, 1989: Basel Convention, which entered into force in 1992, has three key objectives:

- To reduce transboundary movements of hazardous wastes;
- To minimize the creation of such wastes; and
- To prohibit their shipment to countries lacking the capacity to dispose hazardous wastes in an environmentally sound manner.

India ratified the Basel Convention in 1992, shortly after it came into force. The Indian Hazardous Wastes Management Rules Act 1989, encompasses some of the Basel provisions related to the notification of import and export of hazardous waste, illegal traffic, and liability.

UN Framework Convention on Climate Change (UNFCCC), 1992: The primary goals of the UNFCCC were to stabilize greenhouse gas emissions at levels that would prevent dangerous anthropogenic interference with the global climate. The convention embraced the principle of common but differentiated responsibilities which has guided the adoption of a regulatory structure.

India signed the agreement in June 1992, which was ratified in November 1993. As per the convention the reduction/ limitation requirements apply only to developed countries. The only reporting obligation for developing countries relates to the construction of a GHG inventory.

India has initiated the preparation of its First National Communication (base year 1994) that includes an inventory of GHG sources and sinks, potential vulnerability to climate change, adaptation measures and other steps being taken in the country to address climate change. The further details on UNFCC and the Kyoto Protocol are provided in Atmosphere and climate chapter.

Convention on Biological Diversity, 1992: The Convention on Biological Diversity (CBD) is a legally binding, framework treaty that has been ratified until now by 180 countries. The CBD has three main thrust areas: conservation of biodiversity, sustainable use of biological resources and equitable sharing of benefits arising from their sustainable use.

The Convention on Biological Diversity came into force in 1993. Many biodiversity issues are addressed in the convention, including habitat preservation, intellectual property rights, biosafety, and indigenous peoples' rights.

India's initiatives under the Convention are detailed in the chapter on Biodiversity. These include the promulgation of the Wildlife (Protection) Act of 1972, amended in 1991; and participation in several international conventions such as CITES.

UN Convention on Desertification, 1994: Delegates to the 1992 UN Conference on Environment and Development (UNCED) recommended establishment of an intergovernmental negotiating committee for the elaboration of an international convention to combat desertification in countries experiencing serious drought and/or desertification. The UN General Assembly established such a committee in 1992 that later helped formulation of Convention on Desertification in 1994.

The convention is distinctive as it endorses and employs a bottom-up approach to international environmental cooperation. Under the terms of the convention, activities related to the control and alleviation of desertification and its effects are to be closely linked to the needs and participation of local land-users and non-governmental organizations. Seven countries in the South Asian region are signatories to the Convention, which aims at tackling desertification through national, regional and sub-regional action programmes. The Regional Action Programme has six Thematic Programme Networks (TPN's) for the Asian region, each headed by a country task manager. India hosts the network on agroforestry and soil conservation. For details refer to the land resource chapter.

International Tropical Timber Agreement and The International Tropical Timber Organisation (ITTO), 1983, 1994: The ITTO established by the International Tropical Timber Agreement (ITTA), 1983, came into force in 1985 and became operational in 1987. The ITTO facilitates discussion, consultation and international cooperation on issues relating to the international trade and utilization of tropical timber and the sustainable management of its resource base. The successor agreement to the ITTA (1983) was negotiated in 1994, and came into force on 1 January 1997. The organization has 57 member countries. India ratified the ITTA in 1996.

An Assessment of the Legal and Regulatory Framework for Environmental Protection in India: The extent of the environmental legislation network is evident from the above discussion but the enforcement of the laws has been a matter of concern. One commonly cited reason is the prevailing command and control nature of the environmental regime. Coupled with this is the prevalence of the all-or–nothing approach of the law; they do not consider the extent of violation. Fines are levied on a flat basis and in addition, there are no incentives to lower the discharges below prescribed levels.

Some initiatives have addressed these issues in the recent past. The Government of India came out with a Policy Statement for Abatement of Pollution in 1992, before the Rio conference, which declared that market-based approaches would be considered in controlling pollution. It stated that economic instruments will be investigated to encourage the shift from curative to preventive measures, internalise the costs of pollution and conserve resources, particularly water. In 1995, the Ministry of Environment and Forest (MoEF) constituted a task force to evaluate market-based instruments, which strongly advocated their use for the abatement of industrial pollution.

Various economic incentives have been used to supplement the command-and-control policies. Depreciation allowances, exemptions from excise or customs duty payment, and arrangement of soft loans for the adoption of clean technologies are instances of such incentives. Another aspect that is evident is the shift in the focus from end-of-pipe treatment of pollution to treatment at source. The role of remote sensing and geographical information systems in natural resource management and environmental protection has also gained importance over time.

An important recent development is the rise of judicial activism in the enforcement of environmental legislation. This is reflected in the growth of environment-related public litigation cases that have led the courts to take major steps such as ordering the shut-down of polluting factories.

Agenda 21 highlights the need for integration of environmental concerns at all stages of policy, planning and decision-making processes including the use of an effective legal and regulatory framework, economic instruments and other incentives. These very principles were fundamental to guiding environmental protection in the country well before Rio and will be reinforced, drawing on India's own experiences and those of other countries.

Need and Objectives of Conservation

The Department of Environment and Forests was created in the Central Government, which subsequently became the Ministry of Environment and Forests (MoEF) by the mid-1980s. The MoEF is a focal point and a nodal agency in the administrative structure for planning, promotion and implementation of environment, conservation and forestry-related programmes.

The mandates of the Ministry include conservation and survey of flora, fauna, forests and wildlife, prevention and control of pollution, afforestation and regeneration of degraded areas and protection of the environment.

These tasks are being fulfilled by the ministry through environmental impact assessment, eco-regeneration, assistance to organizations implementing environmental and forestry programmes, promotion of environmental and forestry research, extension, education and training to augment the requisite manpower, dissemination of environmental information, international cooperation and creation of environmental awareness among all sectors of the country's population.

Conservation of Water Bodies

National River Conservation Directorate (NRCD): The National River Conservation Directorate, functioning under the Ministry is engaged in implementing the River and Lake Action Plans under the National Lake Conservation Plan

(NLCP) & National River Conservation Plan (NRCP) by providing assistance to the State Governments.

- The objective of NRCP is to improve the water quality of the rivers, which are the major water sources in the country, through the implementation of pollution abatement works, to the level of designated best use. So far a total of 35 rivers have been covered under the programme.
- Major works being taken up under the NRCP include Interception and diversion works to capture the raw sewage flowing into the river through open drains and divert them for treatment. Setting up Sewage Treatment Plants for treating the diverted sewage. Construction of Low Cost sanitation toilets. Construction of Electric crematoria and improved Wood Crematoria to conserve the use of wood, River Front Development, afforestation on the river banks, Public Participation & Awareness etc.
- Works under Ganga Action Plan Phase-II (presently part of National River Conservation Plan) are taken up in 59 towns along the main stem of river Ganga at an approved cost of Rs. 663 crore.
- The Ministry of Environment and Forests have received financial assistance of Yen 13.33 billion from the Japan Bank for International Cooperation (JBIC) for implementation of Yamuna Action Plan (YAP) Phase II, which is part of the National River Conservation Plan (NRCP).
- Under the Gomti Action Plan Phase-I, out of 31 sanctioned schemes, 26 schemes have been completed. A total of 42 mid STPs capacity had already been created under this Plan.
- Besides the river Ganga and its tributaries covered under GAP-I and GAP-II the NRCD has taken up the pollution abatement projects of 14 other States covering 30 rivers and 68 towns.
- The water quality of river Ganga is being monitored at 27 locations from Rishikesh in Uttarakhand to Uluberia

in West Bengal by institutions such as pollution Control Research Institute (Haridwar), CPCB Zonal Office Lucknow, Indian Institute of Technology, Kanpur, Patna Univerity and Bidhan Chandra Krishi Vishwavidyalaya, Kalyani. As a result of the projects completed under Ganga Action Plan, the water quality of river Ganga has shown a general improvement despite tremendous population growth along the river banks.

- The water quality monitoring has also been undertaken for rivers namely, Yamuna, Western Yamuna Canal, Gomti, Hindon, Satluj (Punjab) Cauvery (Tamilnadu), Tunga, Bhadra, Tungbhadara in Karnataka and Waterways of Chennai. The numbers of monitoring stations presently are 158 in 10 rivers which include 27 stations set up in the upper reaches of Ganga and 32 stations of Chennai Waterways.
- A total of 33 projects for conservation of 49 lakes have been sanctioned in 13 States at a total estimated cost of Rs. 632.62 crore. Conservation works for 11 lakes have been completed so far whereas in some cases the project implementation is in last stages of completion. Funding pattern under NLCP (w.e.f. February, 2002) is on a 70:30 cost sharing between the Central and the State Governments.
- The 12th World Lake Conference (Taal 2007), a biennial event under the aegis of international Lake Environment Committee (ILEC) Foundation, was organized by the Ministry, at Jaipur, Rajasthan from 28th October to 2nd November, 2007. The State Govt of Rajasthan was the co-host for this mega event. The central theme of the Conference was 'Conserving lakes & Wetlands for Future'. Other main objectives included identifying the issues concerning lakes and wetlands along with restoration approaches under different conditions adopted by different countries.
- The Conference was inaugurated by Hon'ble President of India, Smt. Pratibha Devisingh Patil on 29th October, 2007 in the presence of other dignitaries including

Hon'ble Governor and Chief Minister of Rajasthan. As many as 600 no. of delegates comprising of nearly 150 overseas delegates from different parts of the world, attended the Conference with their oral or poster presentations on their studies pertaining to the subject matter. The Jaipur Declaration was adopted at the Valedictory session, to work upon as a follow up action of the Conference.

National Wetlands Conservation Programme

The scheme on conservation and management of Wetlands was initiated in 1987 to lay down policy guidelines for implementing programmes of conservation and management of wetlands in the country, to undertake priority wetlands for intensive conservation measures and to monitor Implementation of the Programme of conservation, management and research, and to prepare an inventory of Indian wetlands.

- Number of wetlands under Wetland Conservation Programme increased from 27 in 2004 to 71 in 2005 and to 103 in January 2008.
- A brochure on 'National Wetland Conservation, an approach and Guidelines' was released on the eve of 2nd February, 2007 which has now been published and circulated to all the user agencies.
- Management Action Plans (MAPs) of 36 wetlands have been approved and financial assistance sanctioned. Cases of 10 more M.A.Ps, for newly identified wetlands are being taken up.
- Twenty five sites have already been designated as Ramsar sites in India till date;
- India has been nominated on Board of Directors of wetland International and on request from India. Meeting of Board of Directors of Wetland International was held in New Delhi at Manesar during 19-20 October, 2005, About 23 countries participated. India chaired one of the sessions and efforts made by India in Wetland conservation were highly applauded by all the participating countries.

Environmental Conservation Measures taken in India—Constitutional Amendments Made

Strictly, speaking no constitution deals with a matter such as environmental protection. Because basically any constitution contains only the rules of laws in relation to the power structure, allocation, and manner of exercise. Besides Indian Constitution is already a bulky document and brevity is the character of an ideal Constitution. Hence from the point of view of the principles of the constitutional law as well as, the length of the Constitution it was impossible to have any such provision safeguarding the healthy environment. Therefore till the subsequent amendments the constitutional text of India, was without any specific provision for the protection and promotion of the environment. However the seeds of such provision could be seen in Article 47 of the constitution which command the State to improve the standard of living and public health. To fulfill this constitutional goal, its necessary that the State should provide pollution free environment.

The United Nations Conference on Human Environment held on in June, 1972 at Stockholm placed the issue of the protection of biosphere on the official agenda of international policy and law. The agenda of the conference consisted of the following :

(a) Planning and management of human settlements for environmental quality.
(b) Environmental aspects of natural resources management.
(c) Identifications and control of pollutants and nuisances of broad international significance.
(d) Educational, Information, Social and cultural aspects of environmental issues.
(e) Development and environment.
(f) International Organisational implications of action proposals.

The Stockholm Conference agendas, proclamations, principles and subsequent global, environment protection efforts shows the words realisation of the need to preserve and protect the natural environment. The Conference acclaimed man's fundamental right to adequate conditions of life in an environment of a quality that permitted a life off dignity and well-being. In United Nations Conference on Human Environment, at Stockholm the then Prime Minister of India Mrs. Gandhi while displaying the nations commitment to the protection of environment said:

"The natural resources of the earth, including the air, water, land flora and fauna and especially representative sample of the nature ecosystem must be safeguard for the benefits of present and future generations through careful planning or management, as appropriate... Nature conservation including wildlife must therefore receive importance in planning for economic development".

To comply with the principles of the Stockholm Declarations adopted by the International Conference on Human Environment, the Government of India, by the Constitution 42nd Amendment Act, 1976 made the express provision for the protection and promotion of the environment, by the introduction of Article 48-A and 51-A(g) which form the part of Directive Principles of State Policy and the Fundamental Duties respectively. The amendment provided for the following :

Article 48 A

By the Constitution (42nd Amendment) Act, Section 10 (w.e.f. 3.1.1977). Protection and improvement of environment and safeguarding of forests and wild life:-

"The State shall endeavour to protect and improve the environment and to safeguard the forest and wildlife of the country".

Fundamental Duty

(I) Article 51-A(g) : By Constitution (42nd Amendment) Act, 1976. Section 11 (w.e.f. 3.1.1977)

"It shall be the duty of every citizen of India to protect and improve the natural environment including forests, lakes, rivers and wildlife and to have compassion for living creatures".

Thus the Indian Constitution makes two fold provision.

(a) On the one hand, it gives directive to the State for the protection and improvement of environment.

(b) On the other hand the citizens owe a constitutional duty to protect and improve natural environment.

In protecting the natural environment Article 48-A is of immense importance today. Because with the activist approach of judiciary in India the legal value of Directive Principles jurisprudence has constantly grown up in the Indian Constitutional set-up.

Hence the above provisions are of pivotal significance.

The Government of India to accelerate the pace for environment protection. Further amended the constitutional text by making the following changes.

1. Seventh Schedule of the Constitution:
   (I) In the Concurrent List, 42nd Amendment Inserted.
   (a) Entry 17-A, providing for forests.
   (b) Entry 17-B, for the protection of wild animals and birds.
   (c) Entry 20-A, providing for population control and family planning.
2. Eleventh Schedule of the Constitution.
   (1) This new schedule is added by the Constitution 73rd Amendment Act, 1992. Which received the assent ol' tlic President on 20.4.1993. This schedule has 8 entries (2,3.6.7,11,12,15 and 29) providing for environmental protection and conservation
3. Twelfth Schedule of the Constitution.
   (1) The entry number 8 of this schedule added to the constitutional text by the 74th Amendment Act, 1992, which received the assessment of the President on 20.4.1993 providal for the Urban Local bodies, with the function of environment and promotion of ecological aspects to them.

Due to the above changes the division of legislative power between the Union and the States is spelt out in the following three of the 7th Schedule of the constitution.

List I (Union List) Entries

52. Industries.
53. Regulation and development of oil fields and mineral oil/resources.
54. Regulation of mines and mineral development.
56. Regulation and development of inter-State rivers and river valleys.
57. Fishing and fisheries beyond territorial waters.

List II (State List) Entries

6. Public health and sanitation.
14. Agriculture protection against past and prevention of plant diseases.
18. Land colonisation etc.
21. Fisheries.
23. Regulation of Mines and Mineral development subject to the provisions of
24. Industries subject to the provisions of

List III (Common or Concurrent List) Entries

17-A Forests.

17-B Protection and wild animals and birds.

20. Economic and social planning.

20-A Population control and family planning.

The Eleventh Schedule, added to the Constitution by the constitution 73rd Amendment Act, 1992, assign the functions of soil conservation, water management, social and form forestry, drinking water, fuel and fodder, etc. to the Panchayats with a view to environmental management.

The 12th Schedule of the Constitution added by 74th Amendment Act, 1992 commands the Urban local bodies such as municipalities to perform the functions of Protection of environment and promotion of ecological aspects.

The constitutional changes effected in the 7th Schedule by the 42nd Amendment Act, 1976 is a milestone steps, in the direction of the protection of environment. Because the subject of forests originally was in the State list as entry 19, this resulted into no uniform policy by the State so as to protect the forests. By placing the item 'forest' now in the concurrent list by the entry 17-A, along with the State, Parliament has acquired a law making power.

Because of the above change, in order to have a uniform policy in the forest management the Government of India in the year 1980 set up the Ministry of Environment and Forests. By virtue of this change Parliament also enacted, the central legislation *i.e.* Forest Conservation Act, 1980, which was amended in 1988. The government also adopted the new National Forest Policy in 1988 with a twin object. One to protect the forests and another to consider the needs of the forest dwellers.

Similarly the insertion of the entry 17-B in the concurrent list has empowered the Parliament to enact a law with a view to protection of wild animals and birds. Although we had a comprehensive legislation in the form of Wildlife Protection Act of 1972 the 42nd Amendment has considered the wildlife along with forests. India has also formulated National Action plan for the Protection of wild life. The new entry 20 A in the concurrent list embowers the Parliament to regulate the population explosion one, of the prime cause of the environmental pollution. By these changes, legally and constitutionally it has become possible to lake a uniform action in the matters of proper management of the environment.

Fundamental Rights

The judiciary's dynamic interpretation of fundamental rights have regulated into the rights to healthy environment from the following Articles:

(a) Article 14 : "State shall not deny to any person equality before the law or the equal protection of the laws within the territory of India".

(b) Article 19 (6) : State is empowered to make any law imposing in the interests of the general public, reasonable restrictions on the exercise of freedom to practice any profession, or to carry on any occupation, trade or business. guaranteed by (1) (g).

(c) Article 21 : "No person shall be deprived of his life or personal liberty except according to procedure established by law".

Right Environment

The importation of the 'due process* clause *by the activist approach of the Supreme Court in Maneka Gandhi's case (AIR 1978 SC 597) has revolutionized the ambit and scope of the expression 'right to life* embodied in Article 21 of the Constitution. The right to live in healthy environment is one more golden feather of article 21.

This right connotes that the enjoyment of life and its attainment and fulfillment guaranteed by Article 21 embraces the protection and preservation of nature's gift without which life cannot be enjoyed. The supreme Court of India, in 1980, indirectly conceived this right in a monumental judgment in the case of Ratlam Municipality V/s. Vardichand (AIR 1980 SC 1622).

In this case the Bench of Justice V. R. Krishna lyer and Justice 0. Chinnappa Reddy held the neglect of sanitation of the town of Ratlam by Municipal Council Health hazard. The Court observed:

> *"Even as human rights under Part III of the Constitution have respected by the State regardless provision. Decency and dignity race non-negotiable facts of human rights and are a first charge on local self governing bodies".*

The Court's decision was founded on it's earlier decision in Govind V. Shanti Sarup (AIR 1957 SC 1943), where Section 133 of the code of Criminal procedure was used by the Court to preserve the environment in the interest of "health safety and convenience of public a large".

In the judgment the Supreme Court has no-where referred to Article 21 of the Constitution. But it is simply clear that, the judgment is based on the right to live with decency and dignity as provided in the right to life.

The Court continued, its hidden approach of not referring to Article 21 directly, in another landmark case. Rural litigation and Entitlement Kendra V. State of Uttar Pradesh (AIR 1985 SC p52) although the Court has successfully read Article 21 in Article 48-A of the Part N of the Constitution.

In this case, the Apex Court converted a letter into written petition alleging that the operation of unauthorised and illegal, mining in the Mussorie-Dehradun belt affected the ecology of the areas and led to environment disorder. The Bench consist of Chief Justice P.N.Bhagwati (as he then was), Justice A.N. Sen and Justice Ranganath Misra ordered closing down of mining operations on the ground that lime stone quarries operation causing ecological imbalance and a hazard to healthy environment.

The striking feature of this decision is that, the Court converted a letter in the writ petition under Article 32, without referring to any article from the chapter on fundamental rights.

From the jurists process, it could be submitted that Court restrained itself from invoking Article 21 directly, but regarded the right to live in healthy environment as a part of fundamental right.

In M. C. Mchta V. Shriram Food and Fertilizer Industries and Union of India (Oleum Gas Leak Case-I) (AIR 1987 SC 1965) petitioner filed the write against the oleum gas leakage and for closing down one of the units of Shriram food and Fertilizers industries belonging to Delhi Cloth Mills Ltd.

The Court allowed to restart plant subject to certain stringent conditions laid down in the order. But the notable development is that the Court held that, can enterprise, engaged in any hazardous or inherently dangerous industry which could pose a threat to public health owed an absolutely and non-delidatable duty to the community to ensure that no harm resulted to anyone. Here again Court made no reference to Article 21.

But in III Oleum Gas Leak Case, M. C. Mehta V/s. Union of India (AIR 19P7 SC 1086),Chief Justice P. N. Bhagwati (as he then was) speaking for the Court clearly treated the lights to live in a healthy environment as fundamental right under Article 21 of the Constitution.

This case came before the Apex Court's Judges Bench by a reference made by a Bench of three Judges. On 4th and 6 December, there was leakage of Oleum' Gas from one of the units of Shriram which affected the health of large number of people and death of one person. On behalf of affected people application for compensation came up for hearing. The claim of Article 21 against a private corporation engaged in an activity which has potential to effect the life and health of the people was vehemently argued by counsel for the applicants. On the other hand counsel for Shriram opposed subjecting Shriram to the discipline of Article 21.

In the judgement Chief Justice P. N. Bhagwati (as he then was) speaking for the Court observed:

> *"These applications for compensation are the enforcement of the fundamental rights to life enshrined in Article 2 lot the Constitution and while dealing with such applications, we cannot adopt a hypertechnical approach which would defeat that ends of justice... If this Court is prepared to accept a letter complaining of violation of the fundamental rights of an individual or a class of individuals who cannot approach the Court for justice, there is no reason why these applications for compensation which have been made for the enforcement of the fundamental right of persons affected by oleum gas leak under Article..21 should not be entertained. (AIR 19K7 SC 1089).*

In the judgement. Chief Justice P. N. Bhagwati stressed on the need to develop a law recognising the rule of strict and absolute liability in cases of hazardous or dangerous industries operating at the cost of environment and the human life. The learned Chief Justice observed:

> *"We in India cannot hold our hands back and 1 venture to evolve a new principle of liability which English Courts have not done. We have to develop our law and if we find that it is necessary to construct a new principle of liability to deal with an unusual situation which has arisen and which is likely to arise in future on account of hazardous or inherently dangerous industries which*

are concomitant to an industrial economy, there is no reason why we should hesitate to evolve such principle of liability merely because, it has not been so done England (AIR 1988 SC 1089)".

The significant feature of this litigation is that the Court decided the important issues of liability and quantum of compensation without making a decision on the issue of assumption of jurisdiction in a write petition for orders against Shreeram Enterprises on the ground of violation of Article 21 of the Constitution. The judgement of the Supreme Court had an impact on the various High Court Judgements (AIR 1987A.P.171).

In the case of Subhash Kumar V. State of Bihar (AIR 1991 SC 424) the petitioner by way of public interest litigation, filed a petition for ensuring enjoyment of pollution free water and air. Justice K. N. Singh and Justice N. D. Ojha held:

"Right to live is a fundamental right under Article 21 of the Constitution and it includes the right of enjoyment of life. If anything endangerous or impairs that quality of life in derogation of laws, a citizen has a right to have eerecourse to Article 32 of the Constitution for removing the pollution of water or air which may determined to the quality of life (AIR 1991 SC424).

Since 1980 there is a substantial growth in the case law in environment. In 1987, the Apex Court delivered 13 judgements on the issue. Among the judges. Justice Ranganath Mishra (as he then was). Justice P. N. Bhagawati as judge and then as a Chief Justice, and Justice G. L. Oza decided the maximum cases. Though the Apex Court favoured the balanced approached between the environmental protection and development process. Bhagawati's last judgement on the eve of his retirement in M. C. Mehta's case has opened new horizon in the development of environmental law and also administration of environmental justice (J.I.L.I. Vol.35.PartI.1993).

Any Social process of change must be backed by the social sanction. If it is not then, no Court, no law, no Constitution can enforce it. If it is therefore, although now we find some constitutional provisions protecting the ecological balance it calls for the social sanction through the observance of the constitutional morality, which we lack today, as a national morality. Hence Constitutional directives or decisions fails to produce a desired result.

It is also now being suggested that the Constitution of India must provide a new Article *i.e* Article 21-A stating that, all persons shall have the right to clean and lieveable environment, throughout the territory of India subject to any law imposing reasonable restriction in the interest of general public (C. M. Jariwala, Indian Law Institute International Conference Souvenir, 1994, P.72).

However with due respect to the above views it is humbly submitted that it would be better if such matters are left to the specific legislation or judicial laws rather than accumulating everything in the constitutional text. After all the sanctify of the document called as the fundamental law of the land, the constitution must be upheld so as to distinguish it from any other ordinary legislation. Besides the exploration of the different dimensions of the Article 21 is on going process. The new horizons of the article 21 are coming up from case to case.

In the ultimate analysis of the problem of environmental pollution and its solution it is submitted that, no doubt, the legal, constitutional measures are necessary in the process of management of the proper and better environment. But it is not (he ever lasting solution. The ever lasting solution is that it calls for the people's inner feeling for the protection of environment, the environmental value system, the peoples movement rather than a legal movement.

Hence it calls for the mass education and awareness. This aspect has been very rightly upheld by the summit Court in the case of M.C. Mehta V. Union of India (AIR 1992 SC 382). The peoples collective conscience should wake up before the matter slips out of the hands. Each country now must seriously strive for the maintaining of ecological balance, otherwise tomorrow will be too late.

Relevant Provisions of the Constitution of India

Part IV—Directive Principles of State Policy: 48A Protection and improvement of environment and safeguarding of forests and wild life-The State shall endeavour to protect and improve the environment and to safeguard the forests and wild life of the country.

***Part IVA—Fundamental Duties:* 51A. Fundamental duties**-It shall be the duty of every citizen of India,-

(g) To protect and improve the natural environment including forests, lakes, rivers and wild life, and to have compassion for living creatures;

243G. Powers, authority and responsibilities of Panchayat-Subject to the provisions of the Constitution, the Legislature of a State may, by law, endow the Panchayats with such powers and authority as may be necessary to enable them to function as institutions of self-government and such law contain provisions for the devolution of powers and responsibilities upon Panchayats at the appropriate level, subject to such conditions as may be specified therein, with respect to-

(a) the preparation of plans for economic development and social justice;

(b) the implementation of schemes for economic development and social justice as may be entrusted to them including those in relation to the matters listed in the Eleventh Schedule.

Part IX A—The Municipalities:

243W. Powers, Authority and Responsibilities of Municipalities etc. Subject to the provisions of this Constitutions, the Legislature of a State may, by law, endow—

(a) the Municipalities with such powers and authority as may be necessary to enable them to function as institutions of self-government and such law may contain provisions for the devolution of powers and responsibilities upon Municipalities, subject to such condition as may be specified therein, with respect to-

(i) the preparation of plans for economic development and social justice;

(ii) the performance of functions and the implementation of scheme as may be entrusted to them including those in relation to the matters listed in the Twelfth Schedule;

(b) the Committees with such powers and authority as may be necessary to enable them to carry out the responsibities conferred upon them including those in relation to the matters listed in the Twelfth Schedule

"Eleventh Schedule (Article 243G):

1. Agriculture, including agricultural extension.
2. Land improvement, implementation of land reforms, land consolidation and soil conservation.
3. Minor irrigation, water management and watershed development.
4. Animal husbandry, dairying and poultry.
5. Fisheries.
6. Social forestry and farm forestry.
7. Minor forest produce.
8. Small scale industries, including food processing industries.
9. Khadi, village cottage industries.
10. Rural housing.
11. Drinking Water.
12. Fuel and fodder.
13. Roads, culverts bridges, ferries, waterways and other means of communication.
14. Rural electrification, including distribution of electricity.
15. Non-conventional energy sources.
16. Poverty alleviation programme.
17. Education, including primary and secondary schools.
18. Technical training and vocational education.
19. Adult and non-formal education.
20. Libraries.

21. Cultural activities.
22. Markets and fairs.
23. Health and sanitation, including hospitals, primary health centres and dispensaries.
24. Family welfare.
25. Women and child development.
26. Social welfare, including welfare of the handicapped and mentally retarded.
27. Welfare of the weaker sections, and in particular, of the Scheduled Castes and the Scheduled Tribes.
28. Public distribution system.
29. Maintenance of community assets".

"Twelfth Schedule (Article 243W):

1. Urban planning including town planning.
2. Regulation of land-use and construction of buildings.
3. Planning for economic and social development.
4. Roads and bridges.
5. Water supply for domestic, industrial and commercial purposes.
6. Public health, sanitation conservancy and solid waste management.
7. Fire services.
8. Urban forestry, protection of the environment and promotion of ecological aspects.
9. Safeguarding the interests of weaker sections of society, including the handicapped and mentally retarded.
10. Slum improvement and upgradation.
11. Urban poverty alleviation.
12. Provision of urban amenities and facilities such as parks, garden, play-grounds.
13. Promotion of cultural, educational and aesthetic aspects
14. Burials and burial grounds; cremations, cremation grounds and electric crematoriums
15. Cattle pond; Prevention of cruelty to animals

16. Vital statistics including registration of births and deaths
17. Public amenities including street lighting, parking lots, bus stops and public conveniences.
18. Regulation of slaughter houses and tanneries"

Environmental Laws

In the Constitution of India it is clearly stated that it is the duty of the state to 'protect and improve the environment and to safeguard the forests and wildlife of the country'. It imposes a duty on every citizen 'to protect and improve the natural environment including forests, lakes, rivers, and wildlife'. Reference to the environment has also been made in the Directive Principles of State Policy as well as the Fundamental Rights. The Department of Environment was established in India in 1980 to ensure a healthy environment for the country. This later became the Ministry of Environment and Forests in 1985. The constitutional provisions are backed by a number of laws–acts, rules, and notifications. The EPA (Environment Protection Act), 1986 came into force soon after the Bhopal Gas Tragedy and is considered an umbrella legislation as it fills many gaps in the existing laws. Thereafter a large number of laws came into existence as the problems began arising, for example, Handling and Management of Hazardous Waste Rules in 1989.

General

1986-The Environment (Protection) Act authorizes the central government to protect and improve environmental quality, control and reduce pollution from all sources, and prohibit or restrict the setting and /or operation of any industrial facility on environmental grounds.

1986-The Environment (Protection) Rules lay down procedures for setting standards of emission or discharge of environmental pollutants.

1989-The objective of Hazardous Waste (Management and Handling) Rules is to control the generation, collection, treatment, import, storage, and handling of hazardous waste.

1989-The Manufacture, Storage, and Import of Hazardous Rules define the terms used in this context, and sets up an authority to inspect, once a year, the industrial activity connected with hazardous chemicals and isolated storage facilities.

1989-The Manufacture, Use, Import, Export, and Storage of hazardous Micro-organisms/ Genetically Engineered Organisms or Cells Rules were introduced with a view to protect the environment, nature, and health, in connection with the application of gene technology and microorganisms.

1991-The Public Liability Insurance Act and Rules and Amendment, 1992 was drawn up to provide for public liability insurance for the purpose of providing immediate relief to the persons affected by accident while handling any hazardous substance.

1995-The National Environmental Tribunal Act has been created to award compensation for damages to persons, property, and the environment arising from any activity involving hazardous substances.

1997-The National Environment Appellate Authority Act has been created to hear appeals with respect to restrictions of areas in which classes of industries etc. are carried out or prescribed subject to certain safeguards under the EPA.

1998-The Biomedical waste (Management and Handling) Rules is a legal binding on the health care institutions to streamline the process of proper handling of hospital waste such as segregation, disposal, collection, and treatment.

1999-The Environment (Siting for Industrial Projects) Rules, 1999 lay down detailed provisions relating to areas to be avoided for siting of industries, precautionary measures to be taken for site selecting as also the aspects of environmental protection which should have been incorporated during the implementation of the industrial development projects.

2000-The Municipal Solid Wastes (Management and Handling) Rules, 2000 apply to every municipal authority responsible for the collection, segregation, storage, transportation, processing, and disposal of municipal solid wastes.

2000-The Ozone Depleting Substances (Regulation and Control) Rules have been laid down for the regulation of production and consumption of ozone depleting substances.

2001-The Batteries (Management and Handling) Rules, 2001 rules shall apply to every manufacturer, importer, re-conditioner, assembler, dealer, auctioneer, consumer, and bulk consumer involved in the manufacture, processing, sale, purchase, and use of batteries or components so as to regulate and ensure the environmentally safe disposal of used batteries.

2002-The Noise Pollution (Regulation and Control) (Amendment) Rules lay down

such terms and conditions as are necessary to reduce noise pollution, permit use of loud speakers or public address systems during night hours (between 10:00 p.m. to 12:00 midnight) on or during any cultural or religious festive occasion

2002-The Biological Diversity Act is an act to provide for the conservation of biological diversity, sustainable use of its components, and fair and equitable sharing of the benefits arising out of the use of biological resources and knowledge associated with it

Forest and Wildlife

1927-The Indian Forest Act and Amendment, 1984, is one of the many surviving colonial statutes. It was enacted to 'consolidate the law related to forest, the transit of forest produce, and the duty leviable on timber and other forest produce'.

1972-The Wildlife Protection Act, Rules 1973 and Amendment 1991 provides for the protection of birds and animals and for all matters that are connected to it whether it be their habitat or the waterhole or the forests that sustain them.

1980-The Forest (Conservation) Act and Rules, 1981, provides for the protection of and the conservation of the forests.

Water

1882-The Easement Act allows private rights to use a resource that is, groundwater, by viewing it as an attachment to the land. It also states that all surface water belongs to the state and is a state property.

1897-The Indian Fisheries Act establishes two sets of penal offences whereby the government can sue any person who uses dynamite or other explosive substance in any way (whether coastal or inland) with intent to catch or destroy any fish or poisonous fish in order to kill.

1956-The River Boards Act enables the states to enroll the central government in setting up an Advisory River Board to resolve issues in inter-state cooperation.

1970-The Merchant Shipping Act aims to deal with waste arising from ships along the coastal areas within a specified radius.

1974-The Water (Prevention and Control of Pollution) Act establishes an institutional structure for preventing and abating water pollution. It establishes standards for water quality and effluent. Polluting industries must seek permission to discharge waste into effluent bodies.

The CPCB (Central Pollution Control Board) was constituted under this act.

1977-The Water (Prevention and Control of Pollution) Cess Act provides for the levy and collection of cess or fees on water consuming industries and local authorities.

1978-The Water (Prevention and Control of Pollution) Cess Rules contains the standard definitions and indicate the kind of and location of meters that every consumer of water is required to affix.

1991-The Coastal Regulation Zone Notification puts regulations on various activities, including construction, are regulated. It gives some protection to the backwaters and estuaries.

Air

1948 – The Factories Act and Amendment in 1987 was the first to express concern for the working environment of the workers. The amendment of 1987 has sharpened its environmental focus and expanded its application to hazardous processes.

1981-The Air (Prevention and Control of Pollution) Act provides for the control and abatement of air pollution. It entrusts the power of enforcing this act to the CPCB.

1982-The Air (Prevention and Control of Pollution) Rules defines the procedures of the meetings of the Boards and the powers entrusted to them.

1982-The Atomic Energy Act deals with the radioactive waste.

1987-The Air (Prevention and Control of Pollution) Amendment Act empowers the central and state pollution control boards to meet with grave emergencies of air pollution.

1988-The Motor Vehicles Act states that all hazardous waste is to be properly packaged, labelled, and transported.

UNIT-V

Environmental Movements and Development

Environmental Movements in India

Environmental movements of various countries have emerged due to different reasons. It is basically due to prevailing environmental quality of the locality. The environmental movements in the north are basically on the issue of quality of life. Whereas the environment movements in the south arise due to some other reasons, such as due to conflicts for controling of natural resources and many more. It is being said that the, environmental movements in U.S.A arises, when the book silent spring written by Rachel Carson came in the market in the year 1962. In this book she had written about the impacts of poisonous chemicals, particularly the DDT on the environment. This book had raised the public consciousness. And it leads to the emergence of environmental movements in the U.S.A. The participants of these movements in North are the middle class and upper class people, who have concern for the nature. But in the south the protesters are generally the marginal population–hill peasants, tribal communities, fishermen and other underprivileged people. The different environmental movements in our own country support this argument. The examples could be taken as Chipko, N.B.A., Mitti Bachao Andolan, Koel-Karo Andolan etc. That is why the environmentalism of the North is refereed as "full stomach" environmentalism and the environmentalism of the south is called as "empty–belly" environmentalism.

The Reasons for Emergence of Environmental Movements in India?

Control Over Natural Resources: Control over natural resources is an important reason for emergence of environmental movement in India. Some good examples of these kinds of movements are like Chipko and N.B.A. In the first case, the reason for conflict was control over forest; whereas, in the second the reason was control over water. Let's have a look on the reasons behind the emergence of Chipko movement in the Garwhal Himalyas.

The movement started in the Garhwal Himalaya in April 1973. Between 1973 and 1980, over a dozen instances were recorded where, through an innovative technique of protest, illiterate peasants, men, women and children-threatened to hug forest trees rather than allow then to be logged for export. Notably the peasants were not interested in saving the trees per se, but in using their produce for agricultural and household requirements. In later years, however the movement turned its attention to broader ecological concerns, such as the collective protection and management of forest, and the diffusion of renewable energy technologies.

The Chipko movement was the forerunner of and in some cases the direct inspiration for a series of popular movements in defense of community rights to natural resources. Sometimes these struggles resolved around forest and in other instances, around the control and use of pasture, water, and mineral or fish resources. Most of these conflicts have pitted rich against poor: Logging companies against hill villagers, dam builders against forest tribal communities, multinational corporations deploying trawlers against traditional fisher folk in small boats. Here one party (*e.g.* loggers or trawlers) seek to setup the pace of resource exploitation to service an expanding commercial – industrial economy. A process which often involves the partial, or total dispossession of these communities who earlier had control over the resources in question, and whose own patterns of utilization were less destructive of the environment.

One important factor is that those poor peoples are solely dependent upon those natural resources for there survival hood. So, the changes in control of resources directly hamper their subsistence economy due to which their survival hood came in danger. Therefore the protest of the people rise against those outsiders, which had ultimately taken the shape of environmental movement in many instances.

Political Reasons

Let's see the political scenario of the country after independence; it will answer some part of our question. After independence in 1947 people have great expectation from the indigenous government, it was assumed that the new government which was more aware of the Indian problems and was equally concerned for the people would definitely seek to eradicate all problems, with the installation of new government under the leadership of Nehru, with the observations of industrializations raised hopes but the government policies were only for industrialization without looking the environment and equal sharing of natural resources.

The governmental policies resulted into a lot of displacement of people due to large projects such as dams like Bhakra-Nangal and many others. These policies pushed the local people on the edges more often than not, the agents of resource intensification are given preferential treatment by the states through the grant of generous long leases over mineral or fish stocks, *e.g.*, or the provision of raw materials at an enormously subsidised prices, with the injustice so compounded local communities at the receiving end of this process have no recourse except direct actions, resisting both the state and out side exploiters through a variety of protest techniques. So we can say these struggles might perhaps as seen as manifestation a new kind of 'traditional' class conflict were fought in the cultivated field or in the factory, these new struggles are waged over gifts of nature such as forests, and waters, gifts that are coveted by all but increasingly monopolized by a few.

If we talk in explicitly ecological terms then we can say that history of development in India can be interpreted as being, in essence, a process of resources capture by the omnivorous (individuals and groups with the social power to capture, transform and use natural resources from a much wider catchment area) at the expanse of ecosystem people (those communities which depend very heavily on the natural resources of their own locality). So, we can say the environmental movement is the resistance offered by ecosystem people to the resource capture by omnivorous: as embodied in movements against large dams by tribal communities to be displaced by them or struggles by peasants against diversion of forests and grazing land to industry.

Socio-economic Reaons

The other angles by which we look upon the cause of emergence of environmental movements are the socio-economic reasons. Almost most of the environmental movements in India are some how related with this aspect, also, if we see the location where these movements have started then we would found that most of these areas are tribal dominated. These people have strong beliefs regarding their forests, land and water. At the same time they are also totally dependent upon these resources for their survival hood. Therefore, when these forests or other sources of livelihood get disturbed by the outsiders, their socio-economic conditions get hampered and the ultimate recourse is the movement against those people who were harnessing those resources. Also, women had generally played an important role in these movements, in tribal groups; women are accustomed to responsibility and leadership for community survival. There work involves them directly and daily with forests and natural resources. So, whenever their survival came into risk, they take the lead role for the protection of their community and its resources.

Environmental Degradation/Destruction

Environmental degradation is also an important cause which many time leads to environmental movement. One such *e.g.* was the silent valley case. Here the proposed dam by the Kerala State Electricity Board was supposed to submerge a large tract of virgin forest. Those are one of the few virgin rain forests left in the country. So, the local people of vicinity along with the N.G.O.s resisted this move. In this movement the

K.S.S.P. also get help from scientist community of India and abroad. And the result was withdrawal of this project by the government.

One another *e.g.* of movement which arose due to the degradation of local environment was the movement against the limestone quarrying, in the Doon Valley in the late 1970s and early 1980s. In this case the retired officials and executives of the locality formed the 'friends of the Doon' and the 'Save Mussoorie' committees to safeguard the habitat of the valley. They were joined by hotel owners in Mussoorie, who were worried about the impacts of environmental degradation on the tourist in-flow in this well known ' hill station.' They used different techniques of resistance. Finally they put a Public Interest Litigation (PIL) that resulted in a landmark judgment of the Supreme Court, recommending the closure of all six limestone mines in the Doon Valley.

Environmental Awareness and Media

The spread of environmental awareness and media has also played pivotal role in emergence of environmental movement. People were previously unaware of the importance of the environment. But as the environmental awareness increased due various reasons people started protecting their environment. Some *e.g.* are the local movements to protect the purity of different rivers such as Ganga and Yamuna. The greening of many Indian cities also comes under this category. The Bhagidari movement of Delhi is a good *e.g.* Of this kind of environmental movement. Media has also played an important role in sustaining theses movements.

Conclusion

Now on the above arguments the conclusion could be drawn that the nature based conflicts, the false developmental policies of the government, the marginalization of the tribal and other underprivileged groups and the environmental degradation are the root causes of emergence of environmental movements in India. The lopsided, inequitous, and environmentally destructive processes of development have propelled the people to go against the state in many cases and this leads to the emergence of environmental movements in the country. The risks on the survival hood of the marginal people due to the above mentioned factors had resulted in the emergence of these movements. Therefore the point comes that the environmental movements in different parts of the country grows out of the distribution conflict over the ecological resources needed for livelihood. So we can conclude that environmental movements in India are the resistances by the people for their livelihood and for their survival.

Silent Valley Movement

Save Silent Valley was a social movement aimed at the protection of Silent valley, an evergreen tropical forest in the Palakkad district of Kerala, India. It was started in 1973 to save the Silent Valley Reserve Forest in from being flooded by a hydroelectric project. The valley was declared as Silent Valley National Park in 1985. None the less the controversy surrounding the valley is still on.

Background

Kuntipuzha one of the major rivers takes its origin in the flush green forests of Silent valley. In 1928 the location at Sairandhri on the Kunthipuzha River was identified as an ideal site for electricity generation. A study and survey was conducted in 1958 of the area about the possibility of a hydroelectric project of 120 MV and one costing Rs. 17 Crore was later proposed by the Kerala State Electricity Board.

The Kerala State Electricity Board (KSEB) decided to implement the **Silent Valley Hydro-Electric Project** (SVHEP) centered on a dam across the Kunthipuzha River in 1973. The resulting reservoir would have flood 8.3 km^2 of virgin rainforest. The proposal was enquired by National Committee on Environmental Planning and Co-ordination (NCEPC) and suggested 17 safeguards to be implemented in case the project implemented. A shortage of funds delayed activity. Even then from 1974 to 1975 a very large number of trees were felled in the area. KSEB announced its plan to begin dam construction in 1973.

Beginnings

After the announcement of imminent dam construction the valley became the focal point of "Save Silent Valley", India's fiercest environmental debate of the decade. Because of concern about the endangered lion-tailed macaque, the issue was brought to public attention. Romulus Whitaker, founder of the Madras Snake Park and the Madras Crocodile Bank, was probably the first person to draw public attention to the small and remote area. In 1977 the Kerala Forest Research Institute carried out an Ecological Impact study of the Silent Valley area and proposed that the area be declared a Biosphere Reserve.

In 1978 Smt. Indira Gandhi, the Honorable Prime Minister of India, approved the project, with the condition that the State Government enact Legislation ensuring the necessary safeguards. Also that year the IUCN (Ashkhabad, USSR, 1978) passed a resolution recommending protection of Lion-tailed Macaques in Silent Valley and Kalakkad and the controversy heated up. In 1979 the Government of Kerala passed Legislation regarding the Silent Valley Protection Area (Protection of Ecological balance Act of 1979) and issued a notification declaring the exclusion of the Hydroelectric Project Area from the proposed National Park.

Participants

Kerala Sasthra Sahithya Parishath (KSSP) effectively aroused public opinion on the requirement to save Silent Valley. They also published a Techno-economic and Socio-Political assessment report on the Silent Valley Hydroelectric project. The poet activist Sugathakumari poet activist played an important role in the silent valley protest and her poem "Marathinu Stuthi" (Ode to a Tree) became a symbol for the protest from the intellectual community and was the opening song/prayer of most of the "save the Silent Valley" campaign meetings. Dr. Salim Ali, eminent ornithologist of the Bombay Natural History Society, visited the Valley and appealed for cancellation of the Hydroelectric Project. A petition of writ was filed before the High Court of Kerala, against the clear cutting of forests in the Hydroelectric Project area and the court ordered a stop to the clear cutting.

Dr. M.S. Swaminathan, the renowned Agricultural Scientist, and then Secretary to the Department of Agriculture, called at the Silent Valley region and his suggestion was 389.52 km^2 including the Silent Valley (89.52 km^2), New Amarambalam (80 km^2), Attappadi (120 km^2) in Kerala and Kunda in Tamilnadu (100 km^2) reserve forests, should be made into a National Rainforest Biosphere Reserve, with the aim of "preventing erosion of valuable genes from the area".Listen*:(8:46) to Dr. M. S. Swaminathan speaking on Sustainable Development, p.83, August 27, 2002*

In January 1980 the Hon. High Court of Kerala lifted the ban on clear cutting, but then the Hon. Prime Minister of India requested the Government of Kerala to stop further works in the project area until all aspects were fully discussed. In December, the Government of Kelala declared the Silent Valley area, excluding the Hydroelectric Project area, as a National Park.

In 1982 a multidisciplinary committee with Prof. M. G. K. Menon as chairman, was created to decide if the Hydroelectric Project was feasible without any significant ecological damage. Early in 1983, Prof. Menon's Committee submitted its report. After a careful study of the Menon report, the Hon. Prime Minister of India decided to abandon the Project. On October 31, 1984 Indira Gandhi was assassinated and on November 15 the Silent Valley forests were declared as a National Park, though the boundaries of the Silent Valley Park were limited and no buffer zone was created, despite recommendations by expert committees and scientists.

Park Inaugurated

Ten months later, on September 7, 1985 the Silent Valley National Park was formally inaugurated and a memorial at Sairandhri to Indira Gandhi was unveiled by Shri. Rajiv Gandhi, the new Hon. Prime Minister of India. On September 1, 1986 Silent Valley National Park was designated as the core area of the Nilgiri Biosphere Reserve.

Since then, a long-term conservation effort has been undertaken to preserve the Silent Valley ecosystem.

A New Dam proposal

In 2001 a new Hydro project was proposed and the "Man vs. Monkey debate" was revived. The proposed site of the dam (64.5 m high and 275 m long) is just 3.5 km downstream of the old dam site at Sairandhiri, 500 m outside the National Park boundary.. The 84 km^2 catchment of the project area included 79 km^2 of the Silent Valley National Park.

The Kerala Minister for Electricity called The Pathrakkadavu dam (PHEP) an "eco-friendly alternative" to the old Silent Valley project. The PHEP was designed as a run-off-the-river project with an installed capacity of 70 MW in the first phase (105 MW eventually) and an energy generation of 214 million units (Mu) with a minimal gross storage of 0.872 million cubic metres. The claim was that the submergence area of the PHEP would be a negligible.041 km^2 compared to 8.30 km^2 submergence of the 1970s (SVHEP).. However, The spectacular waterfall between the Neelikkal and Pathrakkadavu hills bordering the Silent Valley will disappear if the proposed Pathrakkadavu hydro-electric project is implemented.-Image

During January to May 2003 a rapid Environmental Impact Assessment (EIA) was carried out during by the Thiruvananthapuram-based Environmental Resources Research Centre and its report was released in December, stating that forest lost due to the project would be just.2216 km^2, not including the 7.4 km approach road and land to be acquired for the powerhouse in Karapadam.

Present Status

- Little more was heard till Nov. 15, 2006 when Kerala Minister for Forest Binoy Viswam said that the proposed buffer zone for Silent Valley would be declared soon.
- On Feb 21, 2007 Chief Minister A. K. Antony told reporters after a cabinet meeting that "*when the Silent Valley proposal was dropped, the centre had promised to give clearance to the Pooyamkutty project. This promise, however, had not been honoured. The Kerala* government has not taken any decision *on reviving the Silent Valley Hydel Project*".

- On Mar 22, 2007 the activist poet Sugathakumari appealed to the Chief Minister of Kerala to restrain the Electricity Minister from reviving the proposal for a hydroelectric project at Pathrakkadavu.
- On April 18, 2007, Kerala Chief Minister V S Achuthanandan and his cabinet approved the Pathrakkadavu Hydro-electric project and sent it to the Union Government for environmental approval.
- The 147.22 km^2 Silent Valley Buffer Zone was formally approved by the Kerala Cabinet on June 6, 2007. The Cabinet also sanctioned 35 staff to protect the area and two new forest stations in Bhavani range at Anavai and Thudukki. The zone is aimed at checking the illicit cultivation of ganja, poaching and illicit brewing in areas adjacent to Silent Valley and help long-term sustainability of the protected area.

Chipko Movement

The Chipko movement or Chipko Andolan (literally "to stick" in Hindi) is a socio-ecological movement that employed the Gandhian methods of satyagraha and non-violent resistance, through the act of hugging trees to protect them from being felled. The modern Chipko movement started in the early 1970s in the Garhwal Himalayas of Uttarakhand, with growing awareness towards rapid deforestation. The landmark event in this struggle took place on March 26, 1974, when a group of female peasants in Reni village, Hemwalghati, in Chamoli district, Uttarakhand, India, acted to prevent the cutting of trees and reclaim their traditional forest rights that were threatened by the contractor system of the state Forest Department, and transpired hundreds of such grassroot level actions, throughout the region. By the 80s, the movement spread throughout India, and led to formulation of people sensitive forest policies and stopping of open felling of trees in regions as far reaching as Vindhyas and the Western Ghats.

The first recorded event of *Chipko* however, took place in village Khejarli, Jodhpur district, in 1730 AD, when 363 Bishnois, led by Amrita Devi sacrificed their lives while protecting green Khejri trees, considered sacred by the community, by hugging them, and braved the axes of loggers sent by the local ruler, today it is seen an inspiration and a precursor for Chipko movement of Garhwal.

The Chipko movement, though primarily a livelihood movement rather than a forest conservation movement, went on to become a rallying point for many future environmentalists, environmental protests and movements the world over and created a precedent for non-violent protest. It occurred at a time when there was hardly any environmental movement in the developing world, and its success meant that the world immediately took notice of this non-violent Tree hugging movement, which was to inspire in time, many such eco-groups, helped in slowing down the rapid deforestation, exposed vested interests, increased ecological awareness, and demonstrated the viability of people power.

Above all, it stirred up existing civil society in India like never before, which started looking towards tribal, and marginalized people and their issues like never before. So much so that, quarter a century later, *India Today* mentioned, the people behind the "forest satyagraha" of the Chipko movement, as amongst "100 people who shaped India". Today, beyond the eco-socialism hue, it is being seen increasingly as an ecofeminism movement, as though many of its leaders were men, women were not just its backbone, but also its mainstay, because they were the ones most affected by the rampant deforestation, leading to lack of firewood and fodder as well as water of drinking and irrigation. Over the years they also became primary stakeholders in majority of the afforestation work that happened under the Chipko movement.

History

The Himalayan region had always been exploited for its natural wealth, be it minerals, or timber, including by the British. The last of nineteenth century, saw implementation of new approaches in forestry, coupled with reservation of forests for commercial forestry, causing disruption in the age-old symbiotic relationship between the natural environment and the rural peasant, both in Kumaon and Garhwal. The few peasant protests that arose during this period were crushed severely. Notable protests in 19th century, were that of 1906, followed by the 1921 protest which was linked with then independence movement imbued with Gandhian ideologies, the 1940s was again marked with a series of protests in Tehri Garhwal region.

Post-independence period, when waves of a resurgent India were hitting even the far reaches of India, the landscape of upper Himalayan region was only slowly changing, and largely remained inaccessible. But all this was to change soon, when an important event in the environmental history of the Garhwal region occurred in the India-China War of 1962, in which India faced heavy losses.

Though, the region was not involved in the war directly, the government wisened by its losses and war casualties, took rapid initiatives to secure its borders, set up army bases, build road network, deep into the upper reaches of Garhwal, on India's border with Chinese-ruled Tibet, an area which was till now all but cut off from the rest of nation. However with construction of roads, and subsequent developments also came mining projects for limestone, magnesium, and potassium, timber merchants and commercial forestry which now had access to forests inaccessible till now.

Soon, the forest cover started deteriorating at an alarming rate, resulting in hardships in labour intensive fodder and firewood collection. This also led to a deterioration in the soil conditions, and soil erosion in the area as the water sources dried up in the hills, and water shortages became rampant. Subsequently, communities gave up the raising livestock, adding to the problems of malnutrition in the region. This crisis was heightened by the fact that Forest conservation policies, like Indian Forest Act, 1927, traditionally restricted the access of local communities to the forests, resulting in scarce farmlands, in an over populated and extremely poor area, despite all its natural wealth. Thus the sharp decline in the local agrarian economy, lead to migration of people into the plains, looking for jobs, which created several de-populated villages in 60s.

Gradually a rising awareness about the ecological crisis, which arose from an immediate loss of livelihood caused by it, resulted in initial activism sparks in the region. Starting in 1964 with the establishment of Dasholi Gram Swarajya Sangh *(DGSS) ("Dasholi Society for Village Self-Rule"), set up by Gandhian social worker, Chandi Prasad Bhatt in Gopeshwar, and inspired Jayaprakash Narayan and the Sarvodaya movement, with an aim to set up small industries using the resources of the forests, their first project was a small workshop making farm tools for local use. Its name was later changed to* Dasholi Gram Swarajya Sangh *(DGSS) from original* Dasholi Gram Swarajya Mandal *(DGSM) in 1980s. Here they had to face the restrictive forest policies, a hangover of colonial era still prevalent and on top of it the "contractor system", in which these pieces of forest land were commodified and auctioned to big contractors, usually from the plains, who brought along their own skilled and semiskilled laborers, leaving only the menial jobs like hauling rocks for the hill people, which paid next meagrely. On the other hand, hill regions saw an influx of new population, which added to already strained ecological balance and cracks started showing everywhere.*

Hastened by increasing hardships, the Garhwal Himalayas soon became centre rising social ecological awareness against reckless deforestation which had denuded much of forest cover, which eventually resulted in the devastating Alaknanda River floods, in July 1970, when a major landslide blocked the river, and effected an area starting from Hanumanchatti, near Badrinath to 350 km downstream till Haridwar, further numerous villages, bridges and roads were washed away. Thereafter incidences of landslides and land subsidence became a common feature in an area which was experiencing rapid civil construction.

"Maatu hamru, paani hamru, hamra hi chhan yi baun bhi... Pitron na lagai baun, hamunahi ta bachon bhi"

Soil ours, water ours, ours are these forests. Our forefathers raised them, it's we who must protect them. — *Old Chipko Song* (Garhwali language)

Soon villagers, especially women had started organizing themselves under several smaller groups, taking up local causes with the authorities, and standing up against commercial logging operations that threatened their livelihoods. In October 1971, the Sangh workers held a demonstration in Gopeshwar to protest against the policies of the Forest Department. More rallies and marches were held in late 1972, but to little effect, that is when the decision to take direct action was taken, and first such occasion arrived when the Forest Department turned down the Sangh's annual request for ten ash trees for its farm tools workshop, and instead a awarded contract for 300 trees to Simon Company, a sports good manufacturer in distant Allahabad, to make Tennis rackets.

In March 1973, the lumberers arrived at Gopeshwar, and after a couple of weeks, they were confronted at village Mandal on April 24, 1973, where about hundred villagers and DGSS workers beating drums and shouting slogans, forced the contractors and their lumberers to retreat. This was the first confrontation of the movement, and finally the contract was cancelled and awarded to the Sangh instead. Though by now, the issue had enlarged from procuring the annual quota of three ash trees, and encompassed a growing concern over the commercial logging, and forest policy of the government, which the villagers saw as unfavourable towards them. The Sangh also decided to resort to hugging the tree, Chipko as a mechanism of non-violent protest.

But the struggle was far from over, as the same company was awarded more ash trees, in the Phata forest, 80 km away from Gopeshwar. Here again, due to local opposition, starting 20 June 1973, the contractors retreated after a stand off that lasted a few days. Thereafter the villagers of Phata and Tarsali, formed a vigil group and watched over the trees till December, when they had another successful stand-off, when the activists reached the site in time, and the lumberers retreated leaving behind the five ash trees felled.

The final flash point began few months, when the government announced an auction scheduled in January 1974, for 2,500 trees near Reni village, overlooking the Alaknanda

River. Bhatt set out for the villages in the Reni area, and enraged the villagers, decided to protested against the move of the government by hugging the trees, over the next few weeks, rallies and meeting continued in the Reni area, and the villagers were prepared for the stand-off.

On March 26, 1974, the day the lumberers were to axe the trees, the men of the Reni village, and DGSS workers, were in Chamoli, diverted by state government and contractors to a fictional compensation payment site, while back home labourers arrived a truckload to the start logging operations. Finally when a girl on seeing them rush to inform Gaura Devi, the head of the village *Mahila Mangal Dal*, at Reni village (Laata was her ancestral home and Reni adopted home). Gaura Devi led 27 women of Reni village, reached the site and confronted the loggers. When all talking failed, and instead loggers started shouting and abusing the women, threatening them with guns, the women resorted to hugging the trees to stop the them from being axed. This went on into late hours, and the women kept a whole night vigil guarding their trees from the cutters, till a few of them relented and left the village. The next day, when with the men and leaders back, the news of the movement spread to the neigbouring Laata and others villages also Henwalghati, and more people joined in. Eventually only after a four-day stand off, the contractors left.

Aftermath

The news reached the state capital, and then state Chief Minister, Hemwati Nandan Bahuguna, set up a committee to look into the issue which eventually, ruled in the favour of the villagers. This then became a turning point in the history eco-development struggles in the region and also across the world.

The struggle soon spread across many parts of the region, and such spontaneous stand-offs between the local community and timber merchants occurred at several locations, with hill women demonstrating their new-found power as non-violent activists. As the movement gathered shape under its leaders, the name Chipko Movement got attached to their activities. As per Chipko historians, the term originally used by Bhatt was the

Garhwali lanaguge word, "angalwaltha", or embrace, which later adapted to Hindi word, Chipko, *which means to stick.*

Subsequently, over the next five years the movement spread to many districts of region, and within a decade throughout the Uttarakhand Himalayas. Larger issues of ecological and economic exploitation of the region were raised. The villagers demanded that no forest-exploiting contracts should be given to outsiders and local communities should have effective control over natural resources like land, water and forests. Thev wanted the government to provide low cost materials to small industries and ensure development of the region without disturbing the ecological balance.

The movement took up economic issues of landless forest workers and asked for guarantees of minimum wage. Globally Chipko demonstrated a clear link between environment concerns till now considered a luxury of the rich, in a new perspective as a matter of life and death for the poor, always the first ones to be devastated by an environmental tragedy, and several scholarly studies were made in the backdrop of the movement. In 1977, in another area, women tied a sacred threads, Rakhi, around trees earmarked for felling, in a Hindu tradition which signifies a bond between brother and sisters.

Women's active participation in the Chipko agitation was a very novel aspect of the movement. The forest contractors of the region usually doubled up as suppliers of alcohol to men. Women held sustained agitations against the habit of alcoholism and broadened the agenda of the movement to cover other social issues.

The movement achieved a victory when the government issued a ban on felling of trees in the Himalayan regions for fifteen years in 1980, by then Prime Minister, Indira Gandhi, until the green cover was fully restored. One of the prominent Chipko leaders, Gandhian Sunderlal Bahuguna took a 5,000 kilometre trans-Himalaya footmarch in 1981-83, spreading the Chipko message to a far greater area. Gradually, women set up cooperatives to guard local forests, and also organized fodder production at rates condusive to local environment. Next, they joined in land rotation schemes for fodder collection, helped replant degraded land, and established and ran nurseries stocked with species they select.

Participants

One of Chipko's most salient features was the mass participation of female villagers. As the backbone of Uttarakhand's agrarian economy, women were most directly affected by environmental degradation and deforestation, and thus connected the issues most easily. How much this participation impacted or derived from the ideology of Chipko, has been fiercely debated in academic circles.

Despite this, both female and male activists did play pivotal roles in the movement including Gaura Devi, Sudesha Devi, Bachni Devi, Chandi Prasad Bhatt, Sundarlal Bahuguna, Govind Singh Rawat, Dhoom Singh Negi, Shamsher Singh Bisht and Ghanasyam Raturi, the Chipko poet, whose songs echo throughout the Himalayas. Out of which, Chandi Prasad Bhatt was awarded the Ramon Magsaysay Award in 1982, and Sundarlal Bahuguna was awarded the Right Livelihood Award in 1987, and Padma Vibhushan in 2009.

Legacy

In Tehri district, Chipko activists would go on to protest limestone mining in the Doon Valley (Dehra Dun) in the 1980s, as the spark spread through the Dehradun district, which had earlier seen devastation of its forest cover leading to heavy loss of flora and fauna. Finally quarrying was banned after years of agitation by Chipko activists, and followed it up with vast public drive of afforestation, which turned around the valley, just in time. Also in the 80s, the activists like Bahuguna took on protest against construction of the Tehri dam on the Bhagirathi River, which went on for the next two decades. Before founding the Beej Bachao Andolan, *Save the Seeds movement that continues to the present day.*

Over time, as a United Nations Environment Programme report mentioned, Chipko activists started "working a socio-economic revolution by winning control of their forest resources from the hands of a distant bureaucracy which is concerned with selling the forest for making urban-oriented products.". It became a benchmark for socio-ecological movements in other forest areas of Himachal Pradesh, Rajasthan and Bihar; in September 1983, Chipko inspired a similar, Appiko movement in Karnataka state of India, tree felling in Western Ghats and Vindhyas was stopped. In Kumaon region, Chipko took on a more radical hue, combining with the general movement for a separate Uttarakhand state, which was eventually achieved in 2000.

In the coming years, the movement not just inspired numerous people to work on practical programmes of water management, energy conservation, afforestation, and recycling, but scholars to start studying issues of environmental degradation and methods of conservation in the Himalayas and throughout India.

On March 26, 2004, Reni and Lata and other villages of the Niti Valley, celebrated the 30th anniversary of the Chipko Movement, where all the surviving original participants united. The celebrations started at Laata, the ancestral home of Gaura Devi, where Pushpa Devi, wife of late Chipko Leader Govind Singh Rawat, Dhoom Singh Negi, Chipko leader of Henwalghati, Tehri Garhwal, and others were felicitated, from here a procession went to Reni, the neighbouring village where the actual Chipko action took place on March 26, 1974.

Narmada Bachao Andolan

Narmada Bachao Andolan (NBA) is a non-governmental organisation (NGO) that mobilised tribal people, *adivasis*, farmers, environmentalists and human rights activists against the Sardar Sarovar Dam being built across the Narmada river, Gujarat, India.

Their mode of campaign includes hunger strikes, mass media publicities, garnering support from noted film and art personalities etc. Narmada Bachao Andolan, together with its leading spokespersons Medha Patkar and Baba Amte, was the 1991 recipient of the Right Livelihood Award.

Background

Post-1947, investigations were carried out to evaluate mechanisms in utilizing water from the Narmada river, which flows into the Arabian Sea after passing through the states of Madhya Pradesh, Gujarat and Maharashtra. Due to inter-state differences in implementing schemes and sharing of water, the Narmada Water Disputes Tribunal was constituted by the Government of India on October 6, 1969 to adjudicate over the water disputes. This Tribunal investigated the matters referred to it and responded after more than 10 years. On December 12, 1979, the decision as given by the Tribunal, with all the parties at dispute binding to it, was released by the Indian Government.

As per the Tribunal's decision, 30 major, 135 medium, and 3000 small dams, were granted approval for construction including raising the height of the Sardar Sarovar dam.

In 1985, after hearing about the Sardar Sarovar dam, Medha Patkar and her colleagues visited the project site and noticed the project work being shelved due to an order by the Ministry of Environment and Forests, Government of India. The reasons for this was cited as "non-fulfillment of basic environmental conditions and the lack of completion of crucial studies and plans". What she noticed was that the people who were going to be affected were given no information, but for the offer for rehabilitation.

Due to this, the villagers had many questions right from why their permission was not taken to whether a good assessment on the ensuing destruction was taken. Furthermore, the officials related to the project had no answers to their questions. While World Bank, the financing agency for this project, came into the picture, Patkar approached the Ministry of Environment to seek clarifications. She realized, after seeking answers from the ministry, that the project was not sanctioned at all, and wondered as to how funds were even sanctioned by the World Bank. After several studies, they realized that the officials had overlooked the post-project problems.

Through Patkar's channel of communication between the government and the residents, she provided critiques to the project authorities and the governments involved. At the same time, her group realized that all those displaced were only given compensation for the immediate standing crop and not for displacement and rehabilitation.

As Patkar remained immersed in the Narmada struggle, she chose to quit her Ph. D. studies and focus entirely on the Narmada activity. Thereafter, she organized a 36-day long, solidarity march among the neighboring states of the Narmada valley from Madhya Pradesh to the Sardar Sarovar dam site. She said that the march was "a path symbolizing the long path of struggle (both immediate and long-term) that [they] really had". This march was resisted by the police, who according to Patkar were "caning the marchers and arresting them and tearing the clothes off women activists".

Formation

There were groups such as Gujarat-based Arch-Vahini (Action Research in Community Health and Development) and Narmada Asargrastha Samiti (Committee for people affected by the Narmada dam), Madhya Pradesh-based Narmada Ghati Nav Nirman Samiti (Committee for a new life in the Narmada Valley) and Maharashtra-based Narmada Dharangrastha Samiti (Committee for Narmada dam-affected people) who either believed in the need for fair rehabilitation plans for the people or who vehemently opposed dam construction despite a resettlement policy.

While Patkar established Narmada Bachao Andolan in 1989, all these groups joined this national coalition of environmental and human rights activists, scientists, academics and project-affected people with a non-violent approach.

Aftermath

Within the focus of Narmada Bachao Andolan towards the stoppage of the Sardar Sarovar dam, she advised addition of World Bank to their propaganda. Using the right to fasting, she undertook a 22 day fast that almost took her life. In 1991, her action brought led to an unprecedented independent review by the World Bank. The Morse Commission, appointed in June

1991 at the recommendation of The World Bank President Barber Coinable, conducted its first independent review of a World Bank project. This independent review stated that "performance under these projects has fallen short of what is called for under Bank policies and guidelines and the policies of the Government of India." This resulted in the Indian Government pulling out of its loan agreement with the World Bank. In response, Patkar said "It is very clear and obvious that they used this as a face-saving device", suggesting that if this were not to happen, the World Bank would eventually would have withdrawn the loan. The World Bank's participation in these projects was eventually cancelled in 1995.

She further undertook a similar fast in 1993 and resisted evacuation from the dam site. In 1994, the Bachao Andolan office was attacked reportedly by a couple of political parties, where Patkar and other activists were physically assaulted and verbally abused. In protest, a few NBA activists and she began a fast and 20 days later, they were arrested and forcibly fed intravenously.

Supreme Court's Decision

Patkar led Narmada Bachao Andolan had filed a written petition with the Supreme Court of India [the nation's apex court] seeking stoppage of construction on the Sardar Sarovar dam. The court initially ruled the decision in the Andolan's favor thereby effecting an immediate stoppage of work at the dam and directing the concerned states to first complete the rehabilitation and replacement process.

The Supreme Court also deliberated on this issue further for several years but finally upheld the Tribunal Award and allowed the construction to proceed, subject to conditions. The court introduced a mechanism to monitor the progress of resettlement pari passu with the raising of the height of the dam through the Grievance Redressal Authorities (GRA) in each of the party states. The court's decision referred in this document, given in the year 2000 after seven years of deliberations, has paved the way for completing the project to attain full envisaged benefits. The court's final line of the order states, "Every endeavour shall be made to see that the project is completed as expeditiously as possible".

Subsequent to the court's verdict, Press Information Bureau (PIB) featured an article which states that "The Narmada Bachao Andolan has rendered a yeoman`s service to the country by creating a high-level of awareness about the environmental and rehabilitation and relief aspects of Sardar Sarovar and other projects on the Narmada. But, after the court verdict it is incumbent on it to adopt a new role. Instead of `damning the dam` any longer, it could assume the role of vigilant observer to see that the resettlement work is as humane and painless as possible and that the environmental aspects are taken due care of".

People Involved

Amongst the major celebrities who have shown their support for Narmada Bachao Andolan are Booker Prize winner, Arundhati Roy and Aamir Khan.. In 1996, veteran documentary film maker, Anand Patwardhan, made an award-winning documentary on this issue, titled: 'A Narmada Diary'.

Criticism

The Narmada dam's benefits include provision drinking water, power generation and irrigation facilities. However, the campaign led by the NBA activists has held up the project's completion, and the NBA supporters have indulged in physical attacks on local people who accepted compensation for moving.

If opponents of the dam had fought for proper resettlement and rehabilitation packages, instead of an unrealistic programme of outright opposition, including the creation of a white elephant of a wildlife sanctuary, then local people would be seeing the benefits of the dam and not contemplating an uncertain future. *—Kirk Leech, The Narmada dambusters are wrong.*

National Test Range at Baliapal, Orissa

In 1985, when the Defence Ministry decided to set up a Nuclear Test Range (NTR) in Baliapal-part of a rich multi-product belt in Balasore, Orissa-the local protests it faced made global news. The protest had women leading from the front. They not only formed the front rung of human barricades to prevent government officials from entering the notified area, the suicide squad that was formed also had a good number of women.

Post-1947, people's protest movements have emerged in every part of India, mainly against displacement owing to dams, mines, industry or wildlife sanctuaries. Between 1951 and 1990, say official figures, 21.3 million people were displaced. Today, the number of displaced people has probably crossed 30 million.

Women-particularly the tribal, landless and rural poor-have participated in great numbers in people's movements because survival issues were at stake: land, water, fuel, fodder and their livelihood from forests. Many of these struggles have catapulted leaders into national prominence but few of these are women. This, even though it is generally accepted that women formed and still form the backbone of such movements.

The feeling of being deprived of due recognition and reward for their contribution to resistance movements has begun to surface among local women participants. Many such women leaders are from Orissa, Jharkhand, Chhattisgarh and Uttaranchal-three mineral-rich, backward states and one forest-rich but neglected state. Together, these states have seen the maximum number of people's movements in the past decade especially after the acceleration of globalisation. And now, women from these four states have got together to try and rectify this historical neglect of their contribution to the polity of their states.

At the recent workshop on 'Women's Role and Participation in Protest Movement against Development Projects' in Bhubaneswar, 40 women leaders shared their frustrations and chalked out future strategies to get their due. The workshop, the first of its kind, was based on studies done in these four states between 2002 and 2003. The studies, as well as the workshop, were conducted by the Institute of Socio-Economic

Development (ISED), a Bhubaneswar-based NGO, and were supported by the Delhi-based Friedrich Ebert Stiftung.

"We were used as numbers and invariably put in the forefront to protect the men from police beatings," recalls Ujalmati of Papal Khunta village about women's participation in the anti-BALCO (Bharat Aluminium Company) agitation in Orissa in the 1980s. "At one point, the police even decided to keep us segregated in the deep Reirakhole jungles because the jails were overflowing. We protested and broke the houses built for the company officials. After this, the company men lost the confidence to carry on work. Ultimately, we won!" recounts the octogenarian.

The female factor thus had its usefulness and was utilised to the hilt by the male leaders. When the armed forces came to quell the agitation in Baliapal, the women said, "We are your mothers, come kill us". The soldiers left them alone and returned.

But when the decision-making time came, these same brave women were given the go-by. In the Baliapal agitation, the decision-making steering committee had a lone woman member- mere tokenism. Jharkhand's Koel Karo hydel power project movement (1950s), and the Netrahat Field Firing Range (1981) struggle also saw women leaders sidetracked when the objectives were achieved.

Underplaying the contribution of women is obviously deeply entrenched. When ISED was studying women's participation in the movements in the four states, it found that most women who actively participated had gone back to domesticity. Besides, they tended to underplay their own invaluable contribution to the struggle, speaking more of the movement than their role in it. In fact, after the Tata Iron and Steel Company (TISCO) withdrew from the proposed Gopalpur steel plant in Orissa after facing fierce opposition, the male leaders told the active women: "Now go back home, your services are no more required."

Laxmi Naudiyal, leader of Bhumi Dhar Sangathan in Tehri Garhwal, Uttaranchal, questions this attitude. "We women are the backbone of our economies. Men either drink or migrate to the plains to earn. We manage the household, children, the aged, cattle, fuel, water-everything. When we join an agitation we have to do all the housework and make time for the protests. It's double duty for women, but who recognises that?"

Through the Chipko movement to save the forests (1970s), the Tehri dam protest and their fight for a separate state for the hilly region, the women of Uttaranchal have proved they have the stuff that leaders are made of. Kadambari Saklani, a leader of the anti-Tehri dam movement illustrates the point. She collected money and constructed a temple at the dam site in 1985. And for 16 long years-until 2001 when the temple was submerged-she sat there in protest every single day, motivating hundreds to do the same.

There were no rewards for these women just as there were none for the women who initiated the protest campaign that led to the formation of the state of Chhattisgarh. The men joined the protests later but the women were kept out when strategies were being formulated to guide the struggle. At the negotiating table, the men did the talking while the women leaders were simply missing! The men, say these local women leaders, pushed aside the women to become spokespersons of the agitating group, eyed (and achieved) political mileage somewhere or sometime. And, at times, the men manoeuvred themselves into a position to extract money from the agitation's opposing group-corporate bodies, contractors or the government.

If the women made this difficult then petty squabbles erupted, egos clashed and these very male comrades-in-arm had false police cases filed against the women. "Patriarchal reassertion in all its glory," spits out Rashmi Diwedi, 37, an Ekta Parishad activist. Diwedi works with the 41 villages of the Baiga tribes against their displacement from the Achanakmar Sanctuary in Bilaspur district, Chhattisgarh. "During the Resistance, we are Durga (Goddess of victory); but when the time comes to sit on the dais, we are illiterates, hence unworthy to sit alongside them!" exclaims Subri Oroam of Jharpahad Mahila Mukti Sangathan of Katari village in Jharkhand.

It goes to the credit of these women that they admit that the lack of a clear ideology in their activism is partly responsible for their current marginalisation. While in Orissa most struggles have been incited and backed by the political opposition (usually the Left parties), in Uttaranchal the Sarvodaya ideology has held sway. In both cases, party affiliates usually reaped the benefit of the toil of the women.

But now these women, a handful though they may be, have decided women should work in unanimity to the extent possible, and despite geo-cultural differences. They intend to project a value system that is humanistic and progressive. In addition, they plan to work towards documenting their past and future participation in movements that have made history but have forgotten to acknowledge women's contribution.

Conditions for Achieving the Gols of Sustainable Development

The role of mining in sustainable development is one issue that decision makers and resource managers have wrestled with for decades. With the development of their income-accounting tool, the TERI researchers have attempted to show how mining activities, which have a finite life span, can be integrated with social and environmental concerns in a way that promotes long-term community development.

The approach adopted by the TERI team places a monetary value on the effects of mining, such as air and water pollution, loss of forests, groundwater depletion, mineral resource use, and reduced agricultural productivity. It also takes into account the direct and indirect benefits to society. In the case of forests, for example, this would include the economic benefits gained from the generation of marketable products and the indirect benefits from watershed protection and other services. These environmental costs can be seen as an additional amount that should be contributed by the mining company to finance environmental rehabilitation using the "polluter pays" principle.

The team used similar accounting practices to place values on the health and social costs of mining. To ensure the economic viability of communities after the resource has been exhausted, money would be set aside to finance human and community development. This could help offset one of the main problems associated with mine closures: the lack of skills and resources for alternate economic development.

A Step Forward

The tools the TERI team have developed are not a panacea. For one thing they do not address the skewed power relationships so common in mining areas. "In Goa, mining is big business and mine owners are politically powerful," says Dr Noronha. "Mining is causing serious environmental problems, but few questions are asked."

She sees the development of these tools as a step forward in redressing this imbalance. "Mining companies are now aware and, more importantly, acknowledge that they have to act responsibly, that their activities are being monitored and assessed," states Dr Noronha. "Communities have information, both positive and negative, about the activity and its impact in relation to certain societal goals or standards if they want to act toward improved conditions for themselves. And government officials know there is access to information if they want to use it to improve governance in mining regions."

What is Sustainable Development?

Sustainable development has become the new catch phrase. Every international agency — from the World Bank to UNICEF — and almost every country is talking about it. But what does this mean? For environmentalists, sustainable development denotes a radical change from the past. But as a Western joke now goes, sustainable development for multinational companies, many of which have also embraced the concept, means simply "sustained growth" or "sustained profits". Every agency now has its own definition of sustainable development.

"Sustainable development is development that meets the needs of the present without compromising the ability of future generations to meet their own needs". This is a definition offered by the famous World Commission on Environment and Development in its report Our Common Future. Economists have also provided a definition of sustainable development as being an economic process in which the quantity and quality of our stocks of natural resources (like forests) and the integrity of biogeochemical cycles (like climate) are sustained and passed on to the future generations unimpaired. In other words, there is no depreciation in the world"s "natural capital", to borrow a concept from financial accounting.

But what is the operational substance behind such definitions? Who is going to ensure the rights of future generations when, given the highly divided world we live in, a large proportion of even the present generation cannot meet all its needs. Given such a social and political context, the above definitions also fail to say whose future generations" needs are being sought to be protected and preserved. Are we talking only of the future generations of the rich or also of the poor? These definitions are all, at best, rhetorical and woolly.

Eminent Indian economist, Sukhamoy Chakravorty, in a lecture that he delivered to the Centre for Science and Environment a few weeks before his demise, had pointed out that the success of the phrase "sustainable development" lies in the fact that it says nothing precise and, therefore, means anything to anybody. For a logging company it can mean sustained projects; for an environmental economist it can mean sustained stocks of natural forests; for a social ecologist it can mean sustained use of the forest; and, for an environmentalist it can mean a clean heritage for our children. But surely confusion cannot be more productive than clarity.

More than these pious definitions, it is important to understand the political content of sustainable development. Sustainability can never be absolute. A society which learns faster from its mistakes and rectifies its behaviour will invariably be more sustainable than another society which takes a longer time. And a society which fails to incorporate the lessons of its mistakes into its behaviour patterns even after the point of irreversibility has been reached, is obviously a society which is pursuing a totally unsustainable process of development. Learning from one"s mistakes is crucial to the process of sustainable development because no society — today, tomorrow or ever in the future—can claim to be so knowledgeable that it will always manage and use its natural resources in a perfectly ecologically sound manner. That will always be a near impossibility. Changing social, political, cultural, technological and ecological conditions will exert new pressures on the natural resource base and the possibility of its misuse or overuse will always remain. It can, therefore, be argued that sustainable development will be the outcome of a political order in which a society is so structured that it will learn fast from its mistakes in the use of its natural resources and rapidly rectify its human-nature relationships in accordance with the knowledge it has gained.

The important question, therefore, is: which political order will lead to conditions which encourage a society to learn fast from its mistakes in the use of its natural resources? It is obvious that such a society will be one in which decision-making is largely the prerogative of those who will also suffer the consequences of those decisions. If decisions are taken by a distant national bureaucracy or a transnational corporation to use a particular resource, and a local community living next to that resource is suffering in the process, it is unlikely that the decision-makers will change their decisions fast. But if the resource is being overused or misused by a local community which is dependent on it for its survival, and cannot easily relocate itself to another environment (in other words, it is a settled community rather than a frontier community), the declining productivity of the resource would sooner or later force the local community to change its ways.

Sustainability, therefore, arises not out of mushy headed concepts like care for future generations but out of hard political issues like, one, patterns of resource control, and, two, levels of democracy within the decision-making group. Greater the participation, openness and democracy within the members of the decision-making group, greater will be the chances of those who are suffering within the decision-making group — whether the decision is taken by a community or a nation as whole — to get a fair hearing and decisions changed accordingly.

Sustainability thus demands the creation of a political order in which, firstly, control of natural resources rests to the maximum extent possible with local communities who are dependent on those resources; and, secondly, decision-making within the community is as participatory, open and democratic as possible. The more this happens, the more we will move towards sustainable development.

The bedrock of sustainable development is composed of freedom and democracy — a system of governance which gives freedom to a community or a nation, within an universally accepted social framework that prescribes penalties for harming another community or nation, to control the use and management of its natural resources so that it can determine its own way of economic and social development. Each society will experiment and learn from its own mistakes. Sustainable development cannot be thrust upon by an external agent — whether it is the World Bank, the United Nations or the forestry department of a government — simply because it believes, at any point in time, that it has learnt all the lessons there are to learn. That will surely be a process towards unsustainable development.

Suggested Strategies for Sustainable Development in India

India's north-east–largely neglected by mainstream media–is a veritable cauldron of lifestyles, issues, practices and contentions. Immensely rich in terms of natural resources and biodiversity, the region offers possibilities of exhaustive research on how the people have (or have not) used these resources to survive through the ages. While most traditional livelihoods and sustainable development models in the region are fighting against annihilation with their backs to the wall, there are those that have withstood the ravages. Novel survival and livelihood strategies have also emerged in response to new challenges.

Through a range of 'Suggested Areas of Focus', the fellowship attempted to raise and–eventually–answer some critical questions: what makes the north east different from the rest of India? What makes the seven states different from each other? How do the people live in these regions, with little development and hence little livelihood opportunities? How does the resource rich region sustain itself? Have the people found an alternative means of livelihood that is sustainable? What has been the relation between the state and the people in terms of resource sharing? The suggested areas of focus were:

- Traditional medicine and its practice
- Customary and traditional laws and their impact on community forest management (CFM) and joint forest management (JFM)
- Floods and watershed management
- Women, livelihoods and governance
- Conservation as a livelihood
- Agricultural transition: from non-cash crops to cash crops
- Economic liberalisation and its impacts on livelihoods
- Livelihood strategies linked to biodiversity

Moreover, issues in north east are seldom covered in the 'mainstream' press; it is confined to the pages in the region or the occasional supplement on the region. Except of course the insurgency stories. Hence the fellowship was an excellent opportunity for people outside the region to observe, understand and report in-depth on the region.

Unit-VI

International Efforts for Environmental Protection

The Stockholm Conference 1972

Report of the United Nations Conference on the Human Environment

Declaration of the United Nations Conference on the Human Environment: The United Nations Conference on the Human Environment, having met at Stockholm from 5 to 16 June 1972, having considered the need for a common outlook and for common principles to inspire and guide the peoples of the world in the preservation and enhancement of the human environment,

Proclaims that:

1. Man is both creature and moulder of his environment, which gives him physical sustenance and affords him the opportunity for intellectual, moral, social and spiritual growth. In the long and tortuous evolution of the human race on this planet a stage has been reached when, through the rapid acceleration of science and technology, man has acquired the power to transform his environment in countless ways and on an unprecedented scale. Both aspects of man's environment, the natural and the man-made, are essential to his well-being and to the enjoyment of basic human rights the right to life itself.

2. The protection and improvement of the human environment is a major issue which affects the well-being of peoples and economic development throughout the world; it is the urgent desire of the peoples of the whole world and the duty of all Governments.
3. Man has constantly to sum up experience and go on discovering, inventing, creating and advancing. In our time, man's capability to transform his surroundings, if used wisely, can bring to all peoples the benefits of development and the opportunity to enhance the quality of life. Wrongly or heedlessly applied, the same power can do incalculable harm to human beings and the human environment. We see around us growing evidence of man-made harm in many regions of the earth: dangerous levels of pollution in water, air, earth and living beings; major and undesirable disturbances to the ecological balance of the biosphere; destruction and depletion of irreplaceable resources; and gross deficiencies, harmful to the physical, mental and social health of man, in the man-made environment, particularly in the living and working environment.
4. In the developing countries most of the environmental problems are caused by under-development. Millions continue to live far below the minimum levels required for a decent human existence, deprived of adequate food and clothing, shelter and education, health and sanitation. Therefore, the developing countries must direct their efforts to development, bearing in mind their priorities and the need to safeguard and improve the environment. For the same purpose, the industrialized countries should make efforts to reduce the gap themselves and the developing countries. In the industrialized countries, environmental problems are generally related to industrialization and technological development.
5. The natural growth of population continuously presents problems for the preservation of the environment, and adequate policies and measures should be adopted, as

appropriate, to face these problems. Of all things in the world, people are the most precious. It is the people that propel social progress, create social wealth, develop science and technology and, through their hard work, continuously transform the human environment. Along with social progress and the advance of production, science and technology, the capability of man to improve the environment increases with each passing day.

6. A point has been reached in history when we must shape our actions throughout the world with a more prudent care for their environmental consequences. Through ignorance or indifference we can do massive and irreversible harm to the earthly environment on which our life and well being depend. Conversely, through fuller knowledge and wiser action, we can achieve for ourselves and our posterity a better life in an environment more in keeping with human needs and hopes. There are broad vistas for the enhancement of environmental quality and the creation of a good life. What is needed is an enthusiastic but calm state of mind and intense but orderly work. For the purpose of attaining freedom in the world of nature, man must use knowledge to build, in collaboration with nature, a better environment. To defend and improve the human environment for present and future generations has become an imperative goal for mankind-a goal to be pursued together with, and in harmony with, the established and fundamental goals of peace and of worldwide economic and social development.
7. To achieve this environmental goal will demand the acceptance of responsibility by citizens and communities and by enterprises and institutions at every level, all sharing equitably in common efforts. Individuals in all walks of life as well as organizations in many fields, by their values and the sum of their actions, will shape the world environment of the future.

Local and national governments will bear the greatest burden for large-scale environmental policy and action within their jurisdictions. International cooperation is also needed in order to raise resources to support the developing countries in carrying out their responsibilities in this field. A growing class of environmental problems, because they are regional or global in extent or because they affect the common international realm, will require extensive cooperation among nations and action by international organizations in the common interest.

The Conference calls upon Governments and peoples to exert common efforts for the preservation and improvement of the human environment, for the benefit of all the people and for their posterity.

Principles

States the common conviction that:

Principle 1

Man has the fundamental right to freedom, equality and adequate conditions of life, in an environment of a quality that permits a life of dignity and well-being, and he bears a solemn responsibility to protect and improve the environment for present and future generations. In this respect, policies promoting or perpetuating apartheid, racial segregation, discrimination, colonial and other forms of oppression and foreign domination stand condemned and must be eliminated.

Principle 2

The natural resources of the earth, including the air, water, land, flora and fauna and especially representative samples of natural ecosystems, must be safeguarded for the benefit of present and future generations through careful planning or management, as appropriate.

Principle 3

The capacity of the earth to produce vital renewable resources must be maintained and, wherever practicable, restored or improved.

Principle 4

Man has a special responsibility to safeguard and wisely manage the heritage of wildlife and its habitat, which are now gravely imperilled by a combination of adverse factors. Nature conservation, including wildlife, must therefore receive importance in planning for economic development.

Principle 5

The non-renewable resources of the earth must be employed in such a way as to guard against the danger of their future exhaustion and to ensure that benefits from such employment are shared by all mankind.

Principle 6

The discharge of toxic substances or of other substances and the release of heat, in such quantities or concentrations as to exceed the capacity of the environment to render them harmless, must be halted in order to ensure that serious or irreversible damage is not inflicted upon ecosystems. The just struggle of the peoples of ill countries against pollution should be supported.

Principle 7

States shall take all possible steps to prevent pollution of the seas by substances that are liable to create hazards to human health, to harm living resources and marine life, to damage amenities or to interfere with other legitimate uses of the sea.

Principle 8

Economic and social development is essential for ensuring a favorable living and working environment for man and for creating conditions on earth that are necessary for the improvement of the quality of life.

Principle 9

Environmental deficiencies generated by the conditions of under-development and natural disasters pose grave problems and can best be remedied by accelerated development through the transfer of substantial quantities of financial and technological assistance as a supplement to the domestic effort of the developing countries and such timely assistance as may be required.

Principle 10

For the developing countries, stability of prices and adequate earnings for primary commodities and raw materials are essential to environmental management, since economic factors as well as ecological processes must be taken into account.

Principle 11

The environmental policies of all States should enhance and not adversely affect the present or future development potential of developing countries, nor should they hamper the attainment of better living conditions for all, and appropriate steps should be taken by States and international organizations with a view to reaching agreement on meeting the possible national and international economic consequences resulting from the application of environmental measures.

Principle 12

Resources should be made available to preserve and improve the environment, taking into account the circumstances and particular requirements of developing countries and any costs which may emanate-from their incorporating environmental safeguards into their development planning and the need for making available to them, upon their request, additional international technical and financial assistance for this purpose.

Principle 13

In order to achieve a more rational management of resources and thus to improve the environment, States should adopt an integrated and coordinated approach to their development planning so as to ensure that development is compatible with the need to protect and improve environment for the benefit of their population.

Principle 14

Rational planning constitutes an essential tool for reconciling any conflict between the needs of development and the need to protect and improve the environment.

Principle 15

Planning must be applied to human settlements and urbanization with a view to avoiding adverse effects on the environment and obtaining maximum social, economic and environmental benefits for all. In this respect projects which arc designed for colonialist and racist domination must be abandoned.

Principle 16

Demographic policies which are without prejudice to basic human rights and which are deemed appropriate by Governments concerned should be applied in those regions where the rate of population growth or excessive population concentrations are likely to have adverse effects on the environment of the human environment and impede development.

Principle 17

Appropriate national institutions must be entrusted with the task of planning, managing or controlling the 9 environmental resources of States with a view to enhancing environmental quality.

Principle 18

Science and technology, as part of their contribution to economic and social development, must be applied to the identification, avoidance and control of environmental risks and the solution of environmental problems and for the common good of mankind.

Principle 19

Education in environmental matters, for the younger generation as well as adults, giving due consideration to the underprivileged, is essential in order to broaden the basis for an enlightened opinion and responsible conduct by individuals, enterprises and communities in protecting and improving the environment in its full human dimension. It is also essential that mass media of communications avoid contributing to the deterioration of the environment, but, on the contrary, disseminates information of an educational nature on the need to project and improve the environment in order to enable mal to develop in every respect.

Principle 20

Scientific research and development in the context of environmental problems, both national and multinational, must be promoted in all countries, especially the developing countries. In this connection, the free flow of up-to-date scientific information and transfer of experience must be supported and assisted, to facilitate the solution of environmental problems; environmental technologies should be made available to developing countries on terms which would encourage their wide dissemination without constituting an economic burden on the developing countries.

Principle 21

States have, in accordance with the Charter of the United Nations and the principles of international law, the sovereign right to exploit their own resources pursuant to their own environmental policies, and the responsibility to ensure that activities within their jurisdiction or control do not cause damage to the environment of other States or of areas beyond the limits of national jurisdiction.

Principle 22

States shall cooperate to develop further the international law regarding liability and compensation for the victims of pollution and other environmental damage caused by activities within the jurisdiction or control of such States to areas beyond their jurisdiction.

Principle 23

Without prejudice to such criteria as may be agreed upon by the international community, or to standards which will have to be determined nationally, it will be essential in all cases to consider the systems of values prevailing in each country, and the extent of the applicability of standards which are valid for the most advanced countries but which may be inappropriate and of unwarranted social cost for the developing countries.

Principle 24

International matters concerning the protection and improvement of the environment should be handled in a cooperative spirit by all countries, big and small, on an equal footing.

Cooperation through multilateral or bilateral arrangements or other appropriate means is essential to effectively control, prevent, reduce and eliminate adverse environmental effects resulting from activities conducted in all spheres, in such a way that due account is taken of the sovereignty and interests of all States.

Principle 25

States shall ensure that international organizations play a coordinated, efficient and dynamic role for the protection and improvement of the environment.

Principle 26

Man and his environment must be spared the effects of nuclear weapons and all other means of mass destruction. States must strive to reach prompt agreement, in the relevant international organs, on the elimination and complete destruction of such weapons.

United Nations Conference on the Human Environment

The United Nations Conference on the Human Environment (also known as the Stockholm Conference) was an international conference convened under United Nations auspices held in Stockholm, Sweden from June 5-16,1972. It was the UN's first major conference on international environmental issues, and marked a turning point in the development of international environmental politics.

When the UN General Assembly decided to convene the Stockholm Conference, at the initiative of the Government of Sweden, UN Secretary-General U Thant invited Maurice Strong to lead it as Secretary-General of the Conference.

The conference was opened and addressed by the Swedish Prime Minister Olof Palme and secretary-general Kurt Waldheim to discuss the state of the global environment. Attended by the representatives of 113 countries, 19 inter-governmental agencies, and more than 400 inter-governmental and non-governmental organizations, it is widely recognized as the beginning of modern political and public awareness of global environmental problems.

The meeting agreed upon a Declaration containing 26 principles concerning the environment and development; an Action Plan with 109 recommendations, and a Resolution.

One of the key issues addressed was the use of CFCs (haloalkanes), which seemed to be responsible for the depletion of the ozone layer. Global warming was mentioned, but in this matter nothing of substance was achieved at this Conference.

Apart from increasing awareness of environmental issues among public and governments (for example, many governments subsequently created Ministries for the Environment and/or national agencies for environmental monitoring and regulation), the Stockholm Conference laid framework for future environmental cooperation; led to the creation of global and regional environmental monitoring networks and the creation of the United Nations Environment Programme.

Some argue that this conference, and more importantly the scientific conferences preceding it, had a real impact on the environmental policies of the European Community (that would later become the European Union). For example, in 1973, the EU created the Environmental and Consumer Protection Directorate, and composed the first Environmental Action Programme. Such increased interest and research collaboration arguably paved the way for further understanding of global warming, which has led to such agreements as the Kyoto Protocol.

Brundtland Commission 1983

The Brundtland Commission, formally the World Commission on Environment and Development (WCED), known by the name of its Chair Gro Harlem Brundtland, was convened by the United Nations in 1983. The commission was created to address growing concern "about the accelerating deterioration of the human environment and natural resources and the consequences of that deterioration for economic and social development." In establishing the commission, the UN General Assembly recognized that environmental problems were global in nature and determined that it was in the common interest of all nations to establish policies for sustainable development.

Resolution Establishing the Commission

The 1983 General Assembly passed Resolution 38/161[1]; "Process of preparation of the Environmental Perspective to the Year 2000 and Beyond" establishing the Commission. In A/RES/38/161, the General Assembly:

"8. Suggests that the Special Commission, when established, should focus mainly on the following terms of reference for its work:

(a) To propose long-term environmental strategies for achieving sustainable development to the year 2000 and beyond;

(b) To recommend ways in which concern for the environment may be translated into greater co-operation among developing countries and between countries at different stages of economic and social development and lead to the achievement of common and mutually supportive objectives which take account of the interrelationships between people, resources, environment and development;

(c) To consider ways and means by which the international community can deal more effectively with environmental concerns, in the light of the other recommendations in its report;

(d) To help to define shared perceptions of long-term environmental issues and of the appropriate efforts needed to deal successfully with the problems of protecting and enhancing the environment, a long-term agenda for action during the coming decades, and aspirational goals for the world community, taking into account the relevant resolutions of the session of a special character of the Governing Council in 1982;"

Brundtland Report

The Report of the Brundtland Commission, Our Common Future, was published by Oxford University Press in 1987. The Report is available in HTML format, one version with links to cited documents, and an easy-to-read full version is available at the Center for a World in Balance. The Report was welcomed by the General Assembly in its resolution 42/187

The report deals with sustainable development and the change of politics needed for achieving that. The definition of this term in the report is quite well known and often cited:

"Sustainable development is development that meets the needs of the present without compromising the ability of future generations to meet their own needs." It contains within it two key concepts:

- the concept of 'needs', in particular the essential needs of the world's poor, to which overriding priority should be given; and
- the idea of limitations imposed by the state of technology and social organization on the environment's ability to meet present and future needs.

Nairobi Conference 1982

The world community of states, assembled in **Nairobi** form 10 to 18 May **1982** to commemorate the tenth anniversary of the United Nations **Conference** on the Human Environment, held in Stockholm, having reviewed the measures taken to implement the Declaration and Action Plan adopted at that **Conference,** solemnly requests Governments and people to build on the progress so far achieved, but expresses its serious concern about the present state of the environment worldwide, and recognizes the urgent necessity of intensifying the efforts at the global, regional and national levels to protect and improve it.

1. The Stockholm **Conference** was a powerful force in increasing public awareness and understanding of the fragility of the human environment. The years since then have witnessed significant progress in environmental sciences; education, information-dissemination and training have expanded considerably; in nearly all countries, environmental legislation has been adopted, and a significant number of countries have incorporated within their constitutions provisions for the protection of the environment. Apart from the United Nations Environment Programme, additional governmental and not-governmental organizations have been established at all levels, and a number of important international agreements in respect of environmental co-operation have been concluded. The principles of the Stockholm Declaration are as valid today as they were in 1972. They provide a basic code of environmental conduct for the years to come.
2. However, the Action Plan has only been partially implemented, and the results cannot be considered as satisfactory, due mainly to inadequate foresight and understanding of the long-term benefits of environmental protection, to inadequate co-ordination of approaches and efforts, and to unavailability and inequitable distribution of resources. For these reasons, the Action Plant has not had sufficient impact on the international community as a whole. Some uncontrolled deterioration, deforestation, soil and water degradation and desertification are reaching alarming proportions, and seriously endanger the living conditions in large parts of the world. Diseases associated with adverse environmental conditions continue to cause human misery. Changes in the atmosphere – such as those in the ozone layer, the increasing concentration of carbon dioxide, and acid rain-pollution of the seas and inland waters, careless use and disposal of hazardous substances and the extinction of animal and plant species constitute further grave threats to the human environment.

3. During the last decade, new perceptions have emerged: the need for environmental management and assessment, the intimation complex interrelationship between environment, development, population and resources and the strain on the environment generated, particularly in urban areas, by increasing population have become widely recognized. A comprehensive and regionally integrated approach emphasizes this interrelationship can lead to environmentally sound and sustainable socio-economic development.
4. Threats to the environment are aggravated by poverty as well as by wasteful consumption patterns: both can lead people to over-exploit their environment. The International Development Strategy for the Third United Nations Development Decade and the establishment of a new international economic order are thus among the major instruments in the global effort to reverse environmental degradation. Combination of market and planning mechanisms can also favour sound development and rational environmental and resource management.
5. The human environment would greatly benefit form an international atmosphere of peace and security, free from the threats of any war, especially nuclear war, and the waste of intellectual and natural resources on armaments, as well as from apartheid, racial segregation and all forms of discrimination, colonial and other forms of oppression and foreign domination.
6. Many environmental problems transcend national boundaries and should, when appropriate, be resolved for the benefit of all through consultation action. Thus, states should promote the progressive development of environmental law, including conventions and agreements, and expand co-operation in scientific research and environmental management.
7. Environment deficiencies generated by conditions of underdevelopment, including external factors beyond the control of the countries concerned, pose grave

problems, which can be combated by a more equitable distribution of technical and economic resources within and among states. Development countries, and other countries in a position to do so, should assist domestic efforts to deal with their most serious environmental problems. Utilization of appropriate technologies, particularly from other developing countries, could make economic and social progress compatible with conservation of natural resources.

8. Further efforts are needed to develop environmentally sound management and methods for the exploitation and utilization of natural resources and to modernize traditional pastoral system. Particular attention should be paid to the role of technical innovation in promoting resources substitution, recycling and conservation. The rapid depletion of traditional and conventional energy sources poses new and demanding challenges for the effective management and conservation of energy and the environment. Rational energy planning among nations or groups of nations could be beneficial. Measures such as the development of new and renewable sources of energy will have a highly beneficial impact on the environment.

9. Prevention of damage to the environment is preferable to the burdensome and extensive repair of damage already done. Preventive action should include proper planning of all activities that have an impact on the environment. It is also important to increase public and political awareness of the importance of the environment through information, education and training. Responsible individual behaviors and involvement are essential in furthering the cause of the environment. Non-governmental organizations have a particularly important and often inspirational role to play in this sphere. All enterprises, including multinational corporations, should rake account of their environmental responsibilities when adopting industrial production methods of technologies, or when exporting to other

countries. Timely and adequate legislation action is important in this regard.

10. The world community of states solemnly reaffirms its commitment to the Stockholm Declaration and Action Plan, as well as to the further strengthening and expansion of national efforts and international co-operation in the field of environmental protection. It also reaffirms its support for strengthening the United Nations Environment Programme as the major catalytic instrument for global environmental co-operation, and calls for increased resources to be made available, in particular through the Environments fund, to address the problems of the environment. It urges all Governments and people of the world to discharge their historical responsibility, collectively and individually, to ensure that our small planet is passed over to future generations in a condition which guarantees a life I human dignity for all.

The Rio Summit 1992

The **United Nations Conference on Environment and Development**, also known as the **Rio Summit, Earth Summit** (or, in Portuguese, **Eco '92**) was a major United Nations conference held in Rio de Janeiro from June 3 to June 14, 1992.

Overview

172 governments participated, with 108 sending their heads of state or government. Some 2,400 representatives of non-governmental organizations (NGOs) attended, with 17,000 people at the parallel NGO "Global Forum", who had so-called Consultative Status.

The issues addressed included:

- systematic scrutiny of patterns of production — particularly the production of toxic components, such as lead in gasoline, or poisonous waste including radioactive chemicals
- alternative sources of energy to replace the use of fossil fuels which are linked to global climate change

- new reliance on public transportation systems in order to reduce vehicle emissions, congestion in cities and the health problems caused by polluted air and smog
- the growing scarcity of water

An important achievement was an agreement on the Climate Change Convention which in turn led to the Kyoto Protocol. Another agreement was to "not carry out any activities on the lands of indigenous peoples that would cause environmental degradation or that would be culturally inappropriate".

The Convention on Biological Diversity was opened for signature at the Earth Summit, and made a start towards redefinition of money supply measures that did not inherently encourage destruction of natural ecoregions and so-called uneconomic growth.

Twelve cities were also honoured by the **Local Government Honours Award** for innovative local environmental programmes.

These included Sudbury, Ontario in Canada for its ambitious programme to rehabilitate environmental damage from the local mining industry, Austin, Texas in the United States for its green building strategy, and Kitakyushu in Japan for incorporating an international education and training component into its municipal pollution control programme.

The Earth Summit resulted in the following documents:

- *Rio Declaration on Environment and Development*
- *Agenda 21*
- *Convention on Biological Diversity*
- *Forest Principles*
- *Framework Convention on Climate Change*

Both *Convention on Biological Diversity* and *Framework Convention on Climate Change* were set as legally binding agreements.

Critics, however, point out that many of the agreements made in Rio have not been realized regarding such fundamental issues as fighting poverty and cleaning up the environment.

Commission for Sustainable Development (CSD)

CSD has served as the UN high-level forum for sustainable development issues since 1992, when it was established by the UN General Assembly to ensure effective follow-up to the Rio Summit. CSD meets annually at UN Headquarters; its focus themes for 2006/2007 are energy for sustainable development, industrial development, air pollution/atmosphere and climate change.

The Rio Declaration on the Earth Charter

The **Rio Declaration on Environment and Development**, often shortened to **Rio Declaration**, was a short document produced at the 1992 United Nations "Conference on Environment and Development" (UNCED), informally known as the Earth Summit. The Rio Declaration consisted of 27 principles intended to guide future sustainable development around the world.

Some of the principles contained in the Rio Declaration may be regarded as third generation rights by European law scholars.

The 27 Principles of the Rio Declaration

Principle 1. The role of humans.

Human beings are at the centre of concern for sustainable development.

Principle 2. State sovereignty

States have, in accordance with the Charter of the United Nations and the principles of international law, the sovereign right to exploit their own resources pursuant to their own environmental and developmental policies, and the responsibility to ensure that activities within their jurisdiction or control do not cause damage to the environment of other States or of areas beyond the limits of national jurisdiction.

Principle 3. The Right to development

The right to development must be fulfilled so as to equitably meet developmental and environmental needs of present and future generations.

Principle 4. Environmental Protection in the Development Process

In order to achieve sustainable development, environmental protection shall constitute an integral part of the development process and cannot be considered in isolation from it

Principle 5. Eradication of Poverty

All States and all people shall cooperate in the essential task of eradicating poverty as an indispensable requirement for sustainable development, in order to decrease the disparities in standards of living and better meet the needs of the majority of the people of the world.

Principle 6. Priority for the Least Developed

The special situation and needs of developing countries, particularly the least developed and those most environmentally vulnerable, shall be given special priority. International actions in the field of environment and development should also address the interests and needs of all countries.

Principle 7. State Cooperation to Protect Ecosystem

States shall cooperate in a spirit of global partnership to conserve, protect and restore the health and integrity of the Earth's ecosystem. In view of the different contributions to global environmental degradation, States have common but differentiated responsibilities. The developed countries acknowledge the responsibility that they bear in the international pursuit of sustainable development in view of the pressures their societies place on the global environment and of the technologies and financial resources they command.

Principle 8. Reduction of Unsustainable Patterns of Production and Consumption

To achieve sustainable development and a higher quality of life for all people, States should reduce and eliminate unsustainable patterns of production and consumption and promote appropriate demographic policies.

Principle 9. Capacity Building for Sustainable Development

States should cooperate to strengthen endogenous capacity-building for sustainable development by improving scientific understanding through exchanges of scientific and technological knowledge, and by enhancing the development, adaptation, diffusion and transfer of technologies, including new and innovative technologies.

Principle 10. Public participation

Environmental issues are best handled with the participation of all concerned citizens, at the relevant level. At the national level, each individual shall have appropriate access to information concerning the environment that is held by public authorities, including information on hazardous materials and activities in their communities, and the opportunity to participate in decision-making processes. States shall facilitate and encourage public awareness and participation by making information widely available. Effective access to judicial and administrative proceedings, including redress and remedy, shall be provided.

Principle 11. National Environmental Legislation

States shall enact effective environmental legislation. Environmental standards, management objectives and priorities should reflect the environmental and developmental context to which they apply. Standards applied by some countries may be inappropriate and of unwarranted economic and social cost to other countries, in particular developing countries.

Principle 12. Supportive and Open International Economic System

States should cooperate to promote a supportive and open international economic system that would lead to economic growth and sustainable development in all countries, to better address the problems of environmental degradation. Trade policy measures for environmental purposes should not constitute a means of arbitrary or unjustifiable discrimination or a disguised restriction on international trade. Unilateral actions to deal with environmental challenges outside the jurisdiction of the importing country should be avoided. Environmental measures addressing transboundary or global environmental problems should, as far as possible, be based on an international consensus.

Principle 13. Compensation for Victims of Pollution and other Environmental Damage

States shall develop national law regarding liability and compensation for the victims of pollution and other environmental damage. States shall also cooperate in an expeditious and more determined manner to develop further international law regarding liability and compensation for adverse effects of environmental damage caused by activities within their jurisdiction or control to areas beyond their jurisdiction.

Principle 14. State Cooperation to Prevent environmental dumping

States should effectively cooperate to discourage or prevent the relocation and transfer to other States of any activities and substances that cause severe environmental degradation or are found to be harmful to human health.

Principle 15. Precautionary principle

In order to protect the environment, the precautionary approach shall be widely applied by States according to their capabilities. Where there are threats of serious or irreversible damage, lack of full scientific certainty shall not be used as a reason for postponing cost-effective measures to prevent environmental degradation.

Principle 16. Internationalization of Environmental Costs

National authorities should endeavour to promote the internalization of environmental costs and the use of economic instruments, taking into account the approach that the polluter should, in principle, bear the cost of pollution, with due regard to the public interest and without distorting international trade and investment.

Principle 17. Environmental Impact Assessments

Environmental impact assessment, as a national instrument, shall be undertaken for proposed activities that are likely to have a significant adverse impact on the environment and are subject to a decision of a competent national authority.

Principle 18. Notification of Natural Disaster

States shall immediately notify other States of any natural disasters or other emergencies that are likely to produce sudden harmful effects on the environment of those States. Every effort shall be made by the international community to help States so afflicted.

Principle 19. Prior and Timely Notification

States shall provide prior and timely notification and relevant information to potentially affected States on activities that may have a significant adverse transboundary environmental effect and shall consult with those States at an early stage and in good faith.

Principle 20. Women have a Vital Role

Women have a vital role in environmental management and development. Their full participation is therefore essential to achieve sustainable development.

Principle 21. Youth Mobilization

The creativity, ideals and courage of the youth of the world should be mobilized to forge a global partnership in order to achieve sustainable development and ensure a better future for all.

Principle 22. Indigenous Peoples have a Vital Role

Indigenous people and their communities and other local communities have a vital role in environmental management and development because of their knowledge and traditional practices. States should recognize and duly support their identity, culture and interests and enable their effective participation in the achievement of sustainable development.

Principle 23. People under Oppression

The environment and natural resources of people under oppression, domination and occupation shall be protected.

Principle 24. Warfare

Warfare is inherently destructive of sustainable development. States shall therefore respect international law providing protection for the environment in times of armed conflict and cooperate in its further development, as necessary.

Principle 25. Peace, Development and Environmental Protection

Peace, development and environmental protection are interdependent and indivisible

Principle 26. Resolution of Environmental Disputes

States shall resolve all their environmental disputes peacefully and by appropriate means in accordance with the Charter of the United Nations.

Principle 27. Cooperation between State and People

States and people shall cooperate in good faith and in a spirit of partnership in the fulfilment of the principles embodied in this Declaration and in the further development of international law in the field of sustainable development.

Major Achievements of the Rio Summit

Five years after the Earth Summit in Rio de Janeiro, treaties to protect the atmosphere and biodiversity are foundering, the world's population is spiraling, and more than one billion people cannot feed themselves, the Worldwatch Institute said on Saturday.

In a downbeat assessment of the world's troubled environment, social and political unrest, and prospects for feeding itself, Worldwatch's annual State of the World report listed a series of problems that have worsened since the landmark world environment summit.

"Since Rio, human numbers have grown by 450 million; vast areas of forest have been stripped of trees, and annual emissions of carbon dioxide from fossil fuels, the leading greenhouse gas, have climbed to all-time highs, altering the very composition of the atmosphere," the report by the Washington-based think tank said.

Two of the key initiatives from Rio—treaties to cut fossil fuel emissions that are warming the atmosphere and to protect biodiversity — have stumbled on a lack of commitment from major nations, the report said.

In particular, it said the United States' environmental leadership has receded in the last five years as it has missed targets set in the climate convention by wide margins and failed to ratify the Convention on Biological Diversity.

The United States is among eight countries with 56 percent of the world's population and 53 percent of its forests that "have the Rio agenda—and the fate of the earth—in their hands," the report said.

Other "environmental heavyweights" are Germany, Japan, Russia, China, India, Indonesia and Brazil, countries that Worldwatch said should play a bigger role in bridging differences between industrialised nations of the Northern Hemisphere and developing nations of the Southern Hemisphere.

China, India and other developing countries increasingly hold the key to reversing the environmental slide, and their burgeoning use of resources may force developed countries to face up to their own unsustainable economies, the report said.

The report also faulted international institutions, and rich countries' flagging commitments to them, for failing to confront environmental threats.

For example, it said government funding of the United Nations Development Programme and the U.N. Environment Programme has been inadequate.

The World Bank, which lends some $20 billion annually to developing nations, has claimed to have expanded its environmental lending since Rio. But the report said, "It continues to lend large sums for development schemes that add to carbon emissions and destroy natural ecosystems—while the broader vision of a sustainable economy is neglected."

The State of the World report—the 14th in the usually grim series—cited some improvements, including the Montreal Protocol to phase out use of ozone-depleting chemicals and slower-than-expected population growth.

But it said, "Too many governments still pursue economic growth at any price, ignoring the fact that damage to global commons such as the atmosphere and the oceans could severely disrupt the world's economies."

Until finance ministers—and more importantly prime ministers—take these problems as seriously as environmental officials do, nations will continue to undermine the natural resource base and ecosystems on which they depend," it said.

While global schemes such as the Montreal Protocol have had some success, the report said Rio likely marked the end of a "Marshall Plan" approach to environmental problems.

"If the world's economies are to be put on a sustainable footing in the 21st century, it is unlikely to be the result of a single top-down plan," Christopher Flavin, one of the report's authors, said.

"The answer is more likely to lie in an eclectic mix of international agreements, sensible government policies, efficient use of private resources, and bold initiatives by grassroots organisations," Flavin said.

But, the report said Rio "energized the efforts of private citizens to promote environmentally sustainable development," and encouraged non-government organisations around the world to "provide ideas as well as pressure for change."

Main Features of the Rio Declaration

"These 10 days could change the history of humankind."

This is what Japanese Foreign minister Keizo Obuchi told the 2,000 delegates at the U.N.-sponsored global climate conference currently meeting in Kyoto, Japan. The delegates, who represent over 150 nations, are trying to forge a treaty that would mandate reductions in the emission of greenhouse gases.

But when historians look back at Kyoto, will they see an opportunity missed?

For the most part, forecasts by foreign policy and environmental experts have been dim. Many predicted that the initial U.S. negotiating position, which calls for a return to 1990 emission levels by 2012 and the inclusion of developing countries in any treaty, would hinder any potential agreement.

"We are perfectly prepared to walk away from an agreement that we don't think will work," Vice President Gore said before heading to Kyoto to join the U.S. delegation. America's participation in any agreement drafted in Kyoto is considered critical because the U.S. emits a quarter of the world's greenhouse gases.

Despite a rocky beginning to the conference, negotiators were able to produce an agreement to reduce greenhouse gases after going into an 11th day of talks. The agreement calls for the 159 countries to reduce their emissions of greenhouse gases by 5.2 percent below 1990 levels by 2012.

Each country will have an individual reduction target to reach the world-wide reducation of 5.2 percent, although there are a few nations that will be allowed to increase their emissions. Under the draft proposal, the U.S. will reduce its emissions by seven percent below 1990 levels, the European Union's emissions will drop by eight percent and Japan's will reduce emmissions by six percent. Australia, on the other hand, is allowed to increase it emmissions by five percent.

Going into the conference, the U.S. had proposed stabilizing emissions at 1990 levels by 2012. The European Union had called for all developed nations to reduce their emissions by 15 percent by 2010, while Japan had called for a five percent reduction. The deal appears to be a compromise between those positions.

Consensus was also reached regarding the gases covered in the treaty. The U.S. had called for any treaty negotiated in Kyoto to cover six greenhouse gases—three natural, three man-made — while Japan and the E.U. only wanted negotiations to cover the three natural gases. It now appears that all six gases will be part of any deal. But only 38 developed nations are mandated to reduce their greenhouse gas emissions; developing nations only have to set voluntary limits. That could doom U.S. ratification of the Kyoto protocol. The U.S. Senate, which will have to ratify the treaty, voted 95-0 to demand the participation of developing nations in any agreement while those countries have strongly resisted such efforts.

Our forum asks: How were the competing proposals in Kyoto be worked out? Should developing nations been included in this treaty? Will the Kyoto conference be judged as a failure or a success?

Kyoto Conference and the part on Global Warming 1997

In the last couple of weeks it's been snowing in Kyoto, snowing in London, snowing in Washington, and snowing all over Mexico—in Guadalajara for the first time since 1881. Early flurries should have given some of the delegates to the Kyoto Global Warming talks reason to pause, but no, by day 5 we knew Americans were in trouble. There in front of the conference hall, on heat-absorbing blacktop, encircled by a "prayer group" pleading for forgiveness, the ice penguins finally started to melt. And brother, it was downhill from then on.

Kyoto, according to S. Fred Singer, economist Thomas Gale Moore, and numerous other hapless observers, was a sea of the silly, the simple, and the sanctimonious.

Kyoto hotels, determined to set a good example, left little notes in all the rooms expressing concern about "destructive climate changes," then asked patrons to get by on one sliver of soap and to have the decency not to request clean towels every day.

Over at the conference center, Greenpeace continued to have trouble with Mother Nature. Having mounted a huge "kitchen of tomorrow" display, complete with a refrigerator powered by $20,000, 15-foot-high solar panels (put THAT under your Christmas tree!), Greenpeace announced plans to offer free solar-brewed coffee to all comers. Of course, the sun didn't shine for the first three days and the coffee pot didn't work, suggesting a serious glitch in their rather expensive system.

Outside the conference center, representatives of the Korean Federation of Environmental Movements was festooning the shrubbery with snappy slogans: "Cool the Earth, Save Us," "Please: Gas Masks!", No Nukes, No Fossil Fuels for Us," and "Silent but Angry." Inside, Korean delegates were refusing to be held to any binding constraints on emissions. Outside, indoctrinated Japanese politicians decreed that all thermostats be turned down to 68 degrees fahrenheit, and later dealt with complaints from chilly conferences by handing out shawls emblazoned with "Smart Life with Energy Saving." Inside, indoctrinated Japanese kiddies, following the trend set by AIDS activists, hung quilts proclaiming their abhorrence of global warming.

Kyoto drew 3,500 registered journalists, who spent most of their time looking for someone to interview. Anyone with the slightest claim to importance was followed around by an entourage of TV cameras and reporters hoping that he or she would say something significant. Failing that, reporters interviewed each other or, if they got really desperate, interviewed those not of the faith, *i.e.* skeptical scientists, unconvinced economists, and others still exhibiting sane behavior.

On the day of the Vice President's long-awaited "16,000 miles for five minutes" address, events were more evocative of a Hollywood movie than an international summit. Reporters relegated to watching Gore's speech on big screen TVs (only a handpicked 50 were allowed inside the conference hall) behaved like the supporting cast in 1984 or Close Encounters of the Third Kind. As Gore's giant image appeared on screen, hordes of reporters crowded around each video projector, taking photographs of the TV, pressing their microphones up to the speakers, and straining to catch every word emanating from this New Age Big Brother.

Inside the conference center, Gore pulled off a remarkable rendition of Elmer Gantry meets Dances with Wolves—in other words, substantively nothing but mesmerizing nonetheless. "The most vulnerable part of the Earth's environment is the very thin layer of air clinging near the surface of the planet," he intoned. "We are altering the relationship between the Earth and the Sun" (the moon and the stars!). Changing our behavior will require "humility because the spiritual roots of our crisis are pridefulness.....Our children's children will read about the 'Spirit of Kyoto' and remember well the place and time where humankind first chose to embark together on a long-term sustainable relationship between our civilization and the Earth's environment."

Gore wrapped it up by comparing those opposing this Kyoto tent meeting to shills for the Tobacco Institute, a line still guaranteed to have most of the delegates, and not a few of the reporters, down on their knees, with their hands in the air, shouting "Hallelujah!" We would only comment that, as in Elmer Gantry, assuming that position is very useful for those intent on going through your pockets.

So, at conference end, with Undersecretary of State Stu Eisenstat, leader of the U.S. delegation, proclaiming "The eyes of the world are upon us!" (Now which film was that?).

Who won and who lost? Well, the Third World won; they agreed to nothing. The European Union won; they've already achieved most of their emissions rollback by shutting down dirty East German industries and closing British coal mines and, according to Finnish TV, plan to make up any shortfall by backdooring electricity through Poland, an exempt country. Norway, Iceland, and Australia won. Though not generally thought of as "developing countries," these three get to increase emissions. The United States and Japan, with national bureaucracies in the grip of Mother Earth fanatics, lost.

Here at home, the U.S. media, ever susceptible to packaged information — and some Kyoto observers were astonished at the huge sums Big Environment spent on packaging information — did their best to sell the deal to the American public, calling it "modest" and "conservative." Tim Lamer notes in a Media Research Center report on network coverage ("Media Reality

Check: Imposing an Energy Crisis Without Debate," Dec. 12) that climate scientists skeptical of global warming were largely missing from news reports. In 16 of the 19 stories broadcast between December 1 and December 11, reporters simply assumed that the talks had broad scientific support.

Meanwhile, at the **Annual Meeting of the American Geophysical Union**, held last week in San Francisco, California, research papers were presented that throw cold water on two of the mainstays of global warming hysteria. First, Harry Lins and James Slack of the U.S. Geological Survey reported that despite devastating floods in recent years — most notably in the upper Great Plains, California's Central Valley, and along the Mississippi River — a review of records dating back to 1914 shows no increase in either the frequency of floods or their size. "We do not see any evidence of a change in large-scale national patterns," says Lins. What may have changed, the researcher s note, is development along flood-prone rivers.

Second, climate modeler Joyce Penner of the University of Michigan, a noted contributor to the IPCC report, announced that new research on aerosols suggest that the 1 degree Fahrenheit warming of the last century may be entirely due to natural variability and not—yet—to human activity.

Finally, to end on an even more positive note, a CNN survey, announced last week, shows that despite all the hoopla there are fewer Americans concerned about global warming in 1997 (24 percent) than there were in 1989 (35 percent), a result that appears to support the recent New York Times survey showing that only 1 percent of Americans thought environment was the most pressing concern for America, and only 7 percent thought global warming was a problem at all.

So as we look ahead to next November's global warming talks in Buenos Aires, where the thermostats will be set at 80 degrees fahrenheit and organizers will be passing out hand-held fans printed with "Smart Life with Energy Saving," let's review three points that mysteriously disappeared from the 1996 IPCC report, Chapter 8, sometime between approval of the draft and publication:

1. "None of the studies cited above has shown clear evidence that we can attribute the observed [climate] changes to the specific cause of increases in greenhouse gases."
2. "No study to date has positively attributed all or part [of the climate change observed to date] to anthropogenic [man-made] causes."
3. "Any claims of positive detection of significant climate change are likely to remain controversial until uncertainties in the total natural variability of the climate system are reduced."

UNIT-VII

Curriculum in Environmental Education

Dimensions of Curriculum in Environmental Education

Place-based education is a relatively new term, appearing only recently in the education literature. However, progressive educators have promoted the concept for more than 100 years. For example, in "The School and Society," John Dewey advocated an experiential approach to student learning in the local environment: "Experience [outside the school] has its geographical aspect, its artistic and its literary, its scientific and its historical sides. All studies arise from aspects of the one earth and the one life lived upon it" (1915, p. 91). Place-based education usually includes conventional outdoor education methodologies as advocated by John Dewey to help students connect with their particular corners of the world. Proponents of place-based education often envision a role for it in achieving local ecological and cultural sustainability (1). This Digest reviews placebased curriculum and instruction, especially as it relates to outdoor and environmental education, and provides examples of K-12 resources and programmes.

Outdoor Education, Environmental Education And Place-based Education: How are They Connected?

The main purpose of "outdoor education" is to provide meaningful contextual experiences—in both natural and constructed environments—that complement and expand classroom instruction, which tends to be dominated by print and electronic media (Knapp, 1996, p. ix). It is a broader term than "environmental education," which can be described as instruction directed toward developing a citizenry prepared to live well in a place without destroying it (Orr, 1994, p. 14). Environmental education can occur both inside and outside the classroom.

Understanding the relationships among place-based education, outdoor education, and environmental education is worthwhile because each concept has been developed somewhat separately by educators who have produced curriculum materials and instructional practices that could be useful within the other concept areas. Further complicating this potential exchange is the variety of labels that have been applied to each of these approaches. For example, as the field of outdoor education matured, it was labeled school camping, camping education, and eventually, outdoor education. Likewise, place-based education has been referred to as "community-oriented schooling," "ecological education," and "bioregional education."

Paul Theobald refers to "place-conscious" elementary and secondary classrooms in his book, "Teaching The Commons" (1997, pp. 132-159). He advocates using the immediate locale as "the lens for disciplinary engagement in all schools across the country" (p. 137). In a later article, Theobald and Curtiss (2000) describe the field as "community-oriented schooling."

Smith and Williams (1999) describe this approach as "ecological education." They write, "The practice of ecological education requires viewing human beings as one part of the natural world and human cultures as an outgrowth of interactions between species and particular places" (p. 3). The authors outline seven principles, two of which directly reflect outdoor education: (1) practical experiences outdoors through the application of an ethic of care, and (2) grounding learning in a sense of place through investigation of surrounding natural and human communities.

Traina and Darley-Hill (1995) extend "locale" to include "bioregional education," encouraging students and teachers to know their place and to consider the impact of lifestyles on the resources of that bioregion. Similarly, Orr's (1994) call for "ecoliteracy" presents principles for rethinking education that clearly relate place-based education to outdoor education: (1) students should understand the effects of this knowledge on real people and their communities; and (2) learning though direct experiences outside the classroom is as important as the content of particular courses.

Thomashow (1995) writes about the goal of achieving "ecological identity" through the examination of four basic questions: What do I know about the place where I live? Where do things come from? How do I connect to the earth? What is my purpose as a human being? He integrates these questions into activities by incorporating reflective learning in the school, home, community, and the workplace (p. xvii). These questions focus curriculum and instruction on understanding and appreciating students' immediate surroundings.

Haymes (1995) speaks directly to a "pedagogy of place" and addresses issues of race and class as they are made manifest in the construction of urban environments and in the power and politics that emerge from those constructs. His work takes a cultural studies perspective and contributes a much-needed complement to more conventional outdoor/environmental curriculum and instruction.

What are The Essential Characteristics of Place-based Education?

A survey of the literature on place-based education reveals characteristic patterns to this still-evolving approach that make it distinctive.

* It emerges from the particular attributes of a place. The content is specific to the geography, ecology, sociology, politics, and other dynamics of that place. This fundamental characteristic establishes the foundation of the concept.
* It is inherently multidisciplinary.
* It is inherently experiential. In many programmes this includes a participatory action or service learning

component; in fact, some advocates insist that action must be a component if ecological and cultural sustainability are to result.

* It is reflective of an educational philosophy that is broader than "learn to earn." Economics of place can be an area of study as a curriculum explores local industry and sustainability; however, all curricula and programmes are designed for broader objectives.
* It connects place with self and community. Because of the ecological lens through which place-based curricula are envisioned, these connections are pervasive. These curricula include multigenerational and multicultural dimensions as they interface with community resources.

Why is Place-based Education Important?

Some critics of place-based education believe that the primary goal of schooling should be to prepare students to work and function in a highly technological and consumer-oriented society. In contrast, place-based educators believe that education should prepare people to live and work to sustain the cultural and ecological integrity of the places they inhabit. To do this, people must have knowledge of ecological patterns, systems of causation, and the long-term effects of human actions on those patterns (Orr, 1994). One of the most compelling reasons to adopt place-based education is to provide students with the knowledge and experiences needed to actively participate in the democratic process.

What are Some Sources of Place-based Curriculum?

Space limitations in this Digest preclude extensive lists and descriptions of place-based programmes. However, the references below will direct the reader to many of them.

Periodicals: For descriptions of exemplary curricula, see the resources and reviews sections of back and future issues of:

"The Active Learner: A Foxfire Journal for Teachers." The Foxfire Fund, Inc. P. O. Box 541, Mountain City, GA 30562-0541. 706-746-5828.

"Clearing: Environmental Education in the Pacific Northwest." Creative Educational Networks/EE Project, P. O. Box 82954, Portland, OR 97282. 503-657-6958 x 2638.

"Green Teacher: Education For Planet Earth." 95 Robert Street, Toronto, Ontario, Canada M5S 2K5. 416-960-1244.

"Orion Afield: Working for Nature and Community." The Orion Society, 195 Main Street, Great Barrington, MA 01230. 413-528-4422. (Especially "In Pursuit of a Bioregional Curriculum," Spring, 1999, Vol. 3, No. 2).

"Taproot: A Publication of The Coalition for Education in the Outdoors." P. O. Box 2000, Park Center, Cortland, NY 13045. 605-753-4971.

Books: In addition to books included in the reference list, see the following:

Bowers, C. A. (1995). "Educating for an ecologically sustainable culture." Albany, NY: State University of New York Press. Describes three curriculum models of community and environmental renewal and profiles the Foxfire Curriculum, the Common Roots Programme, and the Ecoliteracy Project. Bowers notes that the three programmes represent very different approaches, but they all share the common characteristic of having evolved outside schools of education (p. 184).

Cajete, G. (1994). "Look to the mountain: An ecology of indigenous education." Durango, CO: Kivaki Press. Describes Indigenous teaching and learning tied to place. Written by a Tewa Indian specializing in environmental education and multicultural curriculum/programme development in science, social science, and the arts. These concepts and principles are equally adaptable to mainstream institutions.

Haas, T., & Nachtigal, P. (1998). "Place value: An educator's guide to good literature on rural lifeways, environments, and purposes of education." Charleston, WV: ERIC Clearinghouse on Rural Education and Small Schools. Chapter subtitles describe the book's scope: education for living well ecologically, politically, economically, spiritually, and in community.

Extensive annotated bibliographies for each aspect of place-based education are included.

Hart, R. A. (1999). "Children's participation: The theory and practice of including young citizens in community development and environmental care." London: Earthscan Publications Ltd. Outlines a theory and practice leading to sustainable "development that meets the needs of the present without compromising the ability of future generations to meet their own needs" (p. 5). Hart's examples of place-based curricula are provided through several case studies from all over the world.

Kriesberg, D. A. (1999). "A sense of place: Teaching children about the environment with picture books." Englewood, CO: Teacher Ideas Press. Highlights integration of the arts with place, providing teachers with picture book resources and activities for place-based teaching.

Smith, G. A., & Williams, D. R. (Eds.) (1999). "Ecological education in action: On weaving education, culture, and the environment." Albany, NY: State University of New York Press. Kiefer and Demple describe a strategy for building an ecologically sustainable way of learning in the programme, "Common Roots." They conclude, "in creating a context for local curriculum, we have seen the power of unifying the curriculum through the unique story of each community" (p. 43).

Sobel, D. (1993). "Children's special places: Exploring the role of forts, dens, and bush houses in middle childhood." Tucson, AZ: Zephyr Press. Offers several case studies in Chapter 5: "Making a Place in The Curriculum" and demonstrates the importance of childhood experiences around the home and community.

The Orion Society (1998). "Stories in the land: A place-based environmental education anthology." Great Barrington, MA: The Orion Society. John Elder describes four fundamental themes illustrated by the programmes described: attentiveness to students' home landscapes, the convergence of natural sciences and the arts, time spent outdoors, and exploring cultural aspects of the community (pp. 13-14). The authors of this anthology provide examples of place-based curricula.

Conclusion and Recommendations for Future Directions

Place-based education represents a recent trend in the broad field of outdoor education. It recaptures the ancient idea of "listening to the land" and living and learning in harmony with the earth and with each other. As society becomes increasingly urbanized and technologized, educators must continue to adopt and adapt more of the goals, theory, and practice of place-based education.

Natural Resources: Definition and Classification

Natural resources are naturally occurring substances that are considered valuable in their relatively unmodified (natural) form. A natural resource's value rests in the amount of the material available and the demand for it. The latter is determined by its usefulness to production. A commodity is generally considered a natural resource when the primary activities associated with it are extraction and purification, as opposed to creation. Thus, mining, petroleum extraction, fishing, hunting, and forestry are generally considered natural-resource industries, while agriculture is not. The term was introduced to a broad audience by E.F. Schumacher in his 1970s book Small is Beautiful.

Classification of Natural Resources

Natural resources are mostly classified into renewable and non-renewable resources. Renewable resources.

Renewable resources are generally living resources (fish, reindeer, coffee, and forests, for example), which can restock (renew) themselves if they are not over-harvested but used sustainably. Once renewable resources are consumed at a rate that exceeds their natural rate of replacement, the standing stock (see renewable energy) will diminish and eventually run out. The rate of sustainable use of a renewable resource is determined by the replacement rate and amount of standing stock of that particular resource. Non-living renewable natural resources include soil and water.

Flow renewable resources are very much like renewable resources, only they do not need regeneration, unlike renewable resources. Flow renewable resources include renewable energy sources such as the following renewable power sources: solar, geothermal, biomass, landfill gas, tides and wind.

Resources can also be classified on the basis of their origin as biotic and abiotic. Biotic resources are derived from living organisms. Abiotic resources are derived from the non-living world (*e.g.*, land, water, and air). Mineral and power resources are also abiotic resources some of which are derived from nature.

Non-renewable Resources

A non-renewable resource is a natural resource that exists in a fixed amount that cannot be re-made, re-grown or regenerated as fast as it is consumed and used up.

Some non-renewable resources can be renewable but take an extremely long time to renew. Fossil fuels, for example, take millions of years to form and so are not practically considered 'renewable'. Many environmentalists proposed to tax on consumption of non renewable resources.

Natural Capital

Natural resources are natural capital converted to commodity inputs to infrastructural capital processes. They include soil, timber, oil, minerals, and other goods taken more or less from the Earth. Both extraction of the basic resource and refining it into a purer, directly usable form, (*e.g.*, metals, refined oils) are generally considered natural-resource activities, even though the latter may not necessarily occur near the former.

A nation's natural resources often determine its wealth and status in the world economic system, by determining its political influence in. Developed nations are those which are less dependent on natural resources for wealth, due to their greater reliance on infrastructural capital for production. However, some see a resource curse whereby easily obtainable natural resources could actually hurt the prospects of a national economy by fostering political corruption. Political corruption can negatively impact the national economy because time is spent giving bribes or other economically unproductive acts instead of the generation of generative economic activity. There also tends to be concentrations of ownership over specific plots of land that have proven to yield natural resources.

In recent years, the depletion of natural capital and attempts to move to sustainable development have been a major focus of development agencies. This is of particular concern in rainforest regions, which hold most of the Earth's natural biodiversity-irreplaceable genetic natural capital. Conservation of natural resources is the major focus of natural capitalism, environmentalism, the ecology movement, and Green Parties. Some view this depletion as a major source of social unrest and conflicts in developing nations.

Natural Resources in Dantewada District

District Dantewada is rich enough in respect of Natural Resources. Valuable minerals are hidden between the deep green timber forest. Iron, Tin, Kimberlite, corrundum, High quality Granite, Silica, and many other valuable minerals.

Forest

The forest in the district is also very peculier in the manner that where one side it is full of Timber Wood Sal, Teak, on the other side it is full of wild fruit bearing trees which is the lively hood of tribals of the district.

Dantewada boasts of being the oldest forest type under erstwhile Bastar Circle. Spread over an area of 8362.00 Sq. Km. forests of Dantewada are not only an index on nature's bounty, but also a visitior's delight.

Champion & Seth classified these forests in to four groups namely : South Indian Moist Deciduous forests, mainly comprising of teak, Moist Deciduos forests without teak, Mixed forests, subtropical wet hill forests comprising of Bamboo also. It is also worth mentioning here that Sal Forests give way to rich Teak forests here in the district.

For administrative convenience forests of the district have been kept under three Divisions namely-Dantewada, Bijapur & Sukma. The Forests of the district harbour rich fauna in their natural inhabitats. Indravati National Park situated in the western part of the District is the only Project-Tiger-Area in the entire Chattisgarh region, and along with the river Indrawati "Wild Buffaloe" (*bos bubalis*) fighting its last survival is also found in two Sanctuaries-namely Bharamgarh and pamed. Apart from these two mammals, Pather, Spotted Deer, Wild Bear are also not uncommon in these forests.

Main tree spieces of the forests of the district are Teak (*tectona grandis*) Sal, (*shorea robusta)* Saj (*terminalia tomentosa*), Bija *(petrocarpus marsupeun*), Haldu (*adina cardfolia*) and Bamboo (*dendrocalomons strictus)*. Their main "minor forest produce" are Tamarind (*tamarindus indica*), Mahuwa (*mahua indica*), Kosa (cocoons).

Wildlife

Wildlife includes all non-domesticated plants, animals, and other organisms. Domesticating wild plant and animal species for human benefit has occurred many times all over the planet, and has a major impact on the environment, both positive and negative.

Wildlife can be found in all ecosystems, Deserts, rain forests, plains, and other areas—including the most developed urban sites—all have distinct forms of wildlife. While the term in popular culture usually refers to animals that are untouched by human factors, most scientists agree that wildlife around the world is impacted by human activities.

Humans have historically tended to separate civilization from wildlife in a number of ways including the legal, social, and moral sense. This has been a reason for debate throughout recorded history. Religions have often declared certain animals to be sacred, and in modern times concern for the natural environment has provoked activists to protest the exploitation of wildlife for human benefit or entertainment. Literature has also made use of the traditional human separation from wildlife.

Forest

A **forest** is an area with a high density of trees. There are many definitions of a forest, based on the various criteria.

These plant communities presently cover approximately 9.4% of the Earth's surface (or 30% of total land area) and function as habitats for organisms, hydrologic flow modulators, and soil conservers, constituting one of the most important aspects of the Earth's biosphere. Historically, "forest" meant an uncultivated area legally set aside for hunting by feudal nobility, and these hunting forests were not necessarily wooded much if at all (see Royal Forest). However, as hunting forests did often include considerable areas of woodland, the word forest eventually came to mean wooded land more generally. A woodland is ecologically distinct from a forest.

The latitudes 10° north and south of the Equator are mostly covered in tropical rainforest and the latitudes between 53°N and 67°N with boreal forest.

Fishery

Generally, a **fishery** is an entity engaged in raising and/ or harvesting fish, which is determined by some authority to be a fishery. According to the FAO, a fishery is typically defined in terms of the "people involved, species or type of fish, area of water or seabed, method of fishing, class of boats, purpose of the activities or a combination of the foregoing features".

In particular, the term is often applied to a combination of fish and fishers in a region, the latter fishing for similar species with similar gear types. A fishery may involve the capture of wild fish or raising fish through fish farming or aquaculture.

Biodiversity

Biodiversity is the variation of life forms within a given ecosystem, biome, or for the entire Earth. Biodiversity is often used as a measure of the health of biological systems. The biodiversity found on Earth today consists of many millions of distinct biological species, which is the product of nearly 3.5 billion years of evolution.

Evolution and Meaning

Biodiversity is a portmanteau word, from biology and diversity, originating from and used interchangeably with "biological diversity." This term was used first by wildlife scientist and conservationist Raymond F. Dasmann in a lay book advocating nature conservation. It was not widely adopted for more than a decade, when in the 1980s it and "biodiversity" came into common usage in science and environmental policy. Use of the term by Thomas Lovejoy in the Forward to the book credited with launching the field of conservation biology introduced the term along with "conservation biology" to the scientific community. Until then the term "natural diversity" was used in conservation science circles, including by The Science Division of The Nature Conservancy in an important 1975 study, "The Preservation of Natural Diversity." By the early 1980s TNC's Science programme and its head Robert E. Jenkins, Lovejoy, and other leading conservation scientists at the time in America advocated the use of "biological diversity" to embrace the object of biological conservation.

Its contracted form biodiversity *may have been coined by W.G. Rosen in 1985 while planning the* National Forum on Biological Diversity *organized by the National Research Council (NRC) which was to be held in 1986, and first misha appeared in a publication in 1988 when entomologist E. O. Wilson used it as the title of the proceedings of that forum.*

Since this period both terms and the concept have achieved widespread use among biologists, environmentalists, political leaders, and concerned citizens worldwide. It is generally used to equate to a concern for the natural environment and nature conservation. This use has coincided with the expansion of concern over extinction observed in the last decades of the 20th century.

A similar concept in use in the United States, besides natural diversity, is the term "natural heritage." It pre-dates both terms though it is a less scientific term and more easily comprehended in some ways by the wider audience interested in conservation. "Natural Heritage" was used when Jimmy Carter set up the Georgia Heritage Trust while he was governor of Georgia; Carter's trust dealt with both natural and cultural heritage. It would appear that Carter picked the term up from Lyndon Johnson, who used it in a 1966 Message to Congress.

"Natural Heritage" was picked up by the Science Division of the US Nature Conservancy when, under Jenkins, it launched in 1974 the network of State Natural Heritage Programmes. When this network was extended outside the USA, the term "Conservation Data Center" was suggested by Guillermo Mann and came to be preferred.

Definitions

Biologists most often define "biological diversity" or "biodiversity" as the "totality of genes, species, and ecosystems of a region". An advantage of this definition is that it seems to describe most circumstances and present a unified view of the traditional three levels at which biological variety has been identified:

- genetic diversity
- species diversity
- ecosystem diversity

This multilevel conception is consistent with the early use of "biological diversity" in Washington. D.C. and international conservation organizations in the late 1960s through 1970's, by Raymond F. Dasmann who apparently coined the term and Thomas E. Love joy who later introduced it to the wider conservation and science communities. An explicit definition consistent with this interpretation was first given in a paper by Bruce A. Wilcox commissioned by the International Union for the Conservation of Nature and Natural Resources (IUCN) for the 1982 World National Parks Conference in Bali The definition Wilcox gave is "Biological diversity is the variety of life forms...at all levels of biological systems (*i.e.*, molecular, organismic, population, species and ecosystem)..." Subsequently, the 1992 United Nations Earth Summit in Rio de Janeiro defined "biological diversity" as "the variability among living organisms from all sources, including, 'inter alia', terrestrial, marine, and other aquatic ecosystems, and the ecological complexes of which they are part: this includes diversity within species, between species and of ecosystems". This is, in fact, the closest thing to a single legally accepted definition of biodiversity, since it is the definition adopted by the United

Nations Convention on Biological Diversity. The current textbook definition of "biodiversity" is "variation of life at all levels of biological organization".

If the gene is the fundamental unit of natural selection, according to E. O. Wilson, the real biodiversity is genetic diversity. For geneticists, *biodiversity* is the diversity of genes and organisms. They study processes such as mutations, gene exchanges, and genome dynamics that occur at the DNA level and generate evolution. Consistent with this, along with the above definition the Wilcox paper stated "genes are the ultimate source of biological organization at all levels of biological systems..."

Human Ecology

Human ecology is an academic discipline that deals with the relationship between humans, human societies, and their natural, social and created environments.

Establishing the Field of Human Ecology

In the USA, human ecology was established as a sociological field in the 1920s, although geographers used the term much earlier. Amos H. Hawley published Human Ecology — A Theory of Community Structure *in 1950. He dedicated the book to one of the pioneers in the field who had begun writing the work with Hawley, R. D. McKenzie. McKenzie used the term in his paper entitled "The Ecological Approach to the Study of the Human Community," which is Chapter III of the 1925 book,* The City, *by Robert E. Park and Ernest W. Burgess. Hawley contributed other works to the development of the field. In 1961, an important reader,* Studies in Human Ecology, *was published (edited by George A. Theodorson).*

In the 1970s William R. Catton and Riley E. Dunlap built on earlier works by Chicago School's Robert E. Park and Hawley. One main idea of Catton and Dunlap was to go away from the Durkheimian paradigm of explaining social facts only with social facts. Instead, they included physical and biological facts as independent variables influencing social structure and other social phenomena. This change of paradigm can be described as a change from a classical sociological view of human exemptionalism *to a new view (named* new ecological paradigm *by Catton and Dunlap). Humans are no longer seen as an exceptional species that uses culture to adapt to new environments and environmental change, influenced more by social than by biological variables, but rather as one species out of many that interacts with a bounded natural environment.*

In contrast to the Chicago School of Human Ecology developed by Park, Burgess, and Mckenzie during the 1920s, contemporary research in social ecology goes beyond the biological and economic foundations of human ecology to provide a broader, cross-disciplinary perspective on the ways in which human-environment relations are jointly influenced by physical environmental, political, legal, psychological, cultural, and societal forces.

A line of conflict between this new paradigm and the classical sociological approach is the de-valuating of society and culture. Human ecology views human communities and human populations as part of the ecosystem of earth. In this view, sociology would be only a sub-discipline of ecology — the special ecology of the species Homo sapiens sapiens. *Of course, this is seen as an affront by most sociologists.*

Human ecology is variously a sub-discipline of geography, anthropology, psychology, sociology, or ecology. The inclusion or exclusion of human ecology in sociology proper varies between countries and schools of sociological thinking. Environmental sociology is a field of sociology which encompasses the interactions between humans and nature/natural environment, but is rooted in the methodological and theoretical canon of sociology. Sometimes human ecology is seen as part of environmental sociology, sometimes it is seen as something completely separate. Influences can also be seen on occasion between human ecology and the field of political ecology.

Population and its Effects

Population and Economy

The world population has reached an unprecedented 6.7 billion people, and it is continuing to grow by 80 million people every year. 99% of that growth is in the world's poorest countries where people are commonly afflicted by poverty, civil unrest, and scarce resources. These countries are struggling to provide for their existing populations, and even when making strides to improve their infrastructure, they can not keep up with the dramatic population growth. Developing nations now require about $1 trillion per year in new infrastructure development just to accommodate their population growth – a figure that is very far from being met and is effectively impossible for these countries to generate.

Population and Environment

Currently, there is a great deal of concern in the media, government, business, and general public regarding the issue of global warming. However, the impact of rapid human population growth on global warming is often overlooked. Decreasing consumption levels will not be enough if the human population continues to rise. The United Nations Population Division estimates that by the year 2050 the world population will reach 9.2 billion, with most of this increase occurring in the developing world. It is estimated that by 2050 over 50% of carbon emissions will come from developing nations. Not only does population growth significantly contribute to an increase in carbon emissions, but it creates a strain on other resources such as water, food and energy.

Humanity and Population

Improving the status of women is vital to stabilizing population growth and improving the health and well being of humanity. By improving a woman's status in society, she will be able to educate herself and her children, gain access to reproductive health services, and make economic gains to improve her own life along with her family's life. It is also important that men play an active role in maternal health. When men and women are equally valued in society, it is more likely that population numbers will stabilize, resulting in better living standards and a better outlook for the environment.

Population Media Center (PMC) is an international nonprofit organization headquartered in Shelburne, Vermont.

PMC works worldwide to bring about stabilization of human population numbers at a level that can be sustained by the world's natural resources and to lessen the harmful impact of humanity on the earth's environment. PMC uses entertainment broadcasting to change cultural attitudes and individual behavior with regard to health and social issues in various developing countries. To achieve this, PMC adopted the Sabido methodology, which uses long-running serialized melodramas, written and produced in participating countries in local languages, in order to create characters who gradually evolve into positive role models for the audience to bring about use of family planning, adoption of small family norms, avoidance of AIDS, elevation of women's status, protection of children, and related social and health goals, depending upon the relevance of each to the policies of the country in which PMC is working.

PMC has been involved with projects in the following countries: Brazil, Burkina Faso, Ethiopia, Ivory Coast, Jamaica, Mali, Mexico, Niger, Nigeria, the Philippines, Rwanda, Senegal, Sudan, Vietnam, and the United States.

UNIT-VIII

Environmental Education and Educational Technology

Impact of Science and Technology on Environment

New and better technology is being introduced, by each passing day. In every field, new technology is introduced very frequently. This advancement of technology is beneficial, but also has adverse effects on the environment. If we consider advancement of technology in machines, it means more industrialization and poor effect on the environment. Advancement in weapons has also considerable effect on the environment. New technology means more production and more consumption like cars. They create pollution. All these effects are being discussed later. Thus technology, on one hand can be beneficial, but can create a bad impact on the environment.

First of all, we will discuss the effect of machines on environment. More and better machines mean that there would be more industrialization. No doubt industrialization is beneficial for the economy, and as well as for the people living in the country. Industrialization would create pollution including; noise pollution, air pollution and water pollution. When there would be better technology and industrialization then, many areas with natural beauty will be cut down, in order to establish industries, thus the trees will also have been cut. So, bad impact is caused on environment.

Improvement in technology will improve the production of weapons, and when these weapons will be tested and used;

then also the environment will get polluted. Increased use of cars will increase the pollution and destroy the environment. Improvement in technology has also led to pollute children's mind. Media and the computers are the source of technology, and they have led in polluting the mind, and destroying the environment of studies. Children spend more time watching television or using computers, so less time for studies; and there will be no environment of studies left

Technology has also created problem for people. As environment is polluted, different and fatal diseases are being given 'birth'. These diseases are very dangerous for humans. The impact of technology on environment has increased. Due to the cost of health products, pollution and the different diseases, which attack people, health costs have increased. On the other hand, the government will also face problems. As they would have to give health subsides, and try to overcome the fatal diseases, their costs would rise too; Because of people illnesses they would be unable to work, thus again problems for government as per head GDP, would decrease (and production would also fall.)

We discussed about the impact on environment. Now, if we say that is technology beneficial? The answer would most likely be yes! But depends upon the people and government, that how they use the technology. If we consider about machines then as mentioned earlier that it would increase industrialization. Industrialization is most likely beneficial, as production would increase, supply would increase and ultimately the prices would be less. When there would be more production, then it means businesses would expand; thus, employment rate will increase too. Standard of living would thrive of improve as income would be more.

Exports would increase, as production would be more (and imports will fall) Thus betterment for the economy. So, we can say technology can be beneficial, but it depends on the way it has been used. Remedies can be that government should make laws about how to use technology; so that it does not affect the environment. Government apart from making laws should plant more trees for regular air purification.

Teaching Youth about The Environmental Impact of Science and Technology

The life support systems and non-renewable resources on the Earth are being decimated by a burgeoning population which possesses unprecedented power born of science and technology. The impact of technology on the environment has in many ways been devastating. Yet science and technology have also been the greatest forces for beneficient social change in human history and will continue to be needed Lo solve the economic and social problems of the future. Since the future lies in the hands of our youth we must educate them to cope with its environmental problems.

The damage already done to the environment is so great that all education and especially education in science must become imbued with an environmental ethic to reverse the present trend. It is noticed that the solution does not lie in adding environmental ethics courses to the science curriculum but in finding ways to allow ecological and environmental concerns to permeate existing courses and textbooks. This could have the added advantage of making them more relevant and interesting. The environmental ethic must guide all aspects of our lives and will also have to be taught by example outside of formal education.

"How, should the science curriculum be structured and science teaching organized so as to give insights into the ecological and environmental impact of technology in modern society and instill in young people a feeling of global responsibility?" This is the charge to which this paper is addressed. In response we shall consider the ecological problems that confront humanity and how they are related to science and technology. We will give some examples of how to incorporate environmental concerns into basic science courses to achieve not only an awareness of the impact of science and technology but also a motivation on the part of young people to participate in revitalizing the Earth's environment. Introduction of the environmental dimension could, at the very least, make science courses more relevant and interesting.

The Problem: an Earth in Crisis

It has been noticed that the environment is in crisis. All around us it is suffocating and crumbling under the impact of human action. The Worldwatch Institute states: "Our generation is the first to be faced with decisions that will determine whether the Earth our children inherit will be habitable (Brown et al., 1989).

Recital of the major trends has become a litany: the altering of the Earth's asphere by the burning of fossil fuels, the destruction of the protective ozone layer by man-made chemicals, the depletion of tropical rain forests, the extinction of plant and animal species, the spread of deserts, the acid poisoning of lakes and forests, the toxification of air, soil and water and the continuing nuclear threat (WCED, 1987). Concern for the Earth, which found massive expression in the first Earth Day 20 years ago, has been raised to a new level of public awareness by the media. To cite just two examples, Time magazine recently broke from its tradition of celebrating a—Man of the Year— by choosing instead the Earth as—Planet of the Year— and— National Geographic— devoted its last issue in 1988 to the topic of mending the Earth. Its cover was a hologram showing the Earth both whole and shatred. During the past 20 years countless individuals and organizations, large and small, have worked quietly and incessantly towards conservation and ecological sanity to bring about a heightened interest in and concern for a life-sustaining Earth.

Our task as science educators is twofold. One is to clarify the role that science and technology have had in disrupting the Earth's ability to sustain life and the other is to motivate students to use their knowledge, including that of science and technology, to restore the Earth's environment.

Four Related Problems

It now seems clear that the disruption of the ecological balance in the biosphere is due to the impact of—homo sapiens— the culprit species. All the trends mentioned have their origin in human activities. It is no wonder, then, that most of them are exacerbated by the explosive growth of human populations.

A child born today has 5,000 million neighbors. At age 35 they will, according to present projections, number about 10,000 million and close to 20,000 million at age 70. The burgeoning population problem is probably the most serious of the four so-called Ps:—population, pollution, poverty— and the—proliferation— of weapons of mass destruction-chemical, biological and nuclear. A not unique example of the interaction of the first three is to be found in Mexico.

The close to 20 million population of Mexico City, exceeding that of the entire continent of Australia, has a fossil fuel pollution problem that often turns day into night and poverty which belies the fact that Mexico is rich in natural resources, The proliferation of weapons of mass destruction also poses a serious threat to the biosphere. A nuclear holocaust must, of course, be avoided at all costs inasmuch as it represents the ultimate environmental catastrophe but the other weapons of mass destruction-chemical and biological-also pose massive environmental threats. It seems ironic that these weapons bear the imprint and the titles of the three basic sciences: physics, chemistry and biology. Even preparations for conventional war leave ecological scars on the Earth. In a Sierra Club publication titled—Air, Water, Earth, Fire-The Impact of the Military on World Environmental Order— it says: "We should have been alarmed long ago. It is a sad commentary on our powers of foresight that we did not understand sooner that the shadow of Armageddon hovers over mankind."

The list of problems could easily be extended beyond the four Ps but they give us aeasily remembered combination of environmentally related global woes and their common characteristics: they are all interrelated, they all have an impact on the environment and they all tend to deteriorate the quality of life. In varying degrees they are the byproducts of technology.

Technology and Environmental Destruction

Modern technology has given humanity unheard of power to manipulate earth, air, fire and water. With modern bulldozers and power shovels we can move masses of the Earth's surface the size of an Egyptian pyramid in weeks instead of years

(Malone et al., 1984). The effluents of the factories can raise to dangerous levels the temperature of rivers. We can darken the sky with atmospheric pollution, produce temperatures that match those of the sun and destroy a modern city in minutes. Such power has enabd modem man to accelerate all the trends toward the environmental deterioration mentioned earlier. So, even as we acknowledge that technology has yielded benefits and conveniences, we are overwhelmed by its awesome destructive consequences. They now often are out of control and call for action. The relation between science and technology Paul Kirkpatrick (1986), at Stanford University, once wrote: "I think the human race is a hostage of its technology, which is the child of its science. I used to think we were in a noble racket (science) and that the truth should make us free. Now I have to be dubious". Science and technology have grown out of two different but equally important activities. One is the search for knowledge and understanding which characterizes science. The other is the application of knowledge to satisfy human needs which characterizes technology. It is often not recognized that they are fundamentally different modes of activity with the result that the word science is sometimes used loosely and erroneously to describe both (Baez, 1976).

The scientist is motivated by a curiosity which springs from—the longing to know and understand—. The outputs of scientific endeavor include hypotheses, theories and laws which explain the observed phenomena. When the scientist can say, "I understand," his task is done, at least temporarily, even though there are deeper levels of understanding to be pursued.

How about technology? It has been said that science explores what is and technology creates—that which never existed before—.—Creativity— is, therefore, the hallmark of technology the way—curiosity— is the hallmark of science. One cannot generate science without being curious and one cannot generate technology without being creative. Unlike science, whose outputs are—explanations—, the outputs of technology are—things—, such as new devices and procedures. The aim of the technologist is to produce things that satisfy human wants and not necessarily to theorize about the devices and techniques used in the process. The negative aspects of technology stem from one of its objectives which is to—control—the materials and the forces of nature through procedures and devices designed ostensibly to satisfy human needs but often used to proliferate human wants.

The creative aspects of technology have sometimes been downgraded and not given sufficient attention in education. Recent innovative trends in science education have honored and tried to infuse into general education the—spirit of science—, but they have often neglected the—spirit of change through design— which characterizes the creative aspects of technology as practiced by engineers. The need to "mend the Earth" could to a large extent be satisfied if we applied the methodology of technology to it. The technologist tackles problems brought to him by his clients. He builds bridges, skyscrapers, nuclear weapons or Earth satellites for a fee. Much more seldom have technologists been instructed to generate a blueprint for "mending the Earth".

Human Needs—Real or Perceived

Since it is the role of technolo to develop the products that can satisfy human needs it is important to consider what the basic human needs are and how they can be satisfied in ways which exemplify environmental concern.

In developing countries the word need usually means the most basic of survival—needs—food, shelter and clothing. In the affluent countries, on the other hand, it is common to find a host of consumer goods which often represent a response to "advertisement-driven desires" but euphemistically called "needs." Gandhi's remark that there are enough for everyone's need but not enough for everyone's greed comes to mind. The link between the basic human needs and the environment is obvious: our physical needs demand access to natural resources such a land, water and air, which, with the aid of radiant energy from the sun, generate plants and animals-the so called renewable living resources. But human survival and development also require non-renewable resources such as minerals and fossil fuels which are being depleted by an ever increasing human population. All of these resources, renewable and non-renewable, are to be found on a thin layer of the Earth's surface known as the biosphere. In our catalogue of human needs we should, of course, not forget some which go beyond the purely physical. People need meaningful employment, leisure time and the human qualities of respect, care and affection which foster self esteem. They also need to derive aesthetic enjoyment from contact with pristine nature. Deprived of these a prson may languish just as surely as if deprived of food and water. Satisfaction of these needs in the affective domain is very important for the quality of life.

Ecology—The Newest Science

Physics, chemistry and biology, the basic sciences, grew up independently and have traditionally been taught as separate disciplines. But of late it has proven useful to recognize the interrelationships among them and to teach them in integrated ways or at least under the umbrella of an integrating concept. One such concept is that of the sciences of earth and space. Another is the new science of ecology (Buchsbaum et al., 1957) (Bybee, 1979).

The concepts of ecology and environment are closely linked. Ecology is the branch of science concerned with how organisms are interrelated with one another and with the environment. The main tenet of ecology is that all things are interrelated. Ecology is usually considered a branch of biology, because the term—organism— means living body. The concepts of life and life support systems are, therefore, central to ecology (Hardin, 1956). Renewed interest in life and its processes currently finds expression from biological research in the structure of DNA, to concern about the destruction of life support systems anthe csequent extinction of species of plants and animals. Ultimately, of course, it also leads to a consideration of the possible extinction of human life on Earth in a nuclear holocaust. Jonathan Schell (1984) speaks of this as an "awakening". He writes: "In the last few years much of the public having largely ignored the nuclear peril for almost four decades has been discovering a different faith... they have been choosing human survival. This awakening is new, and its consequences are still uncertain but it promises to be one of the great changes of heart in mankind... that alter the psychological and spiritual map of the world." But the scope of ecology goes far beyond that of biology alone. It considers all the factors that make life possible on our planet. It must also consider disciplines such as economics and the social and behavioral sciences which deal with the motivation of people to utilize natural resources.

The resources which sustain life are being destroyed by an increasing world population which tends to use its technology to generate non-sustainable economic development. It is destroying the biological diversity which provides a cushion for possible recovery from an ecological disaster. One has begun to realize that the survival of plants and animals, including people, may depend upon the understanding of the principles of ecology and upon general adoption of an environmental ethic. The reason ecology is so important at this particular time is that humanity is entering a critical era in which the knowledge that comes from physics, chemistry and biology, treated separately, is not sufficient to cope with the problems of human survival. It must be supplemented by and integrated with the knowledge from the other sciences and disciplines. All knowledge must be integrated and treated in the holistic way characteristic of ecology.

Life, Rights and Ethics

The concept of rights has entered the environmental arena from philosophical, religious and scientific considerations. The principles of ecology and the teachings of some Eastern religions are forcing people in modern societies to realize that plants and animals also have a right to exist (Borelli, 1986). The well-known United Nations Declaration of Human Rights has been gaining acceptance among the nations. It is not so well known, however, that in 1982 the United Nations adopted a resolution known as the World Charter for Nature which invites Member States "to conduct their activities in recognition of the suprme importance of protecting natural systems, maintaining the balance and quality of nature and conserving natural resources, in the interests of present and future generations." Ethics deals with right and wrong. It is the author's point of view that activities that tend to destroy or diminish life are wrong and those which enhance life are right. His basis for an environmental ethics is, therefore, "respect and affection for living things" which he prefers to the less controversial "respect and affection for nature (Shrader-Frechette, 1981).

Links between Peace and the Environment

It is obvious that a nuclear holocaust would have a devastating effect on the world's environment. Even preparations for war are destroying parts of our natural heritage. But the massive extinction of species which is taking place due to the rainforest deforestation, for example, will have an equally devastating effect unless it is curbed. Broadly speaking, peace has a benign effect on the environment whereas war and preparations for war have destructive effects. Benito Juares, a Mexican president born of Zapotec Indian parents, once said that "respect for the rights of others is the basis of peace". He had people in mind, of course, but if we grant that other living things-plants, animals and the Earth itself (Lovelock, 1979)-have rights, we have, in an environmental ethic based upon "respect and affection for living things", the basis for both peace with the Earth and peace on the Earth.

Rethinking the Basics. The "Four Cs"

To improve the quality of life, education would have to generate fundamental guidelines for thought and action. These basic guidelines include the four Cs;—curiosity, creativity, competence and compassion— (Baez, 1980).

Children seem to be born with three of these traits: curiosity, creativity and compassion which, unfortunately, seem to be stifled at an early age. Competence, on the other hand, has to be learned. No one is born with the ability to tie a shoe-lace, ride a bicycle or read a book. We have noted that science cannot begin without curiosity; that technology, which depends upon design, cannot develop without creativity and that neither can blossom without special competencies. But both science and technology without the guidance of compassion can lead us into unethical paths. Caring for the Earth growing out of compassion is a prerequisite to prevent the destruction of the life support systems.

The Special Role of Compassion

Stan Croner, the author of—An Introduction to the World Conservation Strategy— (WCS.1980) wrote: "There are... reasons (other than the integration of conservation and development) for preserving the species. Simple human compassion is one. Respecting the rights of other kinds of life to exist is another. Perhaps most importantly, we are obligated to our descendants not to leave the earth less interesting and less wondrous because we have been here." Although compassion is a word that does not enter readily into the discourse of scientists it is interesting to note the writings of several physicists who have used it. Weisskopf (1972) hits written: "Science cannot develop unless it is pursued for the sake of pure knowledgend insight. But it will not survive unless it is used intensely and wisely for the betterment of humanity and not as an instrument of domination by one group over another. There are two powerful elements in human existence: compassion and curiosity. Curiosity without compassion is inhuman; compassion without curiosity is ineffectual." Einstein has written: "... A human being is part of the whole called by us,—Universe—, a part limited in time and space. We experience ourselves, our thoughts and our feelings as something separated from therest, a kind of optical delusion of our consciousness. This delusion is a kind of prison for us, restricting us to our personal desires and to affection for a few persons nearest to us. Our task must be to free ourselves from this prison by widening our circle of compassion to embrace all living creatures and the whole of nature in its beauty." I can think of no stronger endorsement of the idea that compassion lies at the heart of an environmental ethic.

What Can be Done to Infuse an Environmental Ethic into Science and Technology Education?

Courses in environmental ethics can be taught in universities. But no doubt they alone cannot produce the widespread diffusion of an environmental ethic which is needed to "mend the Earth." The time has come to put greater emphasis in all science courses on the "four Es": ecology, entropy, environment and ethics (Rifkin, 1981). Formal education is good at transmitting information but not so good at generating attitudes. There is an important body of knowledge in the sciences upon which the right ecological decisions must be made and this can be the subject of lectures, books, and other publications.

But changes in attitude toward the Earth will probably come about in more subtle ways. For example, during a field trip, a biology teacher can, in passing, make remarks and take actions which illustrate a love and aspect for nature which the student may absorb. In order to change the way teachers teach it will be necessary to generate special seminars and workshops to show them how to infuse environmental and ethical concepts into their teaching. Incentives in the form of pay and/or release time. would have to be administered to potential leaders to run these workshops and to teachers to induce them to participate in these pattern-changing activities. Special chapters will have to be written for science textbooks illustrating the concepts of ecology, environment and environmental ethics. The basic concepts of the various scientific principles need to be illustrated with environmental examples. New graphics in the texts and new problems at the end of chapters in science textbooks will have to be generated to illustrate ecological pincipls. Authors who have demonstrated special talents in this area could be encouraged to run special workshops for potential authors.

The sections which follow contain information on topics dealing with ecology and the environment and suggestions on how to incorporate them into the teaching of the basic sciences.

Selected Resources

Before considering the basic sciences separately we mention several sources which can provide a wealth of information on teaching science in ways that are socially relevant and environmentally responsible. One is the set of nine volumes which came out of the Bangalore Conference, Science and

Technology Education and Future Human Needs. The title of Volume 8—The Environment and Science and Technology Education— (Baez, et al., 1987) contains the word environment but the other volumes also deal with environmentally related topics.

Another source is—Science and Society-Teacher's Guide—(Lewis, 1981). The Science and Society Project was set up in 1976 under the direction of John Lewis to demonstrate the relevance of the science learned in the school and the laboratory to the world outside the classroom. It is not surprising, therefore, to find such topics as—population, food and agriculture, energy, mineral resources, resources of land and water and looking to the future— among the topics covered.

The books published by Unesco in its New Trends Series on the teaching of the basic sciences starting in 1967 have increasingly introduced articles which suggest how to teach science in ways which are relevant to the problems of society including those of the environment. There are two other books I would recommend highly to any one looking for examples of environmental topics and how they are related to the basic sciences. One is—Living in the Environment— by G. Tyler Miller, Jr. (1985). This book has a 28 page bibliography with close to 300 annotated entries. It covers every conceivable topic linking ecology with the basic sciences, economics, sociology, ethics and much more. It has a 15 page glossary which can serve-as we illustrate below-as a starting point in any search of ecological topics related to the basic sciences.

The other is—Biology-Its Human Implications— by Garrett Hardin (1956) which also has an extensive bibliography. Of particular interest is his last part titled—The Web of Life—in which he discusses such topics as the—nature and origin of life, the transformation of matter in nature and energy and population problems. His treatment of the relationship between the laws of thermodynamics and the energy requirements of living organisms is an excellent example of the clarity that can be achieved in an introductory text. Both of these books were designed to be used at the first year university level but any attempt to write materials linking ecology with the basic sciences at the school level would benefit from their study. A recent document which links biology to the goals of conservation is the—World Conservation Strategy—(1980) produced by the International Union for Conservation of Nature and Natural Resources (IUCN). The concepts which could enrich a biology course are found in the objectives of the Strategy which are: (a) to maintain—essential ecological processes and life support systems: (b) to preserve—genetic diversity, and (c) to ensure—sustainable utilization of species and ecosystems. A short and photographically illustrated introduction to the Strategy has been published by IUCN (Croner, 1984) as well as a manual for introducing the concepts of the strategy to students in school (1984).

Infusing Ecological Concerns into the Teaching of the Basic Sciences

Setting up a separate course in ecology or environmental science is an idea but presently probably an impossible alternative because of overcrowded curricula. Under the circumstances perhaps the most practical way to transmit the ecological message to students who are enrolled in school science courses is to infuse physics, chemistry, biology and even mathematics courses with examples, illustrations and problems dealing with ecological concepts and concerns. In this way the students will be environmentally sensitized at the same time they are learning the basic scientific concepts.

One might begin by selecting some key concepts around which to develop the environmental theme. Life, food— and energy— suggest themselves. These are core ideas from biology, chemistry and physics, respectively, but they permeate the substance of all three sciences. What goes on in plants and animals, for example, is a continuous series of chemical transformations. Some examples follow.

Biology

Since we have linked the environmental ethic with respect and affection for living things it is natural to consider first biology-the science of life. Ecological topics which could be covered in a biology course in addition to those already mentioned in connection with Hardin's book include—the genetic aspects of some human problems, interactions of heredity and environment, the conquest of the land by plants, and man: evolution in the future. As an illustration of how to use the glossary in Miller's book to suggest topics from biology related to the environment we list herewith the biologically related entries under A,B,C.: abiotic, aerobic, bacteria. biodegradable, biogas, biogeochemical cycles, biological control, biomass, biome, biosphere, biota, carnivore, carrying capacity, clearcutting, climax ecosystem, climax species, coastal wetlands, commons, community, complete proteins, contour farming, cultural eutriphication. Clearly, perusing the entire glossary would yield many more terms.

Chemistry

Food is the form of energy needed to sustain human life and its analysis belongs to the subject of chemistry. M.S. Swaminathan describes—food, fodder, fuel and fibre—all intimately linked to chemistry-as the basics of livelihood security and the quality of life. In the '70s Isaias Raw (1974) wrote a chemistry laboratory guide titled—What People Eat— and, with collaborators, published a pioneering chemistry programme based on nutrition (Raw et al, 1975).

Again, sampling Miller's glossary, this time under D,E,F, we find the following chemical terms linked with ecology: DDT, decomposer, desalination, deuterium, dissolved oxygen content, emission standard, entropy, essential amino acid, food additive, food chain, food contaminant, fossil fuels, freon. The other letters of the alphabet yield many more.

Food, Agriculture and Education, Volume 6 in the Bangalore Series (Rao, 1987) contains 25 articles and case studies dealing with food and agriculture in biology education. If we consider the ecological disasters that have occurred in recent years we cannot help also mentioning—pollution— as a topic involving chemistry which must be included for consideration.

Physics

The concept of energy springs from physics but cannot be divorced from chemistry or biology. Anything that moves possesses kinetic energy and this, of course includes all animals and some plants. A tall redwood tree possesses obvious gravitational potential energy while food, fodder and fuels possess forms of chemical pottial energy. In dealing with ecology and the environment perhaps no topic in science is more important than the laws of thermodynamics. The first states that energy cannot be created or destroyed-it can only be converted from one form to another. This is the so calle law of conservation of energy. Physicists are sometimes exasperated when environmentalists urge us to "conserve" energy when they really mean we should not waste it. The laws of physics ensure that energy will be "conserved".

Second law of thermodynamics which states that whenever energy, is converted to heat the—availability— of some of the energy is lost. It is no longer available for use because it has, in a sense become "degraded". This degradation is occurring on an enormous scale world-wide especially due, for example, t the widespread use of automobiles. A good bibliographical source on this subject is Volume IV of Unesco's—New Trends in Physics Teaching— (1984). Forthcoming school level Unesco physics education publications will place emphasis on the environment and other topics of societal relevance as revealed in the extensive work being done in Italy, the Philippines, Kenya, Tanzania, the Netherlands ind Israel. Energy Resources in Science Education, Volume 7 in the Bangalore Conference Series (Kirwan, 1987) is rich in articles linking energy with environmental concerns.

Mathematics

Because the impact of an expanding human population is so great the one mathematical topic chosen here as an example is—exponential growth. The human population of the Earth has been doubting recently approximately every 35 years. A simple but important aspect of exponential growth is the formula for doubling time T which obeys the equation T = 70/p. If the yearly percentage population growth p is, for example, 2 per cent, the doubling time is 35 years.

Another characteristic of exponential growth is that the increment during one doubling time is equal to the sum of all the previous doubling time increments. In the recent past, for example, the use of petroleum fuels was doubling every ten years. If the rate of growth had remained constant, the increment in their use during the next decade alone would exceed the sum of the increments in all previous decades. There are ways of dramatizing this property by graphical constructions. Microcomputers are playing an exciting role in the teaching of science-related ecological subjects but we reluctantly leave this topic to another time.

Who Decides What to Teach?

Scientific knowledge continues to grow exponentially. One estimate is that it doubles every 10 years. It is difficult, therefore, to choose what new material should be added to the science curriculum. For this we need the advice of the physicists, chemists and biologists who are doing research in these fields. They are the ones who—do— science and know what the trends are but, to be helpful in educational reform, they must belong to that small category of scientists who are also interested in teaching. And among these we must seek out those who want to link environmental concern with their subject matter.

The teaching of technological subjects lies outside the scope of this paper but it is important to be aware that the environmental impact of science on society comes about through technology. Because technology arises out of human demands rather than out of a systematic search for new knowledge it is not easy to put it into neat categories. Superconductivity, new, approaches to nuclear fusion, new fuel sources and biotechnology come to mind as examples of the newest technologies. But to decide what to teach about technology in school science we must, again, seek out the practitioners. Some of these are research scientists who have been lured into technology through natural interests or by financial rewards. Still others are engineers. Those which practice technology can help us choose the content of technological material to include in our teaching of science.

In the '60s we learned how important it was to involve practicing scientists in deciding what to teach and in the production of teaching materials. At that time some scientists banded together to write new textbooks and produce new teaching materials for schools. These projects stimulated a wave of course content improvement and curriculum reform in science which had global repercussions and is documented in the Unesco publication—Innovation in science education-world-wide (1976). It is well known that the vigorous effort in the U.S.A. in science teaching improvement in the '60s, still remembered through acronyms like PSSC, SMSG, CHEMS, CBAP and BSCS, was motivated ut least in part by the launching of Sputnik. I will digress here briefly to mention three new activities presently being carried out there in response to the new wave of concern for the need to improve science teaching.

One is the effort of the National Science Teachers Association (NSTA) which has set up a task force to consider—Essential Changes in Secondary School Sciences: Scope, Sequence and Coordination. Its principal aim is to increase the number of young people who study science and to spread the instruction out over a longer interval of time. It takes note of the fact that in many European countries, both east and west, science is taught over a period of many years whereas the tendency in the United States has been to concentrate it into one year. Another is—Project 2061-Education for a Changing Future—of the American Association for the Advancement of Science (AAAS). (The number 2061 refers to the year in which Halley's comet will return). It is designed to engage the scientific community in working with educators to improve science education. Their document,—Science for All Americans, will have inputs from several hundred scientists and educators. A new organization called the National Science Resources Center (NSRC) has been set up under the auspices of the Smithsonian institution and the National Academy of Sciences and has obtained financial support from industrial foundations. It is focusing special attention on the needs of urban school systems and has published a well documented reference book called—Science for Children-Resources, for Teachers. These three groups collaborate with one another when their areas of interest coincide. Of these only the NSRC has given noticeable consideration to environmental matters.

Many organizations are devoted to the teaching of a single basic science, but I will mention only the one with which I am we acquainted-the American Association of Physics Teachers (AAPT)-because it sponsored a workshop on—Physics and Ecology. This took place in Monterrey, Mexico, as part of the Inter-American Conference on Physics Education held in Oaxt~pec in 1987. Although the follow-up on physics and ecology has been minimal, interest in the topic was high at the Conference suggesting that further activity along these lines would be welcome in the AAPT and possibly in similar organizations devoted to other sciences. The organizations named can suggest what should be taught but the actual decisions on what to teach to young people are often made by national or state authorities. They have special boards responsible for generating syllabi and curricula with greater or less liberty given to the teachers to follow them, sometimes simply as guidelines. Ideally these authorities would include people who are following closely the work of the organizations named above and the literature of research in science and education.

The ordinary teacher, however, is often guided by the textbooks available, which, in turn, were written to conform to the state guidelines. The textbook writer therefore plays an important role. The best ones are, I imagine, those who have a strong scientific background or at least have degrees in science education. We now seem ready for a new round of innovation. This time the stimulus would not be the apparent need to—compete— with a state which has launched a new era of space exploration but a recognition that all countries have to— cooperate— in stopping an ecological devastation which knows no political or geographic boundaries. We need to collaborate to mend the Earth. If the ecological message is to come across as we teach science all the organizations mentioned above as well as all others involved in curriculum reform will have to give environmental improvement a high priority.

Degradation of Resources

Degradation of Prairie Soil Resources

"Despite its widespread severity and global impact, soil degradation remains an emotional rhetoric rather than a precise and quantifiable scientific entity." Soil is degraded as a result of processes that reduce its productivity. Such processes usually arise from poor management of the resource. Soils are degraded primarily by erosion, loss of organic matter, salinization and acidification. The first two processes are interrelated. Acidification is not a major problem except in areas where cultivation has been extended into previously forested areas. Salinization is more prevalent.

Soil Erosion

Soil erosion reduces soil productivity through losses of nutrients, water storage capacity and organic matter. The losses in terms of productive capacity are significant though presently obscured by the application of fertilizer. Annual top soil losses in terms of lost productivity on the prairies are estimated to be in the millions of dollars. The present value of the accumulated annual losses is measured in hundreds of millions of dollars, the actual losses being difficult to quantify.

Erosion has taken place over the history of cultivation on the prairies. Both wind and water erosion result in the removal of the finer soil particles, thus leading to compaction of the soil and poor soil tilth. Water erosion is a significant problem on long sloping fields, particularly those summer fallowed or left free of cover. The valuable top soil removed is deposited in depressions, road ditches and waterways giving rise to additional costs. Wind erosion is a major problem when there is little cover by crops or residues as in the spring months particularly during dry seasons. Not only are valuable nutrients lost but the soil deposited elsewhere becomes a problem. Indeed, seedling crops may be destroyed.

Dumanski et al have estimated the annual costs of erosion in the prairie provinces to lie in the range of 155-177 million dollars in the case of water and between 213-271 million dollars in the case of wind. Sparrow has expressed annual soil losses in different terms. He estimated the annual soil loss on the prairies by wind to be about 160 million tonnes and that by water to be 117 million tonnes, these losses from erosion greatly exceeding the rate of soil formation. The annual loss in potential grain production arising from soil erosion during the period of cultivation he considered to be 171 million bushels or 4.6 million tonnes of wheat. He argued that 15 percent of the lost production could not be recovered by additions of fertilizer and estimated the value of lost production at $129 million annually, lending credence to the title of his report *Soil at Risk: Canada's Eroding Future*.

The physical effects of erosion are painfully evident on the knolls and sloping segments of the prairie landscape. It has led to a gradual evolution of farming practices from an initial use of the plow, through use of blade type cultivation to use of minimum tillage. This progression has enabled increasing amounts of trash cover to be maintained over time, thereby reducing erosion. Moreover, in more recent years the width of fields has increased as a reflecting the size of the equipment used, which resulted from the economies of size in farm operations. In addition, intensive tillage operations to incorporate herbicides and fertilizers were adopted. These latter events work against the soil conservation otherwise achieved through maintenance of trash cover. Fortunately, a reduction in the cost of suitable chemicals has made the use of chemical fallow more economical, thereby enabling adoption of minimum tillage practices. This change in practice has been driven by the need to minimize production costs, the protection of the land from erosion being a complementary benefit. At the same time, summer fallowing has largely become confined to the brown soil zone as rotations have been extended in the dark brown zone and continuous cropping has become general in the black soil zone. Losses from soil erosion can therefore be expected to be less extensive in the future than in the past.

Decline in Organic Matter

The main chemical constituents of soil organic matter are carbon and nitrogen. The former is the energy source for most soil microbes while the latter is one of the most important nutrients for plants. Other necessary components of organic matter are phosphorous and sulfur. Under the ecosystem prevailing previous to cultivation, mineralization and immobilization processes were closely integrated. Plant growth (immobilization) and mineralization of soil organic matter occurred simultaneously. Therefore losses of nutrients were minimized allowing for the accretion of organic matter over time. Carbon transfer through the soil is basic to the functioning of the soil-plant system. Primary productivity determines the amount of carbon entering the system while the amount leaving is controlled by soil micro-organisms. In natural ecosystems, the amount of carbon transferred by means of both processes appears equal.

Upon cultivation of the soil for the production of annual crops, productivity and mineralization are uncoupled, particularly when the fields are bare of vegetation. Total inputs of carbon to the soil are altered due to differences both in plant characteristics and to allocation of carbon for above and below ground production.

The practice of summer fallowing has hastened the loss of soil organic matter. Frequent tillage during summer fallowing has increased the rate of decomposition of organic matter while at the same time disrupting soil aggregation and increasing its susceptibility to erosion. There has also been a loss of the more readily available nitrogen.

The magnitude of the losses of organic matter under cereal production has been established as being in the range of 20 to 50 percent in the cultivated layer according to the soil classification. McGill estimated in 1981 that organic matter losses in the topmost layer of soil averaged 41 percent in the brown soil zone, 44 percent in the dark brown soil zone, 49 percent in the black soil zone and 36 percent in the grey soil zone. Research has established that by improved cultural practices, the decline in organic matter can be halted and indeed reversed. Nonetheless, additional nitrogen is now required to maintain yields on many prairie soils.

Regardless of the productivity losses identified, annual wheat yields after an initial decline following settlement have trended upward over the last 50 years.

Uncertainty remains, however, as to how soils will behave under such changed cultural practices as snow trapping, minimum tillage, green manuring and chemical follow. This uncertainty arises because soil changes occur slowly and the effects of agronomic practices take years to become evident.

Soil Salinity

Even before cultivation, large areas of the prairies contained saline soils. However, an expansion of these areas has occurred under cultivation. The rate of increase in the salinized area is related in part to the increase in ground water over time. Salinization occurs as water containing soluble salts moves upward through the soil horizon. Evapotranspiration concentrates the salts in the soil solution to reach levels in the root zone that are detrimental to crop growth.

Any technique which removes water from the subsurface such as drainage, use of deep rooted perennials, reducing summer fallow or continuous cropping diminishes the danger of salinization. Once salinization has occurred, the remedy is to leach the salts out of the root zone. The most viable way to accomplish this cleansing is to use all available precipitation to grow crops and thus reduce the accumulation of ground water. This indicates the desirability of reducing the acreage in summer fallow on the prairies. Such a reduction would also lead to a significant decline in the leaching of nitrogen into the subsoil.

Salinization of dryland agricultural soil constitutes a major problem in southern and central regions of Alberta and Saskatchewan and in a few scattered areas of Manitoba. Approximately 2.2 million hectares of improved land are considered to be subject to secondary salinity. The economic impact of this salinity is said to be in the range of $104-$257 million annually.

Soil Acidification

As indicated previously, acidification is not a major problem in other than a limited part of the prairies. Acidification can be overcome by application of lime. However, heavy applications of nitrogen fertilizers over time have been found to result in soil acidification. Consequently, acidification may become a significant problem in parts of the prairie region under intensive cropping practices which require major inputs of nitrogen fertilizer.

Assessment

While degradation of the soil resource can be reduced or halted by changes in cultural practices, unless these are demonstrated to be economic they are unlikely to be adopted even though desirable from the standpoint of society. Producers are more likely to be interested in maximizing profits in the short-run rather than be concerned with conservation of natural resources and protection of the environment. Any sizable shift in cropping practices by producers will depend on their ability to survive difficult economic times.

Ecological Degradation Due to Exploitation of Natural Resources and Development

There is a story related to the environment, in which a boy who was a very good painter made a big painting of a scene. There were big mountains covered with trees, except a few in the far background which looked snow-covered. From one of the mountains flowed a beautiful river. Down in the valley could be seen a few cosy cottages surrounded by gardens, a few butterflies, some birds soaring high in the air and little children playing happily in the open fields. Indeed it was a beautiful painting.

The boy had a little brother. He also wanted to try his hand at painting. As soon as he got the chance, he picked up the brush and painted the mountain all black. The sparkling blue-white water of the river became brown, and with just one stroke of his brush, the flowers and trees and butterflies disappeared. His older brother was heartbroken. The only consolation was that the child who destroyed the painting was so small that he had done it in ignorance. Though it would require a lot of time and effort, the painter could paint another picture.

Something very similar is happening in our lives. How many of us have looked at nature's beauty, a thousand times more beautiful than any painting can ever be, and realised how fragile it is? Just like the child's stroke of the brush, one action of ours can destroy this beauty — be it the mountains with their forest cover or the sparkling streams and rivers of life-giving water, be it the immense sand deserts or our oceans which are teeming with life; be it our lush green rain forests or the stark beauty of our cold deserts. But, and this is an important but, there is a major difference. While the painting was spoiled by an ignorant child, our earth and its environment are being spoiled by adult humans. Even more significant is the possibility that if nature's system or what we call the environment is destroyed, the effect may be fatal for many species.

Environmentalist and social activist Shri Sunderlal Bahuguna once pointed out that the agony of the present-day world is the offshoot of an illogical and indiscriminate spoliation of the sources of the earth and nature by man for his meaningless material development that is leading him fast towards destruction.

Environment: A Concept of Wholeness

The environment is a concept of wholeness (nature), with non-living and living components interdependent among themselves. It is aptly defined as 'the sum total of all conditions and influences that affect the development and life of organisms'. This comprehensive definition stresses totality, and every living organism from the lowest to the highest, including human being, has it own environment. The word 'nature' in the *Gita* also conveys the idea that it does not belong to anyone but everyone belongs to it, like a family does not belong to anyone but everyone belongs to the family. Like in a family, in the environment also interactions between its different constituents are expected, and these interactions sometimes might lead to hazardous situations. Interaction is leading to the faster deterioration of the environment.

Traditionally, our understanding of the environment was holistic. A *shloka* from the *Isha Upanishad* goes, 'the whole universe together with its creatures belongs to the Lord (nature). One can enjoy the bounties of nature by giving up all greed'. Implicit in this thought is that no creature is superior to any other, and human beings should not have absolute power over nature. Let no one species encroach on the rights and privileges of nature. The element of sustainability is ingrained in this, because the emphasis is on using nature without greed. Once the element of greed enters, exploitation starts and we cease to utilise nature for the good of all human beings.

Traditional cultures have always lived in harmony with their natural environments. Nature and humankind (*prakriti* and *purusha*) form inseparable parts of the life support system. This system has five elements: air, water, land, flora and fauna, which are interconnected, interrelated and interdependent. Deterioration in one element affects the others.

Traditional social ethics placed great emphasis on the values, beliefs and attitudes that helped man to live in harmony with nature. The *Bhumi Suktam* in the *Atharvaveda* is said to be the most impressive and eloquent testament of ecological values that can be found anywhere in world literature. These and similar texts from diverse cultural traditions throughout the earth express a world-view which is informed by the spirituality inherent in nature and stress the holistic and harmonious relationship between humanity and nature.

In the *Manusmriti* (5.45) it is written that 'he who injures innoxious beings from a wish to give himself pleasure, never finds happiness, whether living or dead'. Reference to ecological concerns is also found in *Charaka Samhita*, *Vimansthan*, 3.2. 'The destruction of forests is most dangerous for the nation and human beings. *Vanaspati* has a direct relation with the well-being of society. Due to the pollution of the natural environment and the destruction of forests, many diseases crop up to ruin the nation'.

During Ashoka's time (272-232 bc), perhaps for the first time in the history of the world ecological concerns became state concerns. His imperial edicts laid down rules of conduct that had to be obeyed with respect to the environment. Non-compliance was met with punishment.

T.N. Khoshoo writes, quoting Gandhiji in *Mahatma Gandhi: An apostle of applied human ecology*, that 'it is an arrogant assumption to say that human beings are lords and masters of the lower creatures. On the contrary, being endowed with greater things in life, they are the trustees of the lower animal kingdom'. The delicate and holistic balance that exists in nature has to be respected and maintained.

The Himalayas, the proverbial 'Third Pole', have always remained a source of fascination and inspiration for different people and have been deemed to be the cradle of civilisation in the subcontinent. There seems to be general agreement that the ecology of the Himalayas has been endangered. The Himalayas have exercised a great influence on the environmental conditions of northern India and the people living in the Indo-Gangetic plain. They have prevented the monsoon winds from crossing over Tibet and forced them to precipitate most of their moisture on the Indian side in the form of rain and snow. This unique ecology of the Himalayas, which has such an extensive and pervasive influence on the life of our people, needs to be preserved, conserved and qualitatively upgraded.

The developmental activities of man such as the construction of high dams, roads, exploration for minerals and mining activity and the quest for arable land have to face the challenge of intensified dynamic process, commonly referred to as geographical hazards. Natural resources are being exploited in the name of economic development. Indira Gandhi's interpretation is that the real conflict is not between environment and development but between the environment and reckless exploitation by man in the name of efficiency. We have to live a life according to the rhythm of nature. Human inference in natural environmental conditions often gives these dynamic processes catastrophic proportions, leading to disasters and irreparable damage to the natural balance of the ecosystem.

It is not just concern about the extinction of the big cats, but concern for all inhabitants and non-living resources. We have to stop this undeclared war against nature. Human beings are at the crossroads. Careless application of technology is leading to eco-degradation and pollution. Gandhiji emphasised, 'The earth provides enough for every man's need but not for every man's greed'.

Sustainable development is, therefore, a concept of good and sound economic growth that can be maintained indefinitely with damage to the environment. Good environment generally begets good economics.

The words 'economics' and 'ecology' have the same root, *oikos*, which refers to a house. While economics deals with financial housekeeping, ecology deals with environmental housekeeping.

Studies have shown that the perspectives of ecology are different from those of economics in that the former stresses limits rather than continuous growth, stability rather than continuous 'development'. The ecosystem is the basic unit which has biotic and abiotic components that form an interrelated, interconnected and interdependent system. The most important characteristic of an ecosystem is that it is dynamic, evolving and auto-sustainable as long as it remains reasonably undisturbed and there is incoming sunlight. The equilibrium of an ecosystem is disturbed by external stimuli such as natural cataclysmic changes and ever-increasing human activities dictated by socio-economic growth. The basic difference is that the socio-economic system, in contrast, is hitched only to one species, human beings. In an ecosystem, different species of plants and animals including human beings and micro-organisms form an interacting system. Thus, the economic process is unidirectional and human beings can only progress forwards. Conflict between the ecosystem and the socio-economic system arises from unidirectional and unlimited human wants to meet genuine needs as also greed. This has caused ecological crisis, which in other words means human exploitation of resources at a greater rate than can be normally regenerated under natural conditions.

Central Himalayas

The central Himalayas comprise eight hill districts of Uttar Pradesh, namely Chamoli, Pauri, Tehri, Uttarkashi, Dehradoon, Almora, Nainital and Pithoragarh, spread over an area of about 52,000 sq km. The people of the region are poor, ignorant and backward but the environment has made them simple, honest, hard-working, cheerful and courageous. The region is quite rich in religious and cultural heritage. The Hindu shrines of Badrinath, Kedarnath, Gangotri, Yamunotri and the Sikh gurudwara at Hemkund near the famous valley of flowers attracts pilgrims every year. People come not only on pilgrimage but also to escape the stresses and strains of urban life, to relax and to enjoy the beauties of nature.

Forest: A Womb

The term 'forest' applies not only to trees but also to scrub vegetation and grassland. It is aptly defined as 'a peculiar organism of unlimited kindness and extends generously the products of its life activity; it affords protection to all beings, offering shade even to the axeman, who destroys it'. Trees and forests are also important for deep psychological reasons. In returning to the forest, we are returning to the womb, not in psychoanalytical terms but in cosmological terms. We are returning to our origins.

For centuries forests and the people living around have complemented each other, the latter deriving their livelihood from the farmer, who in turn maintained the ecological balance and environmental quality together with conservation of soil and water. The hill people utilise their traditional knowledge to use forest resources without destroying them. From the forest they get fuel for cooking, fodder for their cattle, fruit, timber for building their houses and medicinal herbs for curing diseases. The forest helps in maintaining the flow of perennial springs, in bringing rain, in keeping the soil and water conserved, in preventing landslides, thereby giving protection from this natural calamity. It helps regulate watershed management so as to maintain the fertility of the soil, control droughts and floods, and preserve wildlife.

Massive deforestation in the Himalayan region is the important factor in ecological degradation. Non-availability of certain species, decline of fodder and wood resources, loss of the habitat of wildlife, soil erosion, recurrent floods and drying-up springs and seasonal streams and climatic changes are the consequences of man's activity. It is obvious that there is something wrong with the management of these vital resources.

The deforestation which has taken place due to commercial exploitation of trees for timber, resin, medicinal herbs, etc., the developing of new agricultural fields, over-grazing by animals, the coming up of new habitation (*e.g.* because of the construction of the Tehri dam), the building of roads mainly after the China invasion of 1962, tourism development and other development activities, increase in the population (men as well as animals), all have had an adverse affect on the environment and have brought about ecological imbalance.

The forest has gone away from the villages. It is reported that there is a scarcity of fuel, fodder and fruit. Medicinal herbs are going to be extinct. The adverse affects noticed by us were that due to deforestation in the villages of Garhwal there is watershed failure, which has resulted in both drought and flood conditions, soil erosion, landslides, changes in the microclimate, increase in the silting rate which has caused a rise of the river beds, loss of wildlife, drying up of natural springs on which the villagers depend for drinking water.

The Chipko movement took place in April 1973 in Mandal near Gopeshwar of Chamoli district. It is a grassroots non-violent and non-political movement. It is purely an ecological movement which has brought the women of the region in the mainstream of public life, and it is guided by common rural folk and not by professional leaders. 'Chipko' means to cling to the trees to save them from being cut. It awakened among the people the need for the protection of the forests.

One aspect of the deteriorating forest ecology is the large-scale replacement of natural forests by the plantation of only commercially profitable trees. These man-made forests are not capable of working in the same way as the natural forests for maintaining the ecological balance. In some instances they may do positive harm. For example, in the Himalayan forest, the oak tree is regarded as the farmer's best friend because it absorbs water for a long time and releases it slowly. This gives rise to springs around which hill villages have been established. Its leaves are used as fodder, it has a leafy canopy and a rich undergrowth of grasses which protect the soil from being directly struck by rain, and its wood is used for making agricultural implements.

Now it is being replaced by pine trees because of their commercial use. The pine tree has not the capacity to retain water, which has resulted in the drying up of springs, creating a scarcity of drinking water. It has no canopy and no undergrowth, thus leaving the mountain slopes fully exposed to erosion by rain and wind. Its leaves are not used as fodder, and they are inflammable and acidic, which makes the land infertile. But in order to extract resin from the trees the planting of pines is going on.

Forest Fires

Forest fires are another cause of the destruction of trees, vegetation, thick layer of humus and animals. The two major causes of forest fire are:

a. *Intentional Fire*: The forest is often set on fire by the villagers during the summer season to get a good growth of grass following the rains. The fire burns the debris that is lying on the forest floor and hence the grass is able to grow well in the rainy season. Sometimes it spreads and destroys vast tracts of valuable trees. The forest is also set a fire by the forest department to clear it of dry vegetation in order to avoid the risk of a huge fire. Firing is done from top to bottom by cutting fire-lines at regular intervals to control the fire. Villagers also set fire to pine leaves falling on the surface as they inhibit the undergrowth.

b. *Accidental Fire*: Fire is also caused by man's carelessness. Unextinguished campfires of trekkers and picnickers, forest labourers throwing away burning cigarettes, bidis and matchsticks, villagers burning the unwanted material on their fields during summer, throwing away of torches used by travellers to see their way in the forest at night, and acid applied to increase the yield of resin. This acid may be spilled on the dry needles of a pine forest, thereby leading to forest fires.

The flow of air in the hills is upwards, which is responsible for huge fires, and a fire may go beyond control if it spreads from the bottom of a hill. It is easily controlled if it is from top to bottom. Too much dryness also helps in spreading fires.

There are several traditional methods of controlling fires: by beating the branches of trees on the fire, by throwing soil and water on it, and by cutting a fire-line to prevent its further spread.

Removal of leaf litter by the villagers to spread under their cattle and for use as fuel is responsible for soil erosion, disturbances in the hydrological cycle in the hill areas and of organic manure in the soil. But at the same time too much accumulation of dry leaf litter increases the risk of forest fires.

Soil: an Anchorage for All

Soil is the receptacle of all that lives. The hymn dedicated to the earth in the *Atharvaveda* (12.1.12) sums up the traditional attitude of reverence:

Impart to us those vitalizing forces
that come, O Earth, from deep within your body,
Your central point, your navel; purify us wholly.
The Earth is mother; I am son of Earth,
The rain-giver is my father; may he shower
on us blessings!

Soil is our most valuable material heritage, the basis of all terrestrial life. As an ecological factor, soil is of great significance, for it affords a medium for the anchorage of plants and a depot for minerals and water.

Normally, soil is constantly generated and enriched when an ecosystem is left undisturbed or minimally disturbed. However, due to loss of vegetal cover, there is a progressive loss of soil due to erosion, together with attendant consequences like landslides and siltation.

Water: Flow of Life

Water is yet another important element of the life support system. Water is also the home of aquatic life. The presence of aquatic life is an indication of the well-being of water. The personification of water is integral to the Indian ethos. All rivers are feminine and so associated with fertility (except the Brahmaputra, which is male). Most important of all rivers is the Ganga, and her sacredness is enshrined in the myth of *gangavatarana* or the descent of the Ganges.

According to Indian mythology the Ganges was brought down to the earth and the nether world by the penances of Bhagirath, descendant of Sagara, king of Ayodhya, to atone for the sins of his ancestors and to bring them once more to life. Lord Shiva's matted locks acted as a breakwater to gentle the rush of water which would otherwise have split the world asunder. The ecological message of this myth is as apparent as the physical reality of the course of the Ganga. The rich Deodara forests are associated with the breakwaters of Shiva's matted locks, through which it meanders.

The region receives plenty of rain, but due to deforestation there is a failure of watershed which results in the unchecked flow of water during the monsoon to cause a sudden swelling of streams in rivers so that there are floods in the foothills and even in the plains, and droughts in the villages located on the slope of the mountain. A watershed is a natural drainage area draining off water to a common point which ultimately meets with a river. Integrated development of watersheds thus takes care of water, crops, fuel, fodder and livestock with a view to develop the overall economy. Several NGOs with people's participation are trying to reset watershed management by planting trees on the top of the slope to retain the water, building tanks of cement and alkathene to save rainwater, building check dams on the streams to break the velocity of gushing water which brings silt along with it.

The region has a number of rivers, streams and springs, but the people are unable to use the water since it flows in deep channels. Thus the people used springs for drinking water and *gula*s for irrigation and other daily needs. The skill of the people is reflected in the canals (*gula*s), the gravitational channels which they make to divert stream water to various levels in the difficult hilly terrain. They also run small water mills, using the power of the falling water. The water mill is locally known as *gharrat*, which grinds cereals and spices.

Impact of Development

Development in the region is the other major feature of the ecological crisis, which takes different forms such as the coming up of dams, building of roads, tourism development, etc. Quarrying, mining and blasting operations also give rise to landslides, which not only block traffic on the roads but sometimes form lakes by the temporary blockade of rivers. When the water exerts pressure these burst, causing devastating floods, sweeping away roads, bridges, agricultural land, etc. For example, the Alaknanda flood of 1970 was of a similar type. Such floods are a constant threat to highways, villages, streams, dams, agricultural land and tourists.

The limestone industry in the Doon valley has caused severe damage to the environment — loss of topsoil, lowering of the water table, deposition of dust on plant surfaces, emission of gases from the kilns. Processing of limestone in the kilns leads to the emission of CO_2, CO and SO_2 gases. Plants show defoliation, chlorosis, necrosis, etc.

The coming up of big dams like the Tehri dam, which submerge large fertile areas which are so scarce in the region, and standing on a seismically active zone having many thrust and faults, may also be responsible for an ecological crisis.

The traffic of vehicles alters the composition of vegetation. Building of roadways in the mountain system creates disturbances. This does not mean that roads in the hills are not important, but they need to be constructed in consonance with the nature of geological formation. The construction of a hill road involves felling of existing protective vegetation, cutting and blasting otherwise stable hill slopes, and the rolling down of the resultant debris which in turn destroys vegetation and causes severe erosion resulting in extensive slope failures. These are often termed as landslides. The phenomenon of landslides is not linked with road making alone but also with land use in general.

Tourism

The Himalayan region is considered to be abundantly suited for tourism since it offers all kinds of attractions to tourists. A paradise for anglers and a challenge to hikers. The lush green valleys, emerald meadows, vast icefields have now started showing abrasion due to increasing human activity. Tourism brings a large number of people together, which leads to marked changes that are detrimental to the ecosystem as a whole. Tourism is found in the form of pilgrim tourism and for pleasure and adventure. To accommodate the large tourist influx, hundreds of new buildings are being constructed every year. The tourist activity has to be in consonance with the principles of conservation of nature and with the protection of associated resources. Unplanned development in the Himalayas is causing irreparable damage. The problems of litter, noise, erosion, destruction of fauna and flora have become acute. The garbage problem is another Himalayan task to solve. Litter and garbage piles are all around, as we have noticed during our visit to Gangotri.

Thus tourism development is another big problem in the region. *Dhabas* (roadside hotels) are coming up frequently right from Gangotri to Gomukh, which is responsible for the rise in temperature; grassy trails have started in Rudranath, Madhmaheshwar and Tungnath due to trekkers and mountaineers. A number of people visited the hill stations every year mainly in the months of May, June and October.

Observations

Suggestions which may help in maintaining the ecological balance in the Himalayas are: afforestation should be encouraged by planting mixed trees, both conifers and broad-leaved. Monoculture of trees should be avoided; on the higher slopes cultivation of agricultural crops should be stopped. Instead of agriculture, crop trees should be planted. To stop the over-exploitation of the forest by government contractors for resin, medicinal herbs, timber, etc., there should be a total ban on cutting of trees on mountain slopes and in catchment areas. Instead of big dams, small dams and hydro-electric power stations can be constructed. For a very small village a hydro-electric generator can be installed in the water mill. The region has plenty of water, which can promote the growth of fisheries. Promote horticulture and small-scale industry in the region, which will provide job opportunities to the local people. Promote *sulabh sauchalaya* and bio-gas plants for recycling biodegradable material. To reduce the pressure of the growing population on natural resources, they should be provided LPG gas, kerosene oil, solar cookers. Preventive measures have to be taken to avoid the chances of forest fires. In the summer of 1995 the fire in the central Himalayas has made the air polluted and caused a rise in the temperature, loss of vegetation, animals, etc.

There should be a check on quarrying, mining and blasting operations. Efforts should be made to develop more hill stations as tourist centres in the region to avoid the overcrowding of tourists in the well-known hill stations. Kilns with filter devices and higher chimneys should be constructed to minimise the effect on the environment. Any sort of development should be in harmony with the environment, and renewable resources like ground water and forests should be used at a rate at which they are being replenished by nature.

Depletion and Conservation of Natural Resources-The Role of Forests and Habitat

For millennia humans have left their mark on the world's forests, although it was difficult to see. By the twenty-first century, however, forests that humans once thought were endless are shrinking before their eyes. Forests are not only a source of timber; they perform a wide range of social and ecological functions. They provide a livelihood for forest dwellers, protect and enrich soils, regulate the hydrologic cycle, affect local and regional climate through evaporation, and help stabilize the global climate. Through the process of photosynthesis they absorb carbon dioxide (CO_2) and release the oxygen humans and animals breathe. They provide habitat for half of all known plant and animal species, are the main source of wood for industrial and domestic heating, and are widely used for recreation.

Forests are attractive and accessible sources of natural wealth. They are not, however, unlimited. Deforestation is caused by farmers, ranchers, logging and mining companies, and fuel wood collectors. Governments have often encouraged the settlement of land through cheap credit, land grants, and the building of roads and infrastructure. Much of these activities led to the destruction of forests, causing some governments to reverse their policies.

Forests play a particularly crucial role in the global cycling of carbon. The Earth's vegetation contains two trillion tons of carbon, roughly triple the amount stored in the atmosphere. When trees are cleared, the carbon they contain is oxidized and released into the air, adding to the atmospheric store of carbon dioxide. Many scientists believe that carbon dioxide contributes to global warming. This release happens slowly if the trees are used to manufacture lumber or are allowed to decay naturally. If they are burned as fuel, however, or in order to clear forestland for farming, almost all of their carbon is released rapidly. The clearing for agriculture in North America and Europe has largely stopped, but the burning of tropical forests has taken over the role of producing the bulk of carbon dioxide added to the atmosphere by land use changes.

A 1995 National Oceanic and Atmospheric Administration (NOAA) study found that about half the carbon dioxide emitted by burning fossil fuels is absorbed by plants in the Northern Hemisphere. The finding showed that plants play a role about equal to that of oceans, to which most of the absorption had previously been attributed. The study showed that plants absorb carbon dioxide that is rich in the carbon isotope 12, or C_{12}, while ocean water absorbs C_{12} and C_{13} equally. By determining the ratios of the isotopes, scientists can determine the relative effects of oceans and plants on the atmosphere's carbon dioxide concentration.

Rising Pressures on Forests

According to Janet N. Abramovitz in Taking a Stand: Cultivating a New Relationship with the World's Forests *(Washington, DC: Worldwatch Institute, 1998), the Worldwatch Institute, an independent, nonprofit environmental research organization, reported that between 1980 and 1995 alone at least 494 million acres of forests vanished—an area larger than Mexico.*

According to the United Nations Food and Agriculture Organization (FAO), approximately half the wood cut worldwide is used for fuel and charcoal. Most fuel wood is used in developing countries. In dry countries such as India, the majority of trees cut are for fuel; in moist tropical areas such as Malaysia, most trees are cut for industrial timber.

Tropical Rain Forests

Tropical forests are the most "alive" places on Earth. Although they cover less than 2 percent of the Earth's surface, they are home to as many as 30 million species of plants and animals—more than half of all life forms on the planet. A single acre of tropical rain forest supports 60 to 80 tree species and an enormous number of vines and mosses.

Rain forests also play an essential role in the weather. They absorb solar energy, which affects wind and rainfall worldwide. Regionally, they reduce erosion and act as buffers against flooding. Tropical trees contain huge amounts of carbon which, when they are destroyed, is released into the atmosphere as carbon dioxide.

Of roughly 3,000 plants identified as having cancer-fighting properties, 70 percent grow in the rain forests. One of every three species of birds in the world nest there. In addition to wildlife, more than 1,000 indigenous tribes still survive in tropical forests, just as they have for thousands of years.

The Natural Resources Defense Council (NRDC), a private organization that supports environmental health, reports that nearly half of the forests on the planet have been decimated and every year more than 30 million acres of tropical forests and woodlands are destroyed for agriculture or logging. Exacerbating this problem, global wood consumption is set to double over the next 30 years, according to the NRDC, further stressing the survival of global forests..

In Combined Summaries: Technologies to Sustain Tropical Forest Resources and Biological Diversity *(Washington, DC: U.S. Government Printing Office, 1992) the now-defunct U.S. Office of Technology Assessment concluded that the major underlying cause of deforestation and species extinction is the lack of alternative employment for the growing populations of tropical countries. Logging and the conversion of forestland to short-term, usually unsustainable, agricultural use results in destruction of the land, declining fisheries, erosion, and flooding.*

Species in tropical rain forests possess a high degree of mutuality, in which two species are completely dependent on one another for survival; for example, a species of wasp and a species of fig tree. Such relationships are believed to evolve as a result of the relatively constant conditions in the tropics. Any species dependent on trees therefore becomes imperiled when a tree is cut down.

The Amazon—An Example

The Amazon rain forests, located in South America, are the most famous of the Earth's tropical forests. They serve as a good example of the controversies surrounding rain forests worldwide. This controversy generally centers on the interest of environmentalists (often from developed countries) in stabilizing the environment and the developing world's basic need to cut down its forests for fuel and livelihood. Most developing nations claim that these needs are too great to be set aside for the sake of the environment. They also resent the industrialized world's disdain of practices the developed countries once followed themselves in building their own nations. These poorer, developing countries also wonder why they are expected to pay for the cleanup of a world that they did not contaminate.

There are also international incentives for continuing to cut down the rain forests. Foreign countries, especially Asian nations, are increasingly eyeing the Amazon forests as a source of ancient trees to make plywood, ornamental moldings, and furniture. Granting logging rights to these nations may seem an appealing option for those South American countries desperate for money.

Based on studies of satellite photographs taken over the Amazon, researchers believe that as much as 10 percent of the original Amazon forest has been destroyed.

Location of protected forest and other forest in the United States, 2001 mainly through "slash and burn" methods of clearing land that are used to convert the land to farming use. The cleared land's productivity usually decreases within a few years, and farmers often have to abandon the fields and move on—slashing and burning a new area.

Role of Individual in Conservation of Natural Resources

The eight natural resources are all necessary for providing the basic needs of humans: food, clothing, and shelter. Our very lives depend on clean air and water. Our ability to feed ourselves rests on maintaining the fertility of the soil in which we plant our crops. Crops will grow only if sufficient sunlight and water are available. Modern society depends on fossil fuels for industrial energy. Natural resources form an unbroken chain of support for us, and it is not difficult to imagine the problems that would arise from the loss of any link in this chain.

The wise use of our natural resources is important because our survival depends on these resources. This is why we think this course is important. During your study time with us, we hope to raise questions that provoke real and thoughtful responses from you. No question is more important than how to use our resources. Our population, which grows at a fantastic rate, is what drives many decisions on the use of natural resources. Consider the following statistics:

- From the time of the Romans, it took nearly 1,700 years for the population to reach one billion.
- It took slightly more than 200 years for the population to double to two billion.
- It took less than a century for the population to triple to more than six billion. The supply of most natural resources has remained at a static rate, so a key question is how large a population can our resources support and for how long.

UNIT-IX

Methods of Teaching in Environmental Education

(a) Characteristics of Good Teaching Method

One set of characteristics of good teaching, extracted from research studies and summarised from the individual lecturer's point of view (Ramsden, 2003) includes:

- A desire to share your love of the subject with students
- An ability to make the material being taught stimulating and interesting
- A facility for engaging with students at their level of understanding
- A capacity to explain the material plainly
- A commitment to making it absolutely clear what has to be understood at what level and why
- Showing concern and respect for students
- A commitment to encouraging independence
- An ability to improvise and adapt to new demands
- Using teaching methods and academic tasks that require students to learn actively, responsibly and co-operatively
- Using valid assessment methods
- A focus on key concepts, and students misunderstandings of them, rather than covering the ground
- Giving the highest quality feedback on student work

- A desire to learn from students and other sources about the effects of teaching and how it can be improved.

A similar set of characteristics has been derived from feedback from students at UTS, and is summarised in the following section.

The Students' Choice

The Planning and Quality unit run a Student Feedback System at UTS. The system uses a questionnaire which gathers both numerical ratings and student opinions about teaching strengths and improvements. Systems for generating and analysing student feedback questionnaires have been used at UTS since 1988, although the questionnaires themselves have changed over time.

In the early 1990s, some research was carried out to look at staff who had been very highly rated by students. Highly rated staff come from a wide range of disciplines and teaching situations, but they share a number of characteristics which students consider to be strengths in teaching in lecture and tutorial classes. The following information was obtained from the students' responses and through interviews with the lecturers. A project on 'effective interaction' carried out in 2003 suggested that the qualities which students value have changed little over time.

Teaching Skills and Practices

The most frequent comment made by students was that highly rated lecturers explained in a way which was clear and helped students to understand. They made difficult work comprehensible without oversimplifying, and used simple language. If technical language was used, it was clearly defined. In lectures, visual media, such as overheads, slides, handouts and blackboard diagrams were used to assist in explanation or clarification where appropriate. Abstract concepts were illustrated with examples, and the distinction between concept and example was made clear.

Highly rated lecturers were well prepared, structured their lecture content effectively, and communicated the structure to students. They clearly defined the subject objectives and emphasised important points. They spoke clearly and at an appropriate speed and allowed adequate time for students to both take notes and listen, indicating when note-taking was and was not required. They often provided handouts to assist students to take notes without furious copying. They used questions and activities to engage students' thinking and interest.

They were highly knowledgeable and up to date in their subject area, but did not pretend to "know it all" and were willing to learn from their students, recognising that work experience makes many part-time and senior students a valuable resource.

Students commented that the lecturers tried to make the work interesting. They related new concepts to students' experiences by means of case studies, relevant examples or anecdotes, and placed a high priority on varying student activities during lecture sessions.

Student participation was encouraged, in lectures as well as tutorial or laboratory sessions. These lecturers knew that most students gained a better understanding from active involvement than from passive note-taking. They therefore made a conscious effort to release time from "lecturing" for student analysis, problem solving, questioning, discussion or "buzz group" activities relevant to the topic for the lecture. During lectures, they made frequent opportunities for questions from, or discussion by, students, and attempted to answer all questions promptly and clearly. They treated all student questions seriously and did not intimidate or ridicule. They also asked direct questions of students in order to check understanding before or during a lecture.

Giving time for students to actively engage with the subject matter means reducing time available to cover new content. The lecturers' most frequent strategies for gaining time without compromising course objectives were:

- Providing students with printed subject notes and/or summary handouts, thus reducing note writing, and encouraging students to highlight key points, add comments and note insights generated during class interactions.

- Thoroughly explaining key concepts and examples in short lecture segments, and encouraging students to access texts and references for further details and multiple examples.
- Reducing the content covered in lectures to central areas, and encouraging wider reading and/or the integration of work experience through carefully designed assignments and tutorials.

Attitude Towards Students

Highly rated lecturers genuinely wanted students to learn, understand and develop critical thinking abilities, as well as master content or learn skills. They demonstrated an empathy with student thinking, anticipating misconceptions and allowing students to develop understanding in a variety of ways. They observed students in class for signs that they were failing to keep up, were bored, or were not understanding, and were flexible in responding to student needs. They encouraged student feedback on their teaching, and often sought informal feedback during classes.

Outside class time, they made a point of being approachable and willing to help students. They tried to avoid "spoon-feeding" and encouraged students to take an active role in working through their difficulties, but would take time to work though concepts in detail with those who genuinely had difficulties.

Personal Qualities

Highly rated lecturers showed enthusiasm for their subject, professional area and teaching role. Students found this motivating and commented that they looked forward to coming to classes. The most frequently mentioned personal attribute of the highly rated lecturers was their "easy going", "relaxed" or "open" manner, and the relaxed atmosphere that this brought to the classroom. Students also appreciated appropriate humour and an attitude which suggested that learning was enjoyable.

In Summary...

Highly rated lecturers saw their teaching role as vitally important They worked hard at making the most of their class contact time to maximise student learning and interest in the subject. While some felt that they were fortunate in having "natural" teaching ability, they all emphasised the considerable amount of time they had spent in lecture and resource preparation.

(b) Seminar

Staff Correspondent

NCERT is Organising the Three-day Event

Mysore: Teachers, teacher educators, researchers, administrators and policymakers from the four southern States and the two Union Territories (Puducherry and Lakshadweep) will arrive in Mysore in January 2008 to discuss environmental education. For, the National Council of Educational Research and Training (NCERT) is organising a three-day southern regional seminar on "The recent trends in environmental education" at the Regional Institute of Education (RIE) from January 23. According to RIE, the seminar offers a platform to assess the status of environmental education through research findings; to share experiences, contribution, achievements and problems of environmental education and to draw recommendations towards the future course of environmental education.

N.N. Prahallada, reader, RIE, said teachers, teacher educators, researchers and policymakers can present articles on the following themes: perspectives of environmental education-history, need and nature, philosophical, sociological, psychological bases of environmental education; value orientation of environmental education, curriculum of environmental education, methods of environmental education, informal, non-formal and distance learning of environmental science; evaluation of environmental science, role of students, parents, society and administration in strengthening environmental education and educational technology and community resource for environmental education.

(c) Workshop

In Japan, cranes attract many visitors to the sites. The similar trend is growing in other Asian countries, particularly in China and South Korea. Therefore cranes can be used as flagship species to promote wetland and wildlife conservation if there is a good education programme at the site, and the tourist industry will also generate income to the local community in a sustainable way. However, if the sites are not well managed, an influx of visitors will cause considerable disturbance and damage to these sites, and sometimes things will get worse as the result from inappropriate measures to promote tourism. In the view of this, the North East Asian Crane Site Network (one of the three waterbird networks under the Asia-Pacific Migratory Waterbird Strategy) organised two workshops and invited important sites for cranes to develop a plan on education and ecotourism at sites important for cranes.

The Network is managed by the Wild Bird Society of Japan (BirdLife in Japan) and financed by the Ministry of the Environment, Japan, under the Asia-Pacific Migratory Waterbird Strategy. It aims to encourage international cooperation on conservation of cranes and wetlands and to ensure the long-term survival of all crane species and their habitat in the region. Eighteen important sites (10 of which are Ramsar Sites) for crane conservation in Russia, Mongolia, China, North Korea, South Korea and Japan have joined the Network since its launch in 1997. Another 10 sites are preparing to join the Network.

The first workshop was held in March 2001, at the Yellow River Delta Nature Reserve, China. About 30 participants from six countries attended the workshop. At the workshop, nature reserve workers from different countries were divided into three groups to develop their own simple projects on education or visitor management.

Most participants then returned to this follow-up workshop at Kushiro, Hokkaido, Japan, 27 February-2 March 2002, to report the results and discuss future plans on this main topic. Based on the discussion, a handbook with guidelines and examples on this theme will be published by the time of the Ramsar COP8 (November 2002).

Special study tours had been organized for the 40 participants from seven countries, including two wildlife NGO workers from Bhutan, during their stay in Kushiro. The overseas participants are impressed by the education programmes, management, local community involvement at reserves in eastern Hokkaido. This gives them the inspiration of management at their home reserves.

The workshop has also provided chances for mutual understanding of reserve workers in different Asian countries and given chances for further cooperation: Gumi in South Korea pledged to join the Network, Cholwon in South Korea proposed to hold an international workshop for the Network, China and Russia agreed to strengthen the cooperation of the Lake Khanka-Xingkai international reserve, and Chinese reserve workers plan to come back to Hokkaido and study the experience of crane site management.

Problem Solving

Imagine children cleaning up rivers or beaches in your community. Or starting recycling programmes, conducting water and air quality tests, research over the Internet, establishing a wetland nursery, or saving trees in your neighborhood. Now, imagine what they learned by planning and carrying out these activities!

In my work with over two thousand students from around the world, I have witnessed young minds learning complex things about societal, ecological and biological systems. They learn about the human component involved when you work together as a group to investigate environmental problems and solutions. And most importantly, I observed what they learn about their own capabilities and potential. They inherently understand the power that is harnessed when a group of people combine their gifts and energies towards a common focus. As a result, these children and young adults are able to make significant contributions to the world at large.

Twenty years ago as a young, enthusiastic and very "green teacher," I decided to teach the young children in my charge about the perils facing the environment. Armed with mountains of research and powerful videos and stories, I created a bleak and dim vision of the future of our world in the minds of these young children. During an emotionally charged lecture on our "Endangered Earth"-I looked out on the sea of faces, once so filled with hope, were now clouded over with fear, frustration, and perhaps, did I even see apathy?

I quickly retreated back to the drawing board, and revisited environmental education within the context of the brain research explosion that revolutionized teaching and how we view the learning process. This time, equipped with a deeper understanding of the goals for environmental education, more life experience in facilitating learning, and a variety of tools that actively engage learners in the learning, I was much better prepared. A major impact on my approach was Howard Gardner's theory of Multiple Intelligences and his definition of intelligence as the ability to:

- Solve real-life problems;
- Find and create problems, and
- Offer a product or service that is valued in at least one culture. *(*Howard Gardner, *Frames of Mind* (New York: Basic Books, 1983, 1993*)*

I began to explore the possibility of how environmental education could be introduced to students using a problem solving, action project oriented approach.

I worked with other educators around the world who were interested in applying this approach to environmental education, and with groups of students throughout the US, as well as other countries including Brazil, the former Soviet Union, Canada and countries throughout Europe. These students applied problem solving and action skills as they investigated environmental issues, while emphasizing specific problems in the local community. The goal was to empower kids to take action on issues that directly effect them so not only would they increase their awareness about environmental issues (a desired outcome), but also would be provided with a variety of tools that they could use to effect change, thereby giving them a voice in the world.

The multidisciplinary and interdisciplinary nature of environmental education immediately became apparent. Students conducted scientific research by collecting water samples, worked closely with scientists and local labs to analyze the results, then applied their mathematical skills to graph and tabulate the data. Students enhanced their writing skills by writing letters to the editor, press releases, and research reports. They utilized technology to create computer diagrams or "computer films" to communicate their research data. They used telecommunications to collect information about their chosen issue, exchange data with peers from other states and countries, and as a way to get others involved in their projects (Budd and Curry, 1995.) Many aspects of the arts were employed as students created posters, paintings, models, plays, skits, and songs to let others know about pressing environmental issues. They exercised their communication, cooperation and citizenship skills as they facilitated local town meetings, made presentations to their school board, mayor and city councils. Some groups of students even made presentations to the U.S. Senate, former prime minister Margaret Thatcher and Raisa Gorbachev, all in an effort to effect local and global change.

Using this project centered, problem solving action oriented approach, the sea of young fearful faces I had once seen were quickly replaced with expressions and attitudes of hope, accomplishment, involvement and responsible environmental behavior.

Field Trips and Surveys, Projects, Exhibition and Other Methods

At the "World Conference on Education for All-Meeting Basic Learning Needs", sponsored by UNESCO, UNEP, and UNICEF in the Spring of 1990, Hungerford and Volk presented the findings of their research on the development of responsible environmental behavior in citizens on an individual basis and in societal groups. Embedded within this approach is empowerment as a crucial tool for creating behavioral change. Traditionally, it was believed that people's behavior towards the environment could be changed by making them more aware. Instead, Hungerford and Volk suggested that the following attributes are required:

- Knowledge of an issue is a prerequisite to action.
- Individuals must possess knowledge of those courses of action which are available and which will be most effective in a given situation.
- Individuals benefit from skill development by appropriately applying knowledge of action strategies to a given issue.

This approach is based largely on "The Hines Model of Responsible Environmental Behavior", which goes beyond the linear model for changing behavior: "increased knowledge leads to favorable attitudes...which in turn leads to action promoting better environmental quality" (Ramsey and Rickson, 1977).

The Hines Model stresses two important variables which were considered in the development of the approach outlined in the Grounds and Gardens curriculum.

First of all, people are more willing to do something about an environmental problem if they feel it is an issue of importance. Most often this is a local issue of concern in their community — something that impacts them directly. Secondly, the model emphasizes that people will become empowered to do something about a problem if they have training and knowledge in problem solving strategies and action skills. (Hines, J.M., et al., 1986).

In their research, Volk and Hungerford looked at how responsible environmental behavior might be actualized through environmental education. Many of the answers lie in the objectives for environmental education as defined over two decades ago at the 1977 Tblisi Intergovernmental Conference on Environmental Education:

Awareness —to help social groups and individuals acquire an awareness and sensitivity to the total environment and its allied problems.

Sensitivity—to help social groups and individuals gain a variety of experiences in, and acquire a set of values and feelings of concern for the environment and it associated issues and problems.

Attitudes—to help social groups and individuals acquire a set of values and feelings of concern for the environment and motivation for actively participating in environmental improvement and protection.

Skills—to help individuals acquire skills for identifying on solving environmental issues and problems.

Participation—to provide individuals with an opportunity to be actively involved at all levels in working toward resolution of environmental issues and problems. (You can find a complete listing of the goals and objectives Tblisi conference declaration 1978.)

This framework provides the perfect vehicle for integrating environmental education across all content areas. While it may seem a rather ambitious task—it is feasible and essential. Traditionally, it was believed that we can change behavior by making people more knowledgeable about the environment and its associated issues. The underlying assumption is that the more we know, the more aware we are, and that we then become motivated to act toward the environment in more responsible ways. I tried that and as a result, scared quite a few ten, eleven and twelve year olds. They were overwhelmed and did not posses the skills to create change in their behavior, let alone affect positive change in their community or the world at large. They in fact, felt powerless.

It becomes increasingly apparent that a responsible and effective way is to use "framing" techniques for our environmental education programmes. Framing moves beyond the arbitrary boundaries of traditional disciplines by creating a framework which allows learning to be related and integrated within a student's life (Heimlich, 1992). Using a problem-solving, action-oriented, project approach, teachers and students can identify and investigate issues and problems of concern to them. Using a wide array of strategies and skills to research specific environmental issues and problems, analyze and interpret these problems, propose creative solutions, and act on those solutions achieves many of the goals stated in the Tblisis conference declaration.

In her article, *Global Issues and Environmental Education*, Carmen E. Trisler reminds us that, "whichever approach is used, ('infusion'-content and skills integrated into existing courses, 'insertion'-the addition of specific courses in environmental education, or framing), the relationship of the individual action in regard to global issues must be central to the instruction if the desired outcome is that of responsible environmental behavior. When studying about global issues, the goal needs to be more than merely acquiring scientific knowledge. A relationship must be made between the individual action and responsibility to the global issue."

In 1990, Congress passed the National Environmental Education Act. The Act directs the Federal Government to play a strong role in increasing the public's literacy by focusing on education of youth. Abby Ruskey aptly describes the key objectives for environmental education in her article, "State Profiles in Environmental Education" as:

An awareness and appreciation of the natural and built environment; knowledge of natural systems and ecological concepts; understanding of the range of current environmental issues; and the ability to use investigative, critical thinking, and problem solving skills towards the resolution of environmental issues: These are key traits of an environmentally literate citizenry. It follows that they are the key objectives of environmental education.

Nearly every state in the country currently has some sort of environmental education programme, however Abby Ruskey's report indicates few have a comprehensive programme that infuses or uses framing, combined with a problem-solving and action project oriented approach. We know that problem solving and decision-making are critical for creating meaningful learning experiences and developing ownership on the part of the learners.

Why Environmental Education?

Of course, one major reason is that it is critical to maintaining our quality of life. Whether we are talking about destruction of the tropical forests, global warming, toxic waste disposal, the ocean crisis or air quality-environmental education is essential if we are to participate fully in solving environmental problems facing us today and on into the future. There are also many positive educational outcomes. A comprehensive approach to environmental education:

- offers educators an effective way to integrate curriculum;
- develops critical and creative thinking skills;
- not only teaches but allows students to develop problem solving skills;
- is the perfect arena for exploring attitudes and values interculturally as well as cross-culturally;
- engages multiple intelligences-especially Gardner's eighth identified intelligence, The Naturalist;
- involves students in their communities;
- utilizes teaching strategies which are student centered, actively involving students in the learning process.
- stresses investigative research skills to help understand the social and economic implications underlying environmental issues
- allows educators to easily integrate many of the principles of education reform: real world applications, cooperative learning, teaching for understanding (Gardner), emphasis on concepts, processes and products as opposed to content only.
- acquisiton of technology skills is enhanced by real-life hands-on learning situations.

Most importantly, this type of approach emphasizes life skills that students will continue to use in future work and throughout their lives. Through encouraging community involvement and social responsibility, students learn how to create positive change in their community. They become empowered as learners and as a voice in the world.

Field Instruction in School Settings—ERIC/SMEAC

Field instruction is consistently recommended as a key element for school-based programmes directed toward environmental learning, but rarely do such recommendations progress beyond the platitude stage. In general, published surveys dealing with the instructional practices of classroom teachers in all fields of formal education indicate that they conduct very few field activities off school grounds. The extent of their use of school grounds is less well documented but is generally considered to be less than optimal.

In an extensive survey of classroom earth science teachers, Mason (1980b) identified a number of factors contributing to paucity of field activity: lack of planning time; lack of resource people for assistance; failure of the school to assume trip risk; lack of a satisfactory method for covering classes; restrictions placed on field work by school regulations; lack of administrative leadership, support, and encouragement; lack of funding; limited available transportation; too much "red tape"; and excessive class size. Though this list was compiled with instruction in secondary school earth science as its specific referent, it appears to be applicable to environmental education in its various countenances, and to K-12 formal education situations in general.

Does Teacher Commitment Exist?

Teacher commitment to the concept of field instruction is questionable even in situations where organizational, administrative, and/or budgetary constraints are less critical. All other things being equal, it is clear that field instruction places additional demands on the skills and energies of the teacher, when compared to other instructional devices. It is in fact "easier" to teach in the classroom than to plan and implement outside-the-four-walls initiatives. Generally, pre-service teacher education does not emphasize methodologies for field instruction, nor are role models of effective field teachers commonplace. In a word, many teachers do not know how to plan and conduct effective field instruction, and have little motivation to learn how to do so.

Proponents of field instruction frequently presuppose a premium on its educational values. In doing so, they often convey the impression that, in their view, the need for field instruction is self-evident and needs no verification. If such values were in fact self-evident, one would expect field instruction to be common practice, regardless of constraints. But it is not.

Over the years, a number of researchers have investigated educational values of various modes of field instruction. Summaries of such studies through the late 1970s were published by Koran and Baker (1979) and Mason (1980a). In this Digest, results of several recent studies targeted on field instruction, specifically field trips, are summarized.

What Does Research Say?—Affective Domain

It has long been an article of faith that a major value of field instruction is in the affective realm. For example, a positive relationship between eleventh grade biology students' attitudes toward science and environmental concepts and their exposure to field trip activities was demonstrated in a study by Ignatiuk (1978). Statistically significant differences in such attitudes between pretest and posttest measurements after varying amounts of field work during a 15-week study period were found; the students involved were using the Biological Sciences Curriculum Study (BSCS) text, Green Version.

Working with college students in an introductory level geological science course designed for general education, Kern and Carpenter (1984) found that a field-oriented approach had a pronounced positive influence on the affective responses of participating students. Interest and enjoyment both increased dramatically, and the students involved attached more importance to their work when compared with students in a control-group class employing a more traditional laboratory approach.

Affective factors considered in the study were value (perception of importance of the field of study), interest (in the course itself), and attitude (enjoyment of the course), leading to an increase in student motivation.

What Does Research Say?—Cognitive Domain

Less well-documented over time have been the cognitive-realm educational values of field instruction. However, a number of recent studies have dealt with various aspects of this concern. How well geography facts and skills are learned and how well such learning is retained was the subject of a study involving junior high school students in Australia (Mackenzie and White 1981). Comparing three groups—one treated to an excursion stressing processing of meaning of phenomena observed and experienced during a field trip, another participating in a traditional "passive" excursion, and the third participating in the same basic geography course, but without an excursion—researchers found that students receiving either form of field work outperformed students with no field trips on a test of geography knowledge.

In addition, those students who participated in the field trip stressing knowledge and idea processing outperformed students who participated in the passive field trip. This was true at the conclusion of instruction and again 12 weeks later. Information and skill links such as those encouraged during the exursion described seem to aid recall and retention of facts and skills.

Field experiences can be planned to capitalize on the effects of novelty of setting to meet students' needs, according to a series of studies conducted by personnel associated with the Smithsonian Institution's Chesapeake Bay Center for Environmental Studies (Falk 1983).

Elementary students can learn a great deal from a single-visit, structured tour of a specific area of a zoological park (Falk and Balling 1982). Though field trips typically have been considered of more use in affecting student attitudes and motivation, this study demonstrated that children do learn on well-structured field trips. The study stressed the critical nature of the design and execution of the field trip, including the need for pre-trip orientation.

The most effective pre-trip orientation reported was that conducted by the student's classroom teacher trained by a targeted workshop, as opposed to orientation by a resource person from the zoo or by a classroom teacher supported by mailed printed materials only.

Using pre-trip instructional materials significantly increased student test scores in a cognitive-gain study dealing with a museum field trip experience for junior high school earth science students (Gennaro 1981). In the study, an experimental group showed statistically significant differences in gain score when compared to a control group which made the same field trip, but did not receive pre-visit instruction.

Does "How To" Guidance Exist?

"How to" information for teachers involved in planning and implementing field instruction with and for their classes is available from a number of sources, many of them highly localized (that is, for specific trips to specific places for specific purposes). The fact that many of them are home-made guarantees a wide range of quality and usefulness and often limits their generalizability. However, many are of particular value for their designed purposes. More general "how to" documents are also available and can be of particular use to those needing overall guidance and basic checklists.

For example, a volume developed by Krepel and DuVall (1981) deals with a broad range of concerns— values of field trips as teaching tools, teacher liability, school board policies, administrative support, teacher responsibilities, safety, supervisory assistance, pre-trip activity, follow-up activities, and trip evaluation.

Project

A **project** in business and science is a collaborative enterprise, frequently involving research or design, that is carefully planned to achieve a particular aim.

Overview

The word project *comes from the Latin word* projectum *from the Latin verb* proicere, *"to throw something forwards" which in turn comes from* pro-, *which denotes something that precedes the action of the next part of the word in time (paralleling the Greek onu) and* iacere, *"to throw". The word "project" thus actually originally meant "something that comes before anything else happens".*

When the English language initially adopted the word, it referred to a plan of something, not to the act of actually carrying this plan out. Something performed in accordance with a project became known as an "object".

This use of "project" changed in the 1950s with the introduction of several techniques for project management. Use of the word "project" evolved slightly to cover both projects and objects. However, certain projects continue to include so-called objects object leaders

Contemporary Western business — characterized by a modern matrix organization and a cooperative culture — currently particularly favors project-based approaches. Authoritarian, bureaucratic organizations with rigid, hierarchical structures show less enthusiasm about project-based work, which may not operate as expected in their environment due to conflicts between different cultures.

Specific Uses

School Usage: Within public schools in the United States, a **project** is an assignment given to a student which generally requires a larger amount of effort than normal homework assignments. They can range anywhere from simple written projects to elaborate and well-constructed Science Fair Projects.

Project Management

In project management a project consists of a temporary endeavor undertaken to create a unique product, service or result. An other definition is a management environment that is created for the purpose of delivering one or more business products according to a specified business case.

Project objectives define target status at the end of the project, reaching of which is considered necessary for the achievement of planned benefits. They can be formulated as S.M.A.R.T.E.R: Specific, Measurable (or at least evaluable) achievement, Achievable (recently Acceptable is used regularly as well), realistic (given the current state of organizational resources) and Time terminated (bounded), Ethical and Recorded. The evaluation (measurement) occurs at the project closure. However a continuous guard on the project progress should be kept by monitoring and evaluating. It is also worth noting that SMART or SMARTER is best applied for incremental type innovation projects. For radical type projects it does not apply as well. Goals for such projects tend to be broad, qualitative, stretch/unrealistic and success driven.

The Relative Efficiency and Implementation Costs of Alternative Methods

A useful means for achieving efficient allocation **of** irrigationwater is to put the right price tag on it. This article discussessome **of** the more pervasive pricing **methods** and compares their **efficiency** performance, paying special attention to the impact **of** the cost **of** implementing each method on its **efficiency**. Thearticle uses an empirical example to demonstrate numerically the **relative efficiency of** the different pricing **methods** and the important role **of** implementation costs. The volumetric, output, input, tiered, and two-part tariff **methods** all can achieve efficiency, although the type **of efficiency** varies from one method to another. These **methods** also differ in the amount and type **of** information, and the administrative cost, needed in their implementation. The example indicates that water pricing methods are most pronounced through their effect on the cropping pattern—more so than through their effect on water demand for a given crop. Implementation costs have a large effect on water tariffs and on welfare and hence should have an important role in determining the desirable method to use in any given water situation.

Relative Efficiency of Teaching Methods

Does Environment Education (EE) in primary and secondary schools merely mean a trip to the neighbourhood park? Or does it actually entail substantial understanding of ecological concepts such as biodiversity, natural resources, and pollution? Is the formal educational structure equipped to help school children imbibe important green lessons and grow up to be citizens who are conscious and sensitive to the threats to environment?

A two-year-long study conducted by the Pune-based Bharati Vidyapeeth Institute for Environmental Education and Research (BVIEER) set out to investigate just this – the efficacy of the school curricula at the state and national level in the field of environment education. Based on its findings and recommendations, a pilot study was initiated in eight states in the country, with revised textbooks. A year of implementation later, the BVIEER is embarking on the evaluation of the project, a report of which will be ready by April next year.

"The Ministry of Environment and Forests (MoEF) felt the need for such a study to be undertaken," explains Shamita Kumar of BVIEER, who is the project co-ordinator. "Several well-known organisations in the country were asked to submit a tender for the implementation of this project, and BVIEER was finally selected based on the expertise of its faculty and its experience in EE," she explains. The project, titled 'Study of status of infusion of environmental concepts in school curricula and the effectiveness of its delivery', is a small component of the India Environment Management Capacity Building Project of the World Bank. This project is funded by the WB through the MoEF. It commenced in October 1999 and was completed in July 2001, and this was followed by implementation in 100 schools in each of the eight states of Maharashtra, Goa, Andhra Pradesh, Assam, Jammu and Kashmir, Punjab, Orissa and Uttaranachal. BVIEER is now evaluating the implementation of the project.

The project started out with the aim to not just study the status of EE in India, but also worked on methodologies of teaching them effectively. It also sought to investigate barriers in implementation of effective EE. Its consequent research, listing of findings, and recommendations to state textbook bureaus were in keeping with these objectives.

"Our first step was to identify the existing environmental concepts in the school curricula, and we chose the Languages, General Science, and Social Science (Geography and History and Civics) textbooks from all the states of India," says Kumar. "The concepts were categorised into 108 codes which fall under the sections of Natural Systems and Resources, Biodiversity, Pollution, Energy, People and Environment and Others. The parameters for judging the quality of these concepts were: text content, case studies and examples, visuals, activities and questions for each lesson as well as accuracy, relevance to the text, appropriateness to the age group, comprehensiveness, consistency, bias and action links. An assessment of the language used was also included," she continues.

Next, in order to meet the second objective, an analysis of the teaching methodologies was taken up. A set of 50 sample schools was selected from all across the country, and these included schools with no EE initiatives, schools with special initiatives, and schools where EE activities had been discontinued. Special attention was given to understanding the existing strengths and weaknesses of the present formal and non-formal systems of teaching EE. Teachers from these 50 schools were then interviewed to investigate barriers in implementation of effective EE both at the curricula level and related to teaching methodology.

The results of these studies were not too encouraging. Despite the fact that the Supreme Court has made it imperative for the government to implement an appropriate EE strategy in the school programme, it has not resulted in any heightened concern for the environment. What the BVIEER found was the lack of a holistic approach that integrates teaching of environmental concepts into real life experiences. There was very poor infusion of information on sustainable lifestyles and what individuals could and should do for environmental preservation through their personal daily activities. As happens often with other components of the school curricula, EE too has become a subject to be learnt by rote, without the students understanding or caring enough for the subject matter.

From the content point of view, the researchers found a serious lack of locale-specific information. Even though the NCERT specifies a set of norms, this is not necessarily reflected at the State level. Adequate information seemed to be missing on topics such as the State's biological diversity, its biogeographic regions, its common and endangered species, how ecosystems can be sustainably used and how degraded systems can be restored. Further the need to limit resource consumption, wastage of water, energy etc. had not been highlighted.

According to Kumar, 'gaps' in information was another point to be rectified. She points to an example quoted in the BVIEER report. While air and water pollution have been frequently addressed, the other forms which include noise, oil, thermal, radiation are discussed cursorily. Solar energy finds ample space, but other sources of non-conventional energy have not been dealt with adequately.

Another important area where the BVIEER team suggested improvement was in the lack of updates in the information. For example, DDT, in most books, is mentioned as being used as a common pesticide, even though commercial production and usage of DDT is banned in India.

While the Geography textbooks were found to include information related to natural resource utilisation, lifestyles, occupations of people, description of flora and fauna of the various biogeographic regions, etc, the History and Civics textbooks had extremely few environmental concepts. Contrary to popular belief, the Language textbooks proved quite exemplary in their infusion of environmental concepts. They included chapters that dealt with endangered species, food habits and behavioural patterns of animals and birds, pollution, national parks and sanctuaries, and also contained animal stories with ethical or moral messages.

Having listed their findings, the next step for the BVIEER team was to make certain recommendations based on the lacunae they had found. Helping enhance the status of EE is no new job to the BVIEER team. Right after its establishment in 1993, it had set to work on preparing a Handbook for teachers of classes V to IX in Maharashtra, orienting them in the teaching of EE. In 1998, the Handbook was finally published, and though it was not adopted as the official resource material for teachers by the Maharashtra Textbook Bureau and the SCERT, it has proved to be beneficial for teachers who started using it.

In the World Bank-funded project, different recommendations were made for the three subjects studied. It was suggested that the Geography textbooks focus on the flora, fauna, endangered and endemic species, natural resources and environmental assets and problems of the various biogeographic regions. Important concepts related to conservation of resources and sustainable development needed to be introduced more frequently.

A historical perspective of natural resource use, sustainable life styles along with pro-environmental initiatives taken by traditional societies in our country were recommended for inclusion in the History textbooks, while the Civics chapters needed to highlight the environmental civic duties of individuals. It was also suggested that the names of regulatory bodies to be approached for grievance redressal should not be left out of the Civics books. The Language classes, it was felt, should work in tandem with the relevant Science and Geography curricula, so that the students first understood the ecological principles, and then discussed value-added concepts.

Along with the actual changes in curricula, the researchers considered it equally imperative to motivate the students to act for environmental preservation. This, they consider, is one of the main aims of EE. Biases need to be removed. Similarly, the urban-rural divide in terms of environmental problems needs to be bridged. "The findings were then submitted to the MoEF," says Kumar, explaining the next step in the process. A meeting of the SCERTS was then called to discuss all the material on hand. Eight states were then selected for implementation of the pilot phase of the project. Their respective Textbook bureaus began to incorporate our findings in their Science, Social Sciences (Geography, History and Civics) and the regional language books of standard VI, VII and VIII," she says.

One year has elapsed since the implementation of the project. BVIEER is now gearing itself for the evaluation. While statistics will be calculated later, the fact remains that the study has resulted in 800 schools nurturing the concept of environment and its preservation amongst their students.

UNIT-X

Role of Teaching in Environmental Education

(a) Teacher's Role–National Resource Center for Environmental Education

Despite steps undertaken to incorporate EE in formal education processes, there is still a clear need to 'go beyond the black board' to broaden and deepen the experience and inclovement with the environment.

Some of the suggestions being made include:

- development of organizational frameworks for student mobility, including work-placement.
- structured exchange of students, teachers, trainers and administrators in various types of educational institutions
- joint development of innovative curricula, traching materials, methods, and modules, including those that use new educational technologies
- research internships at university, industry, laboratories, and other places (including NGOs and community groups)
- intensive programmes such as workshops and training
- other innovative approaches such as distance learning, use of new technologies, computer-based education, etc.

Environmental Education Materials: Guidelines for Excellence Summary

1. ***Fairness and Accuracy:*** EE materials should be fair and accurate in describing environmental problems, issues, and conditions, and in reflecting the diversity of perspectives on them.
   - 1.1 Factual accuracy
   - 1.2 Balanced presentation of differing viewpoints and theories.
   - 1.3 Openness to inquiry
   - 1.4 Reflection of diversity
2. ***Depth:*** EE materials should foster awareness of the natural and build environment, an understanding of environmental concepts, conditions, and issues, and an awareness of the feelings, values, attitudes, and perceptions at the heart of environmental issues, as appropriate for different developmental levels.
   - 2.1 Awareness
   - 2.2 Focus on concepts
   - 2.3 Concepts in context
   - 2.4 Attention to different scales
3. ***Emphasis on Skills Building:*** EE materials should build lifelong skills that enable learners to prevent and address environmental issues.
   - 3.1 Critical and creative thinking
   - 3.2 Applying skills to issues
   - 3.3 Action skills
4. ***Action Orientation:*** EE materials should promote civic responsibility, encouraging learners to use their knowledge, personal skills, and assessments of environmental issues as a basis for environmental problem solving and action.
   - 4.1 Sense of personal stake and responsibility
   - 4.2 Self-efficacy

5. ***Instructional Soundness:*** EE materials should rely on instructional techniques that create an effective learning environment.
   - 5.1 Learner-centered instruction
   - 5.2 Different ways of learning
   - 5.3 Connection to learners' everyday lives
   - 5.4 Expanded learning environment
   - 5.5 Interdisciplinary
   - 5.6 Goals and objectives
   - 5.7 Appropriateness for specific learning settings
   - 5.8 Assessment
6. ***Usability:*** EE materials should be well designed and easy to use.
   - 6.1 Clarity and logic
   - 6.2 Easy to use
   - 6.3 Long-lived
   - 6.4 Adaptable
   - 6.5 Accompanied by instruction and support
   - 6.6 Make substantiated claims
   - 6.7 Fit with national, state or local requirements

Framework

A useful framework for environmental education programmes and projects is the triple foci of education, research and practice. **Education** helps in building awareness among the target audience, primarily using knowledge and information as its resources. **Research** helps in assessment of the environment, using a number of problem issues as starting points. **Practice** helps in developing the apporpriate action, using a number of skills and expertise for the purpose.

Step-by-Step

A simple dissemination package-when attempting to 'sell' a message, an organization or an idea, what are the issues to be kept in mind? How can information delivery be designed, step-by-step?

- ***The Message:*** What is the message that is being disseminated? In what format has it been presented? Is it appropriate to the user or level of dissemination?
- ***The Medium:*** What medium is being used to disseminate the message? What means of online and offline events, publications or other means, are being identified as the medium of dissemination?
- ***The Material:*** Through what media or format is the information being packaged and disseminated (both print and electronic)?
- ***The Target:*** Who are the indended target audience for the message? Is the information being procided useful for them? How are the target being identified? Are they individuals or organizations? Is the message appropriately being modified for the purpose?
- ***The Activity:*** When should the dissemination actually take place? Where? This is critical in ensuring that the indended target receives the information.

The 'Multi' Strategy Approach

The myriad range of problems and solutions, of actors and actions, and of resources and strenghts, that cocern the environment clearly requires a 'multi' strategy that takes into account all possible scenarios. The components of this strategy includes-

- ***Multi-Media:*** the use of different means and technologies to tackle a problem or issue
- ***Multi-Level:*** the understanding of issues involved at different scales at the local, regional, national and international levels
- ***Multi-Purpose:*** the use of information and resources for different purposes to achieve different goals and objectives.
- ***Multi-Activity:*** Use of different forms of formal and informal interaction and collaboration to initiate activities

- ***Multi-Dimension:*** Understand the different modes of communications from one-to-one, one-to-many, many-to-one and many-to-many
- ***Multi-Actor:*** Involve the different actors, bringing in different resources and strengths-including community groups, NGOs, businesses etc.
- ***Multi-Time:*** take a prudent timeline in developing policies that are valid and function on the short-term, medium-term and long-term

(b) Role of Information Technology in Environmental and Human Health

In a time of increasing concern over bioterrorist activity, early response to disease outbreaks is a key public health priority and an emerging field of research. Early knowledge of a disease outbreak can improve response time and health outcomes. Recent public health emergencies such as the severe acute respiratory syndrome (SARS) outbreak and the outbreak of monkeypox in the Midwestern United States in the summer of 2003 highlight the important role that early detection plays in mobilizing rapid response.

While traditional disease surveillance relies on often time-consuming laboratory diagnosis, a new breed of syndromic surveillance systems has the potential to significantly speed up detection of disease outbreaks. These new, computer-based surveillance systems offer valuable and timely information to hospitals as well as to State, local, and Federal health officials.

This Issue Brief describes syndromic monitoring systems and how they are used to track trends within patient populations and to establish early warning of disease outbreaks, including potential bioterrorist activity.

Information Technology to Support Bioterrorism Preparedness

- Detection and monitoring systems support disease and threat surveillance and collect national health status indicators.

- Analytical systems facilitate real-time evaluation of live data feeds and turn data into information to identify disease outbreaks.
- Information resources and knowledge management systems provide reference information, distance learning, and decision support.
- Alerting and communications technologies transmit emergency alerts, facilitate routine professional discussions, and support collaborative activities.
- Response systems help manage vaccine distributions, track side effects, and disseminate public health information.

Currently, many public health surveillance systems generate data for public health labs, the clinical community, and State and local health departments. Many of these systems operate in isolation, however, and fail to capitalize on the potential for electronic data exchange. The current public health investigation cycle—from the first hint of trouble to managing a disease outbreak—is lengthy and frequently involves manual exchange of data across many public health organizations. For example, during the anthrax attacks of fall 2001, investigators communicated thousands of environmental test results exclusively by phone and fax.

Bibliography

Adas, Michael : *Machines as the Measure of Men: Science, Technology, and Ideologies of Western Dominance*, Ithaca, Cornell University Press, 1989.

Altbach, Philip G. and Gail Kelly : *New Approaches to Comparative Education,* Chicago, The University of Chicago Press, 1986.

Basta, Nicholas: *The Environmental Career Guide,* John Wiley Press, 1992.

Bateson, Gregory: *Mind and Nature: A Necessary Unity*, New York, Bantam, 1988.

Bennett, Steven J.: *Ecopreneuring: The Complete Guide to Small Business Opportunities from the Environmental Revolution*, John Wiley and Sons, 1992.

Bentley, T. : *Learning beyond the Classroom: Education for a Changing World*, London, Routledge. 1998.

Carr, W. & Kemmis, S. : *Becoming Critical: Education, Knowledge and Action Research*, London, Falmer, 1986.

Cenkner, William : *A Tradition of Teachers: Sankara and the Jagadgurus Today*, Delhi, Motilal Banarsidass, 1983.

Clover, Darlene Elaine: *Global Perspectives in Environmental Adult Education*, New York, Peter Lang, 2003.

Collett, Jonathan and Stephen Karakashian: *Greening the College Curriculum: A Guide to Environmental Teaching in the Liberal Arts*, Washington, D.C.: Island Press, 1996.

Commoner, Barry: *Science and Survival,* New York, Viking, 1967.

Corcoran, Peter Blaze and Arjen E. J. Wals: *Higher Education and the Challenge of Sustainability: Problematics, Promise, and Practice*, Dordrecht, Springer, 2004.

Cotton, Mathew C and Ronald S. Laura: *Empathetic Education: An Ecological Approach*, London, Falmer Press, 1999.

Day, Brian A. and Martha C. Monroe: *Environmental Education and Communication for a Sustainable World: Handbook for International Practitioners*, Washington, DC: Academy for Educational Development, 2000.

Eblen, William and Ruth: *Experiencing the Total Environment*, New York, Scholastic Book Services, 1977.

Elder, James L.: *A Field Guide to Environmental Literacy: Making Strategic Investments in Environmental Education*, Manchester, MA, Environmental Education Coalition, 2003.

Elliott, J. : *Action Research for Educational Change*, Milton Keynes, Open University, 1991.

Filho, W. L., Z. Murphy, and K. O'Loan: *A Sourcebook for Environmental Education: A Practical Review Based on the Belgrade Charter*, New York and West Yorkshire, The Parthenon Group and ERTCEE, 1996.

Filho, Walter Leal: *Innovation, Education, and Communication for Sustainable Development*, New York, Peter Lang Publishing, 2006.

Forrant, Robert and Linda Silka: *Inside and Out: Universities and Education for Sustainable Development*, Amityville, NY, Baywood Publishing Company, 2006.

Foster, Leila Merrell: *The Story of Rachel Carson and the Environmental Movement*, Children's Press, 1990.

Furth, H.G. : *The World of Grown-ups: Children's Conceptions of Society,* New York, Elsevier North Holland, 1980.

Galbraith, M.W. : *Education Through Community Organizations*, San Francisco, Jossey-Bass, 1990.

Galea, Chris: *Teaching Business Sustainability*, Sheffield, UK: Greenleaf, 2004.

Gibson, R. : *Critical Theory and Education*, London, Hodder & Stoughton, 1986.

Goodall, Steve: *Developing Environmental Education in the Curriculum*, London, David Fulton Publishers, 1994.

Goodlad, John I. : *Educational Renewal: Better Teachers, Better Schools*, San Francisco, Jossey-Bass, 1994.

Graulich, Melody and Paul Crumbley: *Search for a Common Language: Environmental Writing and Education*, Logan, Utah State University Press, 2005.

Hale, Monica: *Ecology in Education*, New York, Cambridge University Press, 1993.

Hart, Paul: *Teachers' Thinking in Environmental Education: Consciousness and Responsibility*, New York, Peter Lang, 2003.

Hautecoeur, Jean-Paul: *Ecological Education in Everyday Life: ALPHA 2000*, Toronto, University of Toronto Press, 2002.

Heimlich, Joe E: *Environmental Education: A Resource Handbook*, Bloomington, Phi Delta Kappa Educational Foundation, 2002.

Hernandez, Carlos and Rashmi Mayur: *Pedagogy of the Earth: Education for a Sustainable Future*, Bloomfield, CT: Kumarian Press, 2000.

Hill, Lilian H. and Darlene E. Clover: *Environmental Adult Education: Ecological Learning, Theory, and Practice for Socioenvironmental Change*. San Francisco, Jossey-Bass, 2003.

Hutchison, David: *Growing Up Green: Education for Ecological Renewal*, New York, Teachers College Press, 1998.

Jacobsen, Susan K., Mallory D. McDuff, and Martha C. Monroe: *Conservation Education and Outreach Techniques*, Oxford, Oxford University Press, 2006.

Jeffs, T. and Smith, M. : *Using Informal Education*, Milton Keynes, Open University Press, 1990.

Johnson, Edward A. and Michael J. Mappin: *Environmental Education and Advocacy: Changing Perspectives of Ecology and Education*, New York, Cambridge University Press, 2005.

Lee, Yoonmi : *Modern Education, Textbooks and Image of the Nation: Politics of Modernization and Nationalism in Korean Education, 1800-1910*, New York, Garland, 2000.

Leou, Mary J.: *Readings in Environmental Education: An Urban Model*. Dubuque, IA, Kendall Hunt, 2005.

Louv, Richard: *Last Child in the Woods: Saving our Children from Nature-Deficit Disorder*, Chapel Hill, Algonquin Books, 2005.

M'Gonigle, Michael and Justine Starke: *Planet U: Sustaining the World, Reinventing the University*, New Society Publishers, 2006.

McHarg, Ian: *Design with Nature,* Garden City, NJ, Natural History Press, 1969.

McInnis, Noel: *You Are An Environment.* Evanston, IL: Center for Curriculum Design, 1972.

Miller, Ron: *Renewal of Meaning in Education: Responses to the Cultural and Ecological Crisis of Our Times*, Brandon, Holistic Education Press, 1993.

Palmer, Joy and Philip Neal: *A Handbook of Environmental Education*. London and New York, Routledge, 1994.

Peterson's Guides: *Education for the Earth,* Peterson's Guides, Princeton, NJ, 1993.

Plitz, Albert: *How Your Body Uses Food*, Chicago, National Dairy Council, 1960.

Poster, C. and Kruger, A. : *Community Education in the Western World*, London, Routledge, 1990.

Premi, M.K. : *Educational Planning in India*, New Delhi, Sterling, 1972.

Ranjan, Rahul: *Environmental Education*, New Delhi, Mohit, 2004.

Rappaport, Ann and Sarah Hammond Creighton: *Degrees that Matter: Climate Change and the University*, Cambridge, MIT Press, 2007.

Reardon, Betty and Eva Nordland: *Learning Peace: The Promise of Ecological and Cooperative Education*, Albany, State University of New York Press, 1994.

Rowe, Mary Budd: *Teaching Science as Continuous Inquiry*, New York, McGraw Hill, 1973.

Sanera, Michael and Jane S. Shaw: *Facts, Not Fear: Teaching Children about the Environment*, Washington, DC: Regnery Publishers, 1999.

Scott, William and Stephen Gough: *Sustainable Development and Learning: Framing the Issues*, London and New York, RoutledgeFalmer, 2003.

Seymour, Mike: *Educating for Humanity: Rethinking the Purposes of Education*, Boulder, Paradigm Publishers, 2004.

Sharma, Sanjay Prakash: *Environmental Education*. Delhi, Vista International, 2006.

Shaw, Jane S: *A Blueprint for Environmental Education*, Bozeman, Political Economy Research Center, 1999.

Sisson, Edith: *Nature With Children of All Ages,* Prentice Hall, New York, 1990.

Smith, Gregory: *Education and the Environment: Learning to Live Within Limits*. Albany, State University of New York Press, 1992.

Sterling, Stephen R.: *Sustainable Education: Re-Visioning Learning and Change*, Dartington, Schumacher Society, 2001.

Stone, Michael K. and Zenobia Barlow: *Ecological Literacy: Education Our Children for a Sustainable World*, San Francisco, Sierra Club Books, 2005.

Taylor, Anne and George Vlastos: *School Zones: Learning Environments for Children*, Corrales, NM, School Zones, 1983.

Thomashow, Mitchell: *Ecological Identity: Becoming a Reflective Environmentalist,* Cambridge, MIT Press, 1995.

Van Matre, Steve: *Earth Education: A New Beginning*, Greenville, Institute for Earth Education, 1990.

Warner, David: *Environmental Careers: A Practical Guide to Opportunities in the 90s*. Lewis Publishers, Boca Raton, FL, 1992.

Wheeler, Keith A. and Anne Perraca Bijur: *Education for a Sustainable Future: A Paradigm of Hope for the 21st Century*, New York, Kluwer Academic Publishers, 2000.

Index

□□□